NATIONAL EXTENSION

30 Hour BASIC

by
Clive Prigmore
(Orpington College of Further Education)

This book can be used to learn BASIC on almost any microcomputer. Additionally we have produced free notes on the minor variations needed for the BASIC of the more popular micros. These free notes are available for:

Acorn Atom □ Alpha Micro □ Apple □ CBM □ Compucolor □ DAI □ Dragon 32 □ Electron □ Midwich □ RML 380Z/480Z □ Sharp □ Superbrain □ Tandy TRS-80 □ T199/4A □ VIC 20 □ Video Genie □

Send a stamped addressed envelope with the make and model written clearly on the inside of the envelope flap to the National Extension College, Dept. CMP, 18 Brooklands Avenue, Cambridge CB2 2HN.

Special editions are available for ZX81 and Spectrum.

NATIONAL EXTENSION COLLEGE CORRESPONDENCE TEXTS

COURSE NUMBER M027

ISBN 0 86082 269 9

Designer: Peter Hall
Photographs: Michael Manni, Cambridge.
Cover photograph: Reeve photography, Cambridge.
Printed by NEC Print.
Cover printed by Burlington Press, Foxton, Cambridgeshire.

First printing 1981
Reprinted with corrections 1982 (twice)
Fourth printing with corrections (1982)

Acknowledgements

The author and the National Extension College wish to thank the following for their help in developing the course:

Acorn Computers Ltd for the loan of a prototype of the BBC Computer, for providing a disk of the BBC BASIC and for answering all our queries about the BASIC.

Joyce Cade for typing the manuscript with all its many complications.

Martin Good for the loan of his PET computer for testing the programs.

Robert Horvath for keying in all the programs into the PET and for ironing out the snags.

Contents

How to use this course

Aims of the course
Quite simply, to help you learn to use a microcomputer with confidence. To do that you need to master three things: (a) the BASIC language; (b) planning good program structures; and (c) using the keyboard. This course teaches you the first two. Your computer will teach you the third!

30 Hour BASIC isn't all there is to know about BASIC but it does cover all the essentials. Once you've completed the course, you will be ready to use a textbook on BASIC or for the second stage BASIC course which will shortly be available from NEC.

Do I need a microcomputer?
You can do the course whether or not you have a microcomputer. All you have to do is to choose one of the following ways of working through the course:

Self-instructional use: With a microcomputer: do all the Exercises and self-assessment questions (SAQ's) and key in all the programs marked [K]. Without a microcomputer: do all the Exercises and SAQ's but omit the items marked [K].

FlexiStudy use: With your own microcomputer: do all the Exercises and SAQ's at home and key in at home all the programs marked [K]. Test your assignment answers on your own microcomputer. Then take/send your problems to your local FlexiStudy centre. Without your own microcomputer: do all the Exercises and SAQ's but ignore the items marked [K]. Then do the assignment questions and take these to your local FlexiStudy centre to run on their microcomputers.

NEC correspondence student: With your own microcomputer: do all the Exercises and SAQ's at home and key in all the items marked [K]. Test your assignments on your own microcomputer before sending them to your NEC correspondence tutor. If the assignment programs don't run properly, tell your tutor what response you are getting from your microcomputer. Without your own microcomputer: do all the Exercises and SAQ's at home but ignore the items marked [K]. Do the assignment questions and post these to your NEC tutor.

Which microcomputer should I use?
Most of the course will run on any microcomputer so don't buy a microcomputer specially to fit the course. If you do buy a microcomputer, base your choice on other factors such as the facilities you need. All the programs will run on the BBC Computer and the course includes special guidance on programming this microcomputer.

Which BASIC does the course use?
There are many versions (dialects) of BASIC, each created by a computer manufacturer modifying the original BASIC. As far as possible we have kept to the common core of most microsoft BASICs. Sometimes the programs contain extra lines which are not needed on all computers. Usually these lines are ignored by computers that don't need them.

Structure of the course

The course is in 9 Units (see Contents). Each Unit includes:

Examples: These are problems which we solve completely for you in the text.

Self Assessment Question (SAQ's): We ask you to stop and quickly check that you have understood a new idea that we have introduced. Answers to these always appear at the end of the Unit in which the SAQ occurs.

Exercises: These are longer problems for you to try. Answers appear at the end of the Unit in which the Exercise occurs.

K which stands for key. This is where we think you could find it helpful to key a program into your own microcomputer.

Assignment: These are questions for you to answer and send to your tutor for marking and comment. There are no answers to these in the course.

UNIT 1
Simple statements and commands

1.1 What does a computer do?

In broad terms, a computer is a machine which helps us to solve certain kinds of problems. These usually involve symbols or characters which are familiar to us through every day use, e.g. letters of the alphabet (capital and lower case), numbers, punctuation marks and some special characters such as +, #, ★. The computer allows us to put in one set of symbols or characters and get out a different but related set. If this seems very vague and too general, let's consider some specific examples.

CHARACTERS IN	CHARACTERS OUT
Numbers representing the size of a window.	Cost of double glazing.
List of books borrowed from a library.	List of those books overdue.
A person's name.	The person's telephone number.
Standard notation for a move in a game of chess.	Picture of the chess board with the move accomplished.
Number representing height and acceleration.	Picture of lunar lander.
Pre-determined codes.	Musical sounds.

Figure 1   Some uses of a computer

This course is not about how the computer does these things but about how you can get it to do them by giving it the right instructions. We shan't therefore be going into any detail of the insides of a computer but you will find it helpful to know which are the major parts of a computer. This is quickly dealt with in the next section.

1.2 What is a computer?

A simple model of a computer is shown in Figure 2.

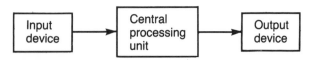

Figure 2   A simple model of a computer

You can see that there are three main parts to a computer:
1 The input device which allows you to enter either instructions or data (information) into the computer. On a microcomputer the input device is a keyboard which looks like a typewriter.

2 The central processing unit (CPU) which, amongst other things, carries out the instructions you have put in. This processing results in a modification of your data giving you the 'answer' or output that you require.

3 An output device which enables you to receive the result of the processing. The output device might be a television screen displaying the output or a printer which actually prints the output onto paper.

All this may sound very mundane. Indeed it would be were it not for the three key characteristics of a computer: (a) its capacity to store very large quantities of data which (b) it is able to process very rapidly and (c) its capacity to store a program which controls its own operation. This last characteristic is by far the most important one and is the one we are going to cover in this course.

Backing store

We shall just mention one other technical detail before looking at programming. If you are using this course you are likely to own or use a microcomputer with a small internal storage capacity. It uses that storage to keep its main running instructions plus the details of the problem it is currently solving. The latter details are erased when you switch the machine off so, if you want to keep your program or data, you have to keep them in a backing store: a separate storage system that you can link to the computer as needed. On small systems this will be an ordinary audio cassette tape and on larger systems, a magnetic disc store.

So, to summarise, the main elements of a computer system are illustrated in Figure 3.

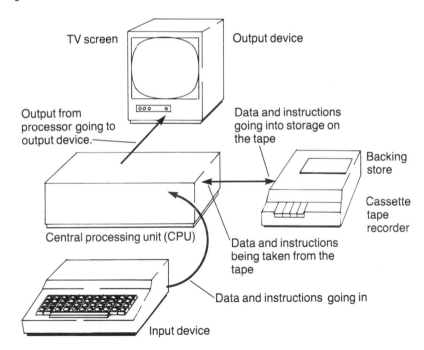

TV screen

Output device

Output from processor going to output device.

Data and instructions going into storage on the tape

Backing store

Cassette tape recorder

Central processing unit (CPU)

Data and instructions being taken from the tape

Data and instructions going in

Input device

Figure 3   A typical computer system

1.3 What is BASIC?

A computer is an electronic device which processes patterns of electrical signals. If you had a problem, you wouldn't be able to feed it into the computer as electrical signals. Nor, if the computer was ready to give you an output, would you be able to understand it if it came as electrical signals. So the computer has a machine code inside it (put there by the manufacturer) to enable it to understand a programming code that you can understand. Machine codes are called low-level programming languages and correspond directly with the patterns of electrical signals in the computer. For obvious reasons, this program is called an interpreter. This course teaches you BASIC which is a high-level programming language. You will then be able to use BASIC to program any computer that contains a BASIC interpreter. BASIC, by the way, stands for Beginners' All-purpose Symbolic Instruction Code.

You may find it useful to note the sequence of events that is taking place when you program a computer.

1 You have a problem.
2 You break down the problem into steps which can be put into BASIC.
3 You write the program in BASIC.
4 You sit at a keyboard and enter your program into the computer.
5 The computer interprets your BASIC instructions into its own code and processes them.
6 The computer prints out the results in the form you specified in the program.

And that is all you need to know about what a computer is. From now on we will assume that all you want to do is to give the computer problems and to get back results so now let's move on to a simple problem which we might want to give to a computer.

1.4 A simple problem

The main activity of programming is breaking down the solution to a problem into simple steps which can be represented by BASIC programming statements.

Imagine that you are playing the part of a computer with a young child. The child might give you two numbers and ask you to tell him their sum. After a short time the child will naturally try you out with large numbers which you cannot add in your head, so you will have to have a paper and pencil at hand. The following could be a typical dialogue.

CHILD: 'Start'
YOU: 'Give me the first number'
CHILD '12 157'
(You write this number on a piece of paper)
YOU: 'Give me the second number'
CHILD: '7 896'
(You write the second number on the piece of paper)
(You perform the addition sum)
YOU: '20 053'

We could describe the computer's part in this process more formally in the following way:

1 Input the first number
2 Input the second number
3 Add the two numbers
4 Output the result

Figure 4   Computer processes in adding two numbers

By this simple analogy we have arrived at a strategy for solving this problem. Broadly speaking, phases 1 and 2 would be concerned with entering numbers into the computer, phase 3 would involve a process in the central processing unit, while phase 4 would involve the output device.

Now, although we have not taught you any BASIC programming yet, we are going to show you what the problem solving sequence would look like when written in BASIC.

Example 1
Write a BASIC program to enter two numbers into the computer and to output their sum.

Solution
We have already worked out an intuitive procedure to solve this problem in Figure 4. A program in BASIC would have the following form.*

```
10   INPUT FIRST
20   INPUT SECOND
30   LET SUM = FIRST+SECOND
40   PRINT SUM
50   END†
```
Program 1

We do not wish to concentrate on the details of the program at this stage, but hope that you can see, without stretching the imagination too far, how the strategy from Figure 4 has been changed into a program. A program then is a 'sequence of instructions composed for solving a given problem by computer'.

SAQ 1
We now come to the first point in the course at which we want you to check your progress through trying this Self-Assessment Question (SAQ). The SAQs are designed to help you find out whether or not you have understood the immediately preceding sections of the course. In each case, the answer to an SAQ appears at the end of the Unit in which the SAQ occurs. If you get all the answers right, just move onto the next section. If you get any wrong, check back to see where you have gone wrong.

---

* You may wish to try the programs in this course on your own microcomputer but there will be complications on some machines until you reach Program 9 on page 19.

† END is not needed on all computers e.g. it may be omitted from programs on the BBC Computer.

Select those phrases from list B which complete correctly the phrases given in A.

A
1 The CPU . . .
2 The main characteristics of a computer system are . . .
3 A machine code is . . .
4 A machine code is an example of a . . . language.
5 BASIC is an example of a . . . language.
6 A BASIC interpreter . . .
7 A computer program is . . .

B
(a)   low-level
(b)   high-level
(c)   . . . holds data and instructions, controls its own processing, and controls the operation of input and output devices.
(d)   . . . a series of instructions or procedural steps for the solution of a specific problem.
(e)   . . . that it is capable of storing large quantities of data, is able to process this data very rapidly and lastly that it is able to store a program which controls its own operation.
(f)   . . . translates code written in BASIC into machine code.
(g)   . . . a code which corresponds directly with the electrical patterns within a computer.

1.5 Statement numbers

Let's have a closer look at Program 1 again:
10   INPUT FIRST
20   INPUT SECOND
30   LET SUM = FIRST+SECOND
40   PRINT SUM
50   END

Program 1 (from p11)

We have said that a program is a sequence of instructions. In the program above each line is an instruction. Thus:

10   INPUT FIRST

is the first instruction of the program, and

50   END

is the last. Instructions in a programming language are sometimes called statements. We will use the two words synonymously.

Entering statements
Until later in the course, we shall restrict ourselves to one instruction per line. When sitting at the keyboard of a micro, the actual process of entering a statement is completed only after the RETURN key has been pressed. So what happens is: You type 10 INPUT FIRST then press RETURN. Then you type 20 INPUT SECOND and press RETURN etc . . .

You see on the screen   10   INPUT FIRST
                           20   INPUT SECOND

You will have noticed that each line begins with a number. These must be whole numbers in the range 1–9999, and they determine the order in which the instructions are processed (executed), i.e. they define the 'sequence' of the instructions. The execution of the instructions starts with the line of the lowest number, and continues in the sense of increasing numbers until instructed otherwise, or until the end of the program is reached. (More about 'until instructed otherwise' and 'ending', later.)

Why then, you may ask, was the program not written as follows?

```
1  INPUT FIRST
2  INPUT SECOND
3  LET SUM = FIRST+SECOND
4  PRINT SUM
5  END                                          Program 2
```

Why not indeed! The program would have done the job perfectly well! However, as you will soon find out when writing programs you need a certain amount of flexibility. In particular you need the opportunity to slip into the program a statement which you have overlooked, or one which will allow you to make an important modification. Numbering our lines 10, 20, 30 and 40 leaves 9 empty lines between statements which may be used to correct or modify the program. When running, the processing proceeds to the next highest line number of the program, so the gap of 9 unused line numbers does not slow down the program execution in any way.

SAQ 2
Look at the line numbers in the following programs and decide which programs would produce a correct sum of FIRST and SECOND.

```
(a)   11  INPUT FIRST
      59  INPUT SECOND
      93  LET SUM = FIRST+SECOND
     401  PRINT SUM
     500  END

(b)   23  INPUT FIRST
      32  INPUT SECOND
      49  LET SUM = FIRST+SECOND
      40  PRINT SUM
      50  END

(c)   10  INPUT FIRST
      20  INPUT SECOND
      15  LET SUM = FIRST+SECOND
      40  PRINT SUM
      50  END

(d)  100  INPUT FIRST
```

```
200  INPUT SECOND
110  LET SUM = FIRST+SECOND
190  PRINT SUM
220  END
```

(e)   100 INPUT FIRST
       50   INPUT SECOND
       407 LET SUM = FIRST+SECOND
       902 PRINT SUM
       1000 END

Programs 3—7

1.6 Executions and commands

The command RUN

Execution? No, it's not the end but the beginning! Let's get on and run our first program before we get tired of it!

```
10  INPUT FIRST
20  INPUT SECOND
30  LET SUM = FIRST+SECOND
40  PRINT SUM
50  END
```
Program 1 (from p11)

And what happens? Nothing. This is because the computor is waiting for us to give instructions to the program as a whole. If you want to execute this program, you must give it the command RUN. This you put on a new line as follows:

```
10  INPUT FIRST
20  INPUT SECOND
30  LET SUM = FIRST+SECOND
40  PRINT SUM
50  END
RUN
```
Program 1 (from p11)

(Don't worry about RUN not having a line number – we'll explain that shortly.)

Then press RET (RETURN on some machines). You will then see ? on the screen which is the computer's way of asking for data. Give it your first number; then press RET; another ? appears because the computer needs your second number. Give it the second number and press RET The answer should now appear. Here is our version of this run:

```
10  INPUT FIRST
20  INPUT SECOND
30  LET SUM = FIRST+SECOND
40  PRINT SUM
50  END
RUN
? 12157
```

? 7896
20053

>READY

Figure 5   A complete run of a program

What we are doing therefore is to distinguish between the entry of a program and its execution. Let's go back to the dialogue between you and the child playing computers. A very explicit infant may have said 'I am going to give you two numbers, I want you to write them down, add them together, and then tell me their sum'. At this point you know exactly what to do, but you haven't yet done anything. You've got the instructions though, you've been programmed. The dialogue may proceed thus:

CHILD: 'Start'
YOU: 'Give me the first number'.
CHILD: '12157'
YOU: 'Give me the second number'.
CHILD: '7896'
YOU: '20053'

Now these instructions have been carried out (run). A program then is just a set of instructions for the computer. When the program is run or executed these instructions are carried out.

Other commands: LIST, SAVE, LOAD
RUN is not the only command which you can give to a program as a whole. You can also use LIST, SAVE and LOAD as follows.

LIST
For example, you may spend quite a lot of time typing a program into your machine and during that process make several corrections. You may then wish to see a fair copy of the program as a whole on the screen. If you type the word LIST, a complete copy of the program in line number order will appear on the screen.

SAVE
Having developed a program to a satisfactory stage you may wish to take a copy of it on to tape or disc; the word SAVE will do this for you. (Your computer will, of course, have to be connected to a back-up store such as a cassette tape recorder.)

LOAD
Later you may wish to use one of your stored programs; the command LOAD will enter the program from your back-up store back into your computer.

Words like LIST, RUN, SAVE and LOAD which allow us to handle the program as a single entity are called commands and are provided by the BASIC interpreter. A command occupies a line on its own and generally does not have a line number, e.g. the word RUN after line 50 causes the program to start to execute, and is equivalent to the child's command 'start' in the dialogue above. Commands will be discussed in greater detail in a later unit, but the four that we have already looked at will allow us to get by for a start.

15

Computer response
After a command has been successfully carried out the interpreter informs the user of this fact by writing a message on the screen, e.g.

READY
or >READY
or OK
or **K** (not to be confused with our K in this course).

Keywords
These are the BASIC words which go in the program to specify what action is to occur. e.g. INPUT, PRINT, LET.

1.7 Execution and data

You will have realised that we have written a program which will add any two numbers in a quite general way, for it is immaterial to the program what numbers we enter when we receive prompts ? on the screen. As the computer executes the program it must be able to request that we input actual numbers for its particular task, i.e. it must have the facility to demand specific data to do the job in hand. You need to be able to distinguish clearly between the program, as a set of more or less general instructions, and the data which are the actual numbers which must be input when the program is executing, in order to solve a particular problem. You can, of course, run your program repeatedly with many pairs of numbers, as you will see later.

Another way of looking at these instructions is to visualize the situation as an umpire gathers the runners at the start of a race in order to give them certain instructions: 'Go down the right-hand side of the field to the furthest corner, over the stile and turn left down the lane . . .' The umpire's instructions are analogous to a program. If the runners understand what he is saying then they know what to do; but they are still at the starting line. They haven't actually started. This is analogous to the program having been entered into the machine. Then the umpire says 'Go!' and the race starts. This is analogous to the computer starting to execute the program. Let's extend the analogy and consider the cross-country race as a novelty race. Imagine that the umpire did not give enough instructions for the runners to complete the course but he said something like 'When you get to the bottom of the lane you will find further instructions pinned to the oak tree . . .' These instructions should be sufficient to guide the runners over the next part of the course, i.e. on to the next clue, and so on until the end of the race. These clues are analogous to giving the program more data during the course of its execution. This analogy may help you to see the important distinction between entering a program into the machine, executing the program, and then inputting data during the course of its execution.

SAQ 3
Below is a print out from a computer. It contains keywords, commands, responses from the system and items of data. It also contains sections that are concerned with entry, execution and listing. Identify as many of these items as possible as follows:

16

Mark keywords with   K
Mark commands with   C
Mark system responses with R
Mark data items with   D
Bracket lines concerned with entry
Bracket lines concerned with execution
Bracket lines concerned with list

```
10  INPUT FIRST
20  INPUT SECOND
30  LET SUM = FIRST+SECOND
40  PRINT SUM
50  END
RUN
?  -37
?  -46
-83

>READY
LIST

10  INPUT FIRST
20  INPUT SECOND
30  LET SUM = FIRST+SECOND
40  PRINT SUM
50  END

>READY
RUN
?  12.83
?  48.95
 61.78
```

Program 1 (from p11)

1.8 INPUT, PRINT and LET

You have seen that a program is a sequence of statements, and we have given you an intuitive idea of how each statement works. You may also have noticed that each of the three types of statement used so far (INPUT, LET and PRINT) corresponds to one of the three main devices which comprise the computer system (input, central processor and output devices). We will now look at each statement in more detail.

INPUT

The word INPUT is a signal to the computer that during execution, an item of data must be entered at the input device. We saw this happen when we ran our first program: after the ? we entered 12157, pressed RETURN to complete the input procedure and then found ourselves confronted by another ? requesting the input of the next number. What, then, happened to 12157, the first item of data? The answer is that it has been stored for later use in the program's execution in the storage location labelled FIRST. The word FIRST has two main functions in the program, (a) when written and later referred to by the programmer it reminds him that at this point in the program the first item of data should be input, and (b) when written in the statement 10 INPUT FIRST the word FIRST is the name or label of a location in the computer's memory. So 10 INPUT FIRST means enter a number at the input device and store it in the location labelled FIRST .

PRINT

The statement 40 PRINT SUM has almost the reverse effect to statements 10 and 20, in that it allows us to output information from the machine. It is a signal to the machine to take a copy of the contents of the store location labelled SUM and pass it to the output device which for most users of this course will be a television screen. Notice that PRINT will literally result in a printed output if a printer is attached to your microcomputer but you still use the command PRINT when your microcomputer is attached to a television set for its output device.

LET

30 LET SUM = FIRST+SECOND is an example of an assignment statement. It is in this type of statement that the processing takes place. As you can see, it is a mixture of store names (SUM, FIRST, SECOND) and arithmetic operators (= and +). If you read it forwards, it says

> Let the store location SUM be made equal to the contents of the location FIRST added to the contents of the location named SECOND.

However, like many mathematical expressions, it is often clearer when read from right to left of the '=' as follows

> Add the contents of the location FIRST to the contents of the location SECOND and store the result in the location labelled SUM.

Generally the assignment statement has the form:
LET store location name = expression.

This means find the value of the expression of the right-hand side of the '=' and store this value in the store location named on the left-hand side of the '='.

The tricky point about LET . . . = . . . is that it is easily confused with . . . = . . . in mathematical equations. An example will demonstrate the difference. Suppose you have stored a number in location L and you want to make the number in that store 5 greater than it now is. You write:

LET L = L+5

Now obviously this doesn't mean:

L = L+5

since there is no value for L which could make this true. What it does mean is that the computer has added 5 to the number that is in store location L.

18

1.9 Store locations

As we have already said, one of the main characteristics of a computer system is its capacity for storing large quantities of data. We must now consider how the BASIC language allows us to allocate store location names. If you look at our first program and recall that a computer is capable of only doing one thing at a time, it is fairly obvious that when we reach line 20 and wish to input our second number, the number that we entered in line 10 must have been stored somewhere! In this case the first number was stored in the location labelled FIRST. We can think of the storage locations as being like a set of pigeon-holes where we distinguish clearly between the label or address or name on each pigeon-hole and the contents of the hole.

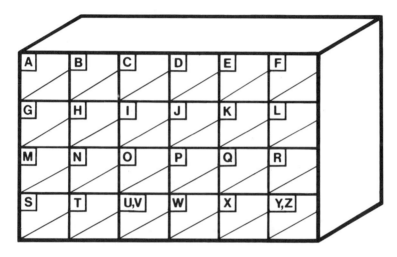

Figure 6   A model of the store locations in a very small computer

You will see that in our model of possible store locations we have used the labels A, B, C . . . On the other hand, in the program we have been studying we have used words of up to six characters to label our stores, e.g. FIRST, SECOND. This brings us to our first major point of difference between the interpreters for the various micro-computers now available. Some BASIC interpreters allow a much wider range of storage names than others. Some machines limit your variable name to a few characters. Others allow longer variable names or even names of unrestricted length. The BBC machine allows variable names of unlimited length.

Choosing store location names
Clearly it makes life a lot easier for the programmer if he chooses store location names which remind him of what he is storing. That is why we chose FIRST, SECOND and SUM. We could have used A, B and S so that our program would have been:

```
10   INPUT A
20   INPUT B
30   LET S = A+B
```

```
40   PRINT S
50   END
```

Program 9

K When you see this symbol it means we suggest you try this program on your own microcomputer if you have one. To do this, key in the lines, press RET and then press RUN. Your computer will ask you for a number. Give it one and press RET. It then asks you for the second number. Give it the second number, press RET and the sum will appear on your screen.

If we had done this, then after inputting 12157 and 7896, the store locations would be:

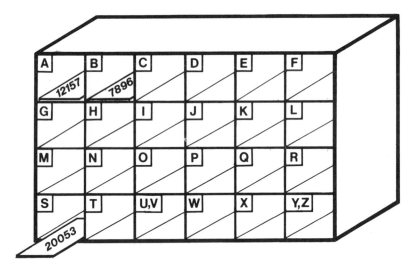

Figure 7   State of the store locations after Program 9.

The common system of location names
Since long store location names are not available on many microcomputers, we will, from now on, use the system of location names that works on practically every microcomputer until we come to lists in a later unit. The system we shall use labels a location by a capital letter by itself or a capital letter followed by a digit. This gives us 286 possible locations as shown in Figure 8.

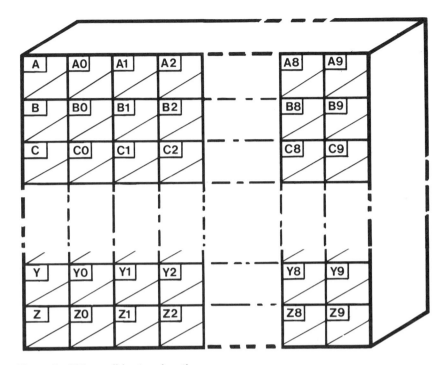

Figure 8   286 possible store locations

1.10 Copying and overwriting

BASIC statements can have two different effects on the contents of a store location. Or rather a statement can either have no effect on the contents of the location or it can change the contents. This is illustrated below.

Effect of copying

Suppose we have the number 53 stored in location A. What happens after LET B = A and after PRINT A? In each case A still stores the number 53 after the statement has been executed:

Before	Statement executed	After

STORE   STORE

53 A	B	C
D	E	F

LET B = A

53 A	53 B	C
D	E	F

| | Before | Statement executed | After | Monitor |

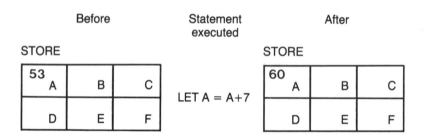

STORE

53 A	B	C
D	E	F

PRINT A

STORE

53 A	B	C
D	E	F

53

In each case the copying statements leave the original store location unchanged. It's just like getting a statement of your bank account: the piece of paper copies your account but your account still has your money in it!

Effect of overwriting

Suppose now that we still have the number 53 stored in location A but this time execute the statement LET A = A+7. The result is:

| | Before | Statement executed | After |

STORE

53 A	B	C
D	E	F

LET A = A+7

STORE

60 A	B	C
D	E	F

The statement LET A = A+7 overwrites the contents of A. That is, the original contents disappears and is replaced by the new contents, which is in this case, 60. Of course we could have made the new contents of A to be 60 in many ways, e.g. by, say: LET A = 60.

SAQ 4

Which of the following are valid store location names for numbers, according to the rules given on pages 20–21.

(a) N3
(b) 3N
(c) W10
(d) B#
(e) QJ
(f) M
(g) M5
(h) M-5
(i) M+5
(j) U0

Give reasons for discarding those names which you reject.

1.11 Arithmetic operators

When you do arithmetic you use four main operators: +, −, × and ÷. BASIC has the same operators, although two are printed differently:

Every day symbol	Meaning	BASIC symbol
+	add	+
−	subtract	−
×	multiply	★
÷	divide	/

SAQ 5

Write the following expressions using BASIC symbols for the arithmetic operators. (Where the expressions use brackets, leave the brackets in your answers.)

(a) 3+7   (e) 30÷(3+2)
(b) 3×7   (f) 24−(4×3)
(c) 8÷4   (g) 5×6×7
(d) 5×(2+8)   (h) 81−(27×2)

SAQ 6

If A has the value of 2, B has the value of 5 and C has the value of 10, calculate the values of the following:

(a) A+B+C   (e) C/(B−A)
(b) A★B   (f) A★A
(c) A★B★C   (g) (B★C)/(B−A)
(d) C/A   (h) (C−B)★(C+B)

The arithmetic is actually done (executed) in BASIC through assignment statements (LET statements) which tell the computer's arithmetic unit (part of the central processor) what to do. We can illustrate this with the following computer model.

Effect of LET A = B−C   STORE AT START

A	15 B	10 C
D	E	F

LET A = B−C

Remember to read this from the right to the left of the "=" sign. It says take the number in location B, subtract from it the number in location C and put the result in location A. So the result is:

Result of LET A = B−C   STORE AT FINISH

Notice that the contents of B and C are unchanged.

5 A	15 B	10 C
D	E	F

Effect of LET A = B★C

STORE AT START

A	15 B	10 C
D	E	F

STORE AT FINISH

150 A	15 B	10 C
D	E	F

SAQ 7
Fill in the values in the store locations A, B and C after each line has been executed in these programs.

1. Program

    10 LET A = 12

    20 LET B = 5

    30 LET C = A★(A+B)

    40 LET A = A+10

Store location values

A	B	C
□	□	□
□	□	□
□	□	□
□	□	□

2. Program

    10 LET A = 20

    20 LET B = A★3

    30 LET C = A/4

    40 LET A = B+C

Store location values

A	B	C
□	□	□
□	□	□
□	□	□
□	□	□

What you have just done isn't (we hope) difficult and it doesn't get any more difficult when we move on to more complicated store location names. We have to make the names more complicated because A, B, C . . . only gives us 26 stores and, as we said on page 21, we are going to use location names A, A0, A1, etc. So,

LET P4 = Q1★R1

is no different from LET A = B★C. P4, Q1 and R1 are simply store location names. P4 is one name, just as XYZ 823A is one car number.

We are now ready to use the arithmetic capacity of a computer.

Example 2

Write a BASIC program to enter two numbers into the computer and then output their sum, difference, product and quotient.

Solution

This may look complicated but we've really solved this already. We had a program (*Program 9*) to output the sum of two numbers, so to output their difference, product and quotient, we only need to change the arithmetic operator in line 30 which reads

30 LET SUM = FIRST+SECOND

First, however, we will rewrite the program using the shorter store location names:

Original version	**New version**
10 INPUT FIRST	10 INPUT N1
20 INPUT SECOND	20 INPUT N2
30 LET SUM = FIRST+SECOND	30 LET S = N1+N2
40 PRINT SUM	40 PRINT S
50 END	50 END

Program 10

Now what we need is three extra versions of the new version, each with a different line 30:

10 INPUT N1 20 INPUT N2 30 LET S = N1+N2 40 PRINT S	" " " " " D = N1−N2 " D	" " " " " P = N1★N2 " P	" " " " " Q = N1/N2 " Q

(Using D for the location for difference, P for the location for product and Q for the location for quotient.)

Do we need to write four programs? Fortunately no, because when we copy the numbers from locations N1 and N2, we don't destroy these contents so we can use them four times over in one program:

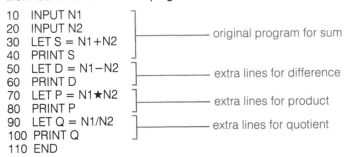

```
10   INPUT N1
20   INPUT N2             ┐
30   LET S = N1+N2        ├────────── original program for sum
40   PRINT S              ┘
50   LET D = N1−N2        ┐
60   PRINT D              ├────────── extra lines for difference
70   LET P = N1★N2        ┐
80   PRINT P              ├────────── extra lines for product
90   LET Q = N1/N2        ┐
100  PRINT Q              ├────────── extra lines for quotient
110  END                  ┘
```

Program 11   Sum, difference, product and quotient of two numbers

K Key Program 11 into your microcomputer. Then key RUN and input two numbers. A typical print out should look like:

```
RUN
? 57.82
? 19.11
  76.93
  38.71
1104.94
3.02564

>READY
```

1.12 Numerical constants

Earlier in this unit we saw that our first BASIC program was capable of manipulating whole, decimal and negative numbers. At this stage we won't go into detail on how numbers are represented in BASIC, but just show you that we can use numbers directly in assignment statements.

The statement LET P = 427★R means create the number 427, multiply it by the number found in store location R and then store the result in location P. (Don't be put off by thinking that computers only handle binary numbers. The computer's interpreter enables us to input ordinary decimal numbers.)

Similarly, the statement LET Y4 = 3.142+Z8 creates the number 3.142 and adds it to the contents of location Z8, and then stores the sum in location Y4.

And the statement LET A = −48.93/B creates the number −48.93 and divides it by the number found in location B and then stores the result of this calculation in location A.

Exercise preamble
Progress in metrication has been slow and life still abounds with irritating little conversions which occasionally tease us, e.g. pounds weight to kilogrammes, yards to metres, pints to litres, a knitting pattern with balls of wool in ounces which must be bought in grammes, etc. . . . If we go on holiday we mentally convert kilometres into miles, and pounds sterling into other currency. Most of us still think of body and weather temperatures in terms of degrees Fahrenheit rather than Centigrade or Celsius. We can imagine the home microcomputer of the future having a general conversion program in it which will do all these diverse conversions for us. The next two exercises are on writing programs to do conversions. You only need the ideas introduced in the earlier programs in this Unit.

Exercise 1
Write programs in BASIC to carry out each of the following conversions:
(a)   Input a number representing a length in inches, and output this length in centimetres, given that one inch is equivalent to 2.54 centimetres.
(b)   Input a number representing a weight in ounces, and output that weight in grammes, given that one ounce is equivalent to 28.375 grammes.
(Answers to Exercises appear at the end of each unit with the SAQ answers.)

Exercise 2

Any conversion involves 'conversion factor × number to be converted' so it is possible to write a general conversion program where you input two numbers each time you use it: the conversion factor and the number to be converted. Write a general conversion program which will do this.

1.13 The remark statement: REM

The statement REM is the remark statement. It allows us to give a title to a program or make some other meaningful remark about the program. For example, within the body of a program it helps us identify what the program or section of the program does. The REM statement is not executed by the computer and is there purely for the benefit of either the programmer or user, i.e. when the computer sees REM at the beginning of a line it ignores everything on that line. The next program is concerned with calculating percentages and so as a title to the program our first statement will be 10 REM ★★PERCENTAGE CALCULATION★★. (The ★★ have no function other than to emphasise the title.)

Example 3

Write a BASIC program to input two numbers and output the second as a percentage of the first.

Reminder   Percentage = (second÷first)×100.

Solution

```
10   REM★★PERCENTAGE CALCULATION★★   (program title using
                                      REM statement)
20   INPUT F
30   INPUT S
40   LET P = (S/F)★100
50   PRINT P
60   END
```
Program 12 Percentage calculation

Typical runs

```
RUN
? 57
? 74
 129.825

>READY
RUN
? 74
? 57
 77.027

>READY
```

K Program 12.

1.14 More complicated arithmetic

We have reached the stage when we can use the computer like a simple four-function calculating machine, but we will soon wish to do slightly more complicated arithmetic. Generally BASIC allows us to set out equations in a familiar way. We can use brackets, i.e. ( ) to group together certain values, and when BASIC evaluates an expression it deals with the values *inside* the brackets first. Next come values involving multiplication or division and finally, addition and subtraction.

This order of preference for performing arithmetic operations is discussed more fully in a later unit, but you will soon see that this order just formalises the way we naturally go about arithmetic calculations.

Let's show you what we mean.

Example 4
Write the following expressions in BASIC:

1. $ab+c$ 2. $a(b+c)$ 3. $\dfrac{a}{b+c}$

Solutions
1. A★B+C
    The order of precedence rules tell us that A★B will be evaluated first and the C added. If you were worried about this you could write (A★B)+C but the brackets aren't essential here.
2. A★(B+C)
    Notice that, just as a bracket is needed in a(b+c) so it is needed in A★(B+C).
3. A/(B+C)

Now try some for yourself.

SAQ 8
Write the following as BASIC expressions:
1. abc
2. $\dfrac{ab}{c}$
3. $\dfrac{a+b}{c}$

Exercise 3
Now that you have written the expressions in SAQ 8 as BASIC expressions, write a program that will allow you to input three numbers (A, B and C) and print out the values of the expressions in SAQ 8.

1.15 Literal printing

You have seen already that we can print out the values from store locations. You will find as the course progresses that the PRINT function is very versatile. One use of this statement is to print messages on the monitor screen which will be helpful to the user when the program is running. These messages are usually referred to as prompts. We have seen already that when an input statement is encountered during the execution of a program, a ? appears on the screen to remind us that an input is required. In even slightly complicated programs, a series of question marks on the screen is confusing to the user since he may not know which input value the question mark is prompting. Prompts generated by PRINT statements are very useful in these circumstances.

It is very easy to get a computer to print a reminder or message on the screen. All you need is a line such as:

20   PRINT "MESSAGE"

This simply prints

MESSAGE

on your screen.

In other words, whatever appears between quotes thus " " after the word PRINT will be printed out exactly as it stands. Notice that, as in the case of the REM statement, the computer doesn't execute the words in the quotes. Thus

20   PRINT "A+B"

results in

A+B

on your screen and the computer does not add the value in location A to the value in location B.

The following example demonstrates the use of PRINT " " to remind the programmer and user of what the program is doing.

Example 5
Write a BASIC program to convert a temperature value given in degrees C into degrees F.
Remember $°F = \frac{9}{5} \times °C + 32$

Solution
```
10   REM★★CENTIGRADE TO FAHRENHEIT★★
20   PRINT"ENTER NEXT TEMP IN DEGREES C"
30   INPUT C
40   LET F = (9/5)★C+32
50   PRINT"THIS TEMP IN DEGREES F IS"
60   PRINT F
70   END
```
print message precedes input statement so that the message is printed before ? appears

Program 13   Temperature conversion

Typical run

```
RUN
ENTER NEXT TEMP IN DEGREES C
? 16
THIS TEMP IN DEGREES F IS
  60.8

>READY
```

K Program 13.

Assignment 1

NEC students: your solution to this assignment should be sent to your NEC tutor for marking. If you own your own microcomputer, write your own assignment in the BASIC for that computer and tell your tutor what make of microcomputer it is. FlexiStudy students: complete the assignments according to the instructions given to you by your FlexiStudy centre.

Remember to make good use of remark and literal print statements when writing your programs.

1.   If you deposit £D in an account paying P% rate of interest for one year, then the yield at the end of the first year is given by the equation

$$Y = D \times \frac{P}{100}$$

(a)   Write a BASIC program to input values for D and P and to output the yield, Y.
(b)   If the original deposit together with the accrued interest is left in the account for a further year at the same rate of interest then the compound interest after the second year will be given by the equation

$$C = (D+Y) \times \frac{P}{100}$$

Extend your program for (a) to calculate and output this compound interest.

2.   Consider the problem of estimating the cost of installing replacement aluminium double glazed windows. The windows comprise 3 parts:

(a) a hardwood surround, (b) aluminium frame and (c) glass. If the height of the window is H metres and the width is W metres, then the total lengths of both hardwood and aluminium required are given approximately by the expression (2H+2W) metres; and the area of glass required by the expression (H×W) square metres.

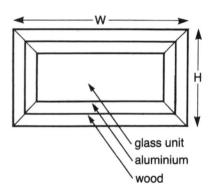

glass unit
aluminium
wood

Figure 9

Write three separate BASIC programs which, on being given values for height and width in metres, will output the cost of
(a)   the hardwood surround if the wood costs £3 per metre;
(b)   the aluminium surround if the aluminium costs £4 per metre;
(c)   the glass unit if the glass unit costs £40 per square metre.

Now link these three into one program to estimate and output the total cost of installation, if the labour cost is £50 per window.

Objectives of Unit 1
Now that you have completed this Unit, check that you are able to:

Write simple programs using:
Line numbers ☐
INPUT ☐
LET ☐
PRINT ☐
Store locations identified by a single letter or a letter followed by a single digit ☐
Copying from one location to another ☐
Overwriting ☐
$+, -, \star, /$ ☐
( ) ☐
Numerical constants ☐
REM ☐
PRINT " " ☐

Know when to use:
RET ☐
RUN ☐

Know how to respond to:
>READY ☐
?, >, etc. ☐

Answers to SAQ's and Exercises

SAQ 1

A	B
1	(c)
2	(e)
3	(g)
4	(a)
5	(b)
6	(f)
7	(d)

SAQ 2
(a) and (e) would run as Program 1.
(b) is asked to print SUM before SUM has been calculated.
(c) and (d) are asked to calculate SUM before SECOND has been inputted.

SAQ 3

```
            (K)
     10  INPUT FIRST
     20  INPUT SECOND          ]
     30  LET SUM = FIRST+SECOND   entry
     40  PRINT SUM             ]
  C── 50  END
  C── RUN
  R── ? −37────────────────────D ]
```

31

```
R ——— ? −46 ————————————————————— D  ⎤
       −83 ————————————————————————— R  ⎦  execution

R ——— >READY
C ——— LIST        (K)
       10  INPUT FIRST                          ⎤
       20  INPUT SECOND                         ⎥
       30  LET SUM = FIRST+SECOND               ⎥  listing
       40  PRINT SUM                            ⎥
K ——— 50  END                                   ⎦

R ——— >READY
C ——— RUN
R ——— ? 12.83 ————————————————————— D  ⎤
R ——— ? 48.95 ————————————————————— D  ⎥  execution
       61.78 ————————————————————————— R  ⎦

R ——— >READY
C ——— RUN
R ——— ? 17.0009 ——————————————————— D  ⎤
R ——— ? −29.2629 —————————————————— D  ⎥  execution
       −12.362 ——————————————————————— R  ⎦

R ——— >READY
```

(Have you noticed that this program has coped with negative and decimal fractional numbers?)

SAQ 4

(a) OK
(b) No, begins with a digit instead of a letter.
(c) Not allowed on all systems. (10 is two digits, not 1 as in, say, W8.)
(d) No, # is not an acceptable symbol in a variable name.
(e) No, uses two letters. (This will, of course, work on some machines.)
(f) OK
(g) OK
(h) No, '-' is not an acceptable symbol.
(i) No, '+' is not an acceptable symbol.
(j) OK

SAQ 5

(a) 3+7   (b) 3★7   (c) 8/4   (d) 5★(2+8)   (e) 30/(3+2)
(f) 24−(4★3)   (g) 5★6★7   (h) 81−(27★2)

SAQ 6

(a) 17   (b) 10   (c) 100   (d) 5   (e) 10/3 or 3⅓ or 3.33 . . .
(f) 4   (g) 50/3 or 16⅔ or 16.66 . . .   (h) 75

SAQ 7

1.

12		
12	5	

2.

20		
20	60	

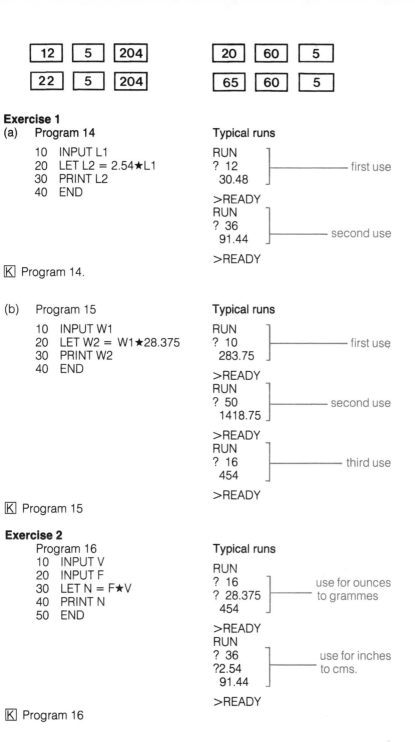

| 12 | 5 | 204 |

| 22 | 5 | 204 |

| 20 | 60 | 5 |

| 65 | 60 | 5 |

Exercise 1
(a)   Program 14

```
10   INPUT L1
20   LET L2 = 2.54★L1
30   PRINT L2
40   END
```

Ⓚ Program 14.

Typical runs

```
RUN
? 12
  30.48
```
——— first use

```
>READY
RUN
? 36
  91.44
```
——— second use

```
>READY
```

(b)   Program 15

```
10   INPUT W1
20   LET W2 = W1★28.375
30   PRINT W2
40   END
```

Ⓚ Program 15

Typical runs

```
RUN
? 10
  283.75
```
——— first use

```
>READY
RUN
? 50
  1418.75
```
——— second use

```
>READY
RUN
? 16
  454
```
——— third use

```
>READY
```

Exercise 2
```
Program 16
10   INPUT V
20   INPUT F
30   LET N = F★V
40   PRINT N
50   END
```

Ⓚ Program 16

Typical runs

```
RUN
? 16
? 28.375
  454
```
use for ounces to grammes

```
>READY
RUN
? 36
?2.54
  91.44
```
use for inches to cms.

```
>READY
```

SAQ 8

1.   A★B★C
2.   A★B/C [(A★B)/C is also correct]
3.   (A+B)/C

Exercise 3

Program 17

```
10   INPUT A
20   INPUT B
30   INPUT C
40   LET R = A★B★C ⎤———— calculates first expression and prints it out
50   PRINT R        ⎦
60   LET R = (A★B)/C ⎤———— calculates second expression and prints it out
70   PRINT R         ⎦
80   LET R = (A+B)/C ⎤———— calculates third expression and prints it out
90   PRINT R         ⎦
100  END
```

Notice that we can use R as the location for all three answers because we copy (print out) each answer in turn before we overwrite with the next answer.

Typical runs

```
RUN              RUN
? 13             ? 13
? −27            ? 13
? 55.2           ? 13
−19375.1         2197
−6.3587          13
−.253623         2

READY            READY
```

K Program 17

UNIT 2
Making decisions

2.1 Introduction

The programs which we considered in Unit 1 were quite straightforward. They started their processing at the statement with the lowest number and continued in line number order until execution finished at the line with the highest line number. One thing that computers are very good at is lots of repetitive calculations; another is their ability to make decisions. Both of these features involve changing the sequence in which a program is executed. This Unit will introduce you to some of the statements which enable you to write programs of this type. But first we are going to introduce you to a new type of PRINT statement.

2.2 PRINT . . . ,

In Unit 1 we wrote a program (Example 3) to output one number as a percentage of another. On the screen, the calculation and result appeared in the format:

```
RUN
? 57
? 74
 129.825
```

Obviously it would be better if the answer included the word Percentage so that it was clearer what was happening. This can easily be done by changing line 50 from 50 PRINT P to

```
50   PRINT "PERCENTAGE", P
```

The effect of this is:

Version of line 50	Result on screen
50 PRINT P	129.825
50 PRINT "PERCENTAGE", P	PERCENTAGE 129.825

The statement PRINT "PERCENTAGE", P has four items in it.

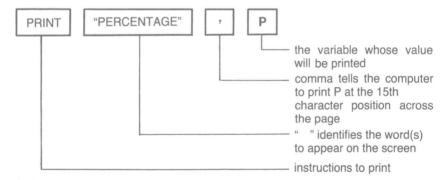

We can use PRINT . . ., to improve the percentage program from Unit 1. At the same time we can improve the appearance of the program by making use of the literal print statement PRINT "   " which we introduced in section 1.15.

Original program

```
10  REM★★PERCENTAGE CALCULATION★★.
20  INPUT F
30  INPUT S
40  LET P = (S/F)★100
50  PRINT P
60  END
```

New program

```
10  REM★★PERCENTAGE★★
20  PRINT "INPUT THE FIRST NUMBER"
30  INPUT F
40  PRINT "INPUT THE SECOND NUMBER"
50  INPUT S
60  LET P = (S/F)★100
70  PRINT "PERCENTAGE",P
80  END
```

Program 1 Improved percentage program

Original program: typical run

```
RUN
? 80
? 37
   46.25
```

New program: typical run

```
RUN
INPUT THE FIRST NUMBER ──────── effect of line 20
? 80
INPUT THE SECOND NUMBER ─────── effect of line 40
? 37
PERCENTAGE          46.25 ───── effect of line 70
```

        └──────── 16th position

        └──────── 15th position reserved for
                  '−' sign with numbers

Notice how the use of literal print at lines 20 and 40, together with PRINT " ", makes the program much more friendly and understandable when in use.
K̲ Program 1.

Commas in PRINT statements
You can use more commas in print statements to space out your results on the screen. BASIC usually has 5 print zones across the screen:* (see p 38):

72 characters

Zone 1	Zone 2	Zone 3	Zone 4	Zone 5
0 to 14	15 to 29	30 to 44	45 to 59	60 to 71

Each successive comma in the print line moves the item after it one zone to the right. Thus

PRINT "ZONE 1", "ZONE 2", "ZONE 3"

results in

ZONE 1   ZONE 2   ZONE 3

and

PRINT "PERCENTAGE", P gave PERCENTAGE   46.25

whereas

PRINT "PERCENTAGE" P would give PERCENTAGE 46.25†

SAQ 1
What would appear on the screen as a result of these print lines?
(Assume A=48, B=8, C=6 in these questions.)
(a)   PRINT "AREA" A
(b)   PRINT "LENGTH" B, "WIDTH" C, "AREA" A
(c)   PRINT "LENGTH", "WIDTH", "AREA"
      PRINT B, C, A

Write PRINT lines in BASIC which would print on the screen the following words in the zones shown:

	Zone 1	Zone 2	Zone 3	Zone 4
(d)	LENGTH	8	WIDTH	6
(e)	LENGTH	8		
	WIDTH	6		
	AREA	48		
(f)	LENGTH	WIDTH		AREA

2.3 Repetitions and GOTO

Suppose now that you wanted to use Program 1 to calculate all the percentages for a test taken by a whole class of pupils. You would have to use the program over and over again, starting at RUN each time, e.g.:

```
>READY
RUN
INPUT THE FIRST NUMBER
? 80
INPUT THE SECOND NUMBER
```

*The BBC Computer has four print zones of 10 characters each so its text spacing using commas will look slightly different from these examples.
†But not on the BBC Computer. To print the value of P next to PERCENTAGE you insert ';'.
Thus PRINT "PERCENTAGE"; P on the BBC Computer is the same as PRINT "PERCEN-TAGE" P on most other computers.

```
? 42
PERCENTAGE         52.5

>READY
RUN
INPUT THE FIRST NUMBER
? 80
INPUT THE SECOND NUMBER
? 19
PERCENTAGE         23.75

>READY
```

Figure 1   Repeated use of percentage program

It would be much easier if, after the computer has calculated the first percentage, it went back to the beginning of its calculation and asked us for the next mark. This we can make it do using the statement

GOTO line number

which redirects the program to whichever line number we insert. Here is the percentage program re-written in this way:

```
10   REM★MARKS INTO PERCENTAGES★
20   PRINT "INPUT THE TOTAL POSSIBLE MARKS"
30   INPUT T
40   PRINT "INPUT THE NEXT MARK"
50   INPUT M
60   LET P=(M/T)★100
70   PRINT"PERCENTAGE",P
80   GOTO 40
```
Program 2 Percentage program for repeated use

Notice the new lines 20 and 30 which ensure that we only have to enter the maximum mark on the test once. The calculation is carried out in lines 50 to 70 and, in reading line 80, the program returns to line 40 to ask us for another mark. A typical run is:

```
RUN
INPUT THE TOTAL POSSIBLE MARKS
? 80
INPUT THE NEXT MARK
? 42
PERCENTAGE         52.5
INPUT THE NEXT MARK
? 67
PERCENTAGE         83.75
INPUT THE NEXT MARK
? 19
```

```
PERCENTAGE      23.75
? 55
PERCENTAGE      68.75
INPUT THE NEXT MARK
?
```

The GOTO statement interrupts the program's normal execution in line number order. As soon as the program reads GOTO, it unconditionally transfers control to the line number in the statement. It is sometimes called an 'unconditional jump'.
Ⓚ Program 2. (Press ESCAPE – or equivalent – when you are fed up with it!)

SAQ 2
The following program squares numbers (i.e. multiplies a number by itself). Add a GOTO line to allow you to use the program over and over again to square successive numbers.

```
10  INPUT N
20  LET S = N★N
30  PRINT S
40  END
```
Program 3   Calculating squares

Ⓚ key and run lines 10 to 40.
Add your extra line and run your new program.

2.4 Programming style

The use of the GOTO statement helped in some ways. However, it still left some loose ends, such as the ? at the end of the run. On reaching line 80 in Program 2 control is always returned to line 40 which then generates the demand for a further input; hence the ?. The program then is locked in a perpetual loop from which it cannot escape. The only way to stop this program is to break out of it which is usually accomplished by pressing the control key together with another key on the keyboard on the microcomputer. (The way of breaking out of a program differs for each micro system and you will have to check up on how this may be accomplished for the particular micro system that you are using. Use ESCAPE on the BBC Computer.)

To have the execution of the program left as it were in mid-air is obviously bad style, but we will sort this out in a little while. More importantly, we ought to warn you of the dangers of using GOTO. As we have said, this statement allows you to jump or branch to virtually any position in the program, which may at this stage seem to be a useful facility. But because GOTO allows us to jump rather at random to any point in the program, it is often used in such a way that the logical structure of the solution is broken up by 'jumps of convenience' to other parts of the program rather than by following the logical structure of the analysis of the problem. We will, therefore, use the GOTO statement sparingly throughout this course. We shall only use it when we think that the clarity of the program will be marred if it is not used. We hope that you will also try and follow our example and use the GOTO statement as little as possible. Though we will avoid its indiscriminate use, you will find it more widely used in some text-books and computer magazines.

2.5 IF ... THEN ...

The problem that we have just left is how to signal to the computer that we have reached the end of the list of marks. When doing a manual calculation, we can see that we have reached the end, or, if not, we would have carried out some sort of counting procedure. In a little while we will see how the computer may be used to count for us, but first we will introduce a means of signalling that the end of the list has been reached.

One method is to end the list of numbers that you put in with a special number that will 'stick out like a sore thumb', eg −9999. We would hardly expect a pupil to have obtained −9999 marks in any test! This value is called a dummy or terminating value, or sometimes a rogue value. We want the program to run as normal when 'proper' marks are inputted but to stop when the mark −9999 is inputted. In other words, we want to be able to write a program with the following logical structure:

1. Start.
2. Input the total marks.
3. Input the next mark.
4. If this value is equal to −9999 then go to line 8 otherwise carry on to line 5.
5. Calculate the percentage.
6. Output the percentage.
7. Go to line 3.
8. Stop.

Figure 2   Stopping the percentage calculation

Fortunately there is a BASIC statement which will carry out the decision in line 4. It is:

IF . . . . . . THEN line number

└── condition to be satisfied for program to jump to given line number

So all we need to do is to translate statement 4 in Figure 2 as

40   IF M = −9999 THEN 80

and insert it into Program 4. This statement means: if the value found in M is equal to −9999, then go to line 80, otherwise continue executing the next statement after 40. The statement in Figure 2 'otherwise carry on to line 5' is not translated into BASIC but is implied: either jump out of sequence or carry on in sequence. We can do this very conveniently by using some new line numbers between the ones we have been using. (You will remember that we deliberately spread out statements 10, 20, 30 . . . so as to leave room to put extra statements in later.) This gives us:

```
10   REM★★PERCENTAGES★★
20   PRINT"INPUT THE TOTAL MARKS"
25   INPUT T
30   PRINT "INPUT THE NEXT MARK"
35   INPUT M
40   IF M = −9999 THEN 80
50   LET P = (M/T)★100
```

```
60   PRINT"PERCENTAGE",P
70   GOTO 30
80   END
```

Program 4   Percentage calculation with a terminating value

You use Program 4 in exactly the same way as Program 2 until you have put in the last mark to be converted to a percentage. Then you enter the mark −9999 and the program ends.

Here is a typical run.

```
RUN
INPUT THE TOTAL MARKS
? 80
INPUT THE NEXT MARK
? 43
PERCENTAGE        53.75
INPUT THE NEXT MARK
? 29
PERCENTAGE        36.25
INPUT THE NEXT MARK
? 62
PERCENTAGE        77.5
INPUT THE NEXT MARK
? −9999 ──────────────────── terminating mark

>READY
```

K̲ Program 4 and use it to convert some marks of your own. Terminate your run with −9999.

SAQ 3
You ended SAQ 2 with the program:

```
10   INPUT N
20   LET S = N★N
30   PRINT S
35   GOTO 10
40   END
```

but like the percentage program, this never stops. Modify the program to include a dummy value for terminating the program.

2.6 Inequalities

It was helpful to be able to use the expression $M = -9999$ in the IF . . . THEN . . . statement to determine whether or not the branch should occur. The statement means if $M = -9999$ is true then branch, otherwise carry on. The $=$ states a relationship between M and −9999.

42

BASIC allows expressions to include relationships:

Relationship	Example	Meaning
>	A>B	the value in store location A is greater than the value in B
<	X<Y	the value in store location X is less than the value in Y

True or false?

Consider the expression A<B. If A = 2 and B = 5 then A<B is true, because 2 is less than 5. Consider the same expression with values A = 2 and B = 1. Now A<B is false, because 2 is not less than I. Similarly if A = 2 and B = 2 then A<B is false, for 2 is not less than 2. In writing programs we often find it useful to be able to know whether a statement involving = or < or > will be true or false. This is called the logical state of the assertion, e.g.

Assertion	Logical state
3>2	True
7<7	False

You will probably find this easy enough for positive whole numbers but may be less sure of what happens in other cases. If in doubt, remember the number line:

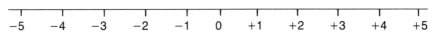

$$-5 \quad -4 \quad -3 \quad -2 \quad -1 \quad 0 \quad +1 \quad +2 \quad +3 \quad +4 \quad +5$$

Figure 3   The number line

If a number is found on this line to be to the left of a second number, then the first is less than the second number; if to the right then the first is greater than the second.

Example 1

Test whether the following expressions are true or false for the given values of A and B.

Values A	B	Expression
2	5	A>B
2	-5	A>B
-2	-5	A>B
-2	-1	A>B
-5	2	A<B
5	-2	A<B
-3	3	A=B

Solution

To do this we work out the value of each expression using the values given and then use the number line to decide whether or not the assertion is true or false for those particular values. So the solution is:

Values		Assertion		
A	B	Expression	Its value	Its logical state
2	5	A>B	2> 5	F
2	−5	A>B	2>−5	T
−2	−5	A>B	−2>−5	T
−2	−1	A>B	−2>−1	F
−5	2	A<B	−5< 2	T
5	−2	A<B	5<−2	F
−3	3	A=B	−3= 3	F

F = false   T = true

SAQ 4
Complete the following table to determine whether the given expressions are true or false for the values given.

Values		Assertion		
A	B	Expression	Its value	Its logical state
3	7	A>B		
5	3	A>B		
−3	5	A>B		
8	5	A<B		
3	9	A<B		
8	−2	A<B		

We are now in a position to use relationships to allow control of a program to jump to a new line when certain conditions are satisfied.

Example 2
In the following program segment after executing line 30, will control pass to line 40 or line 100?

```
10  LET A = −3
20  LET B = 2
30  IF A+B>0 THEN 100
40
```

Program 5

Solution
−3+2>0 is false, so the branch to 100 will not occur and control will just pass on to line 40.

44

SAQ 5

In the following program segments after executing line 30, will control pass to line 40 or to line 100?

(a)
```
10  LET A = 7
20  LET B = -8
30  IF A-B<0 THEN 100
40
```

(b)
```
10  LET X = 3
20  LET Y = -3
30  IF X/Y = -1 THEN 100
40
```

(c)
```
10  LET P = -1
20  LET Q = 3
30  IF P+Q>Q THEN 100
40
```

(d)
```
10  LET M = 3
15  LET N = -4
20  LET P = -2
30  IF M-N<N-P THEN 100
40
```

(e)
```
10  LET R = 1
20  LET S = -2
30  IF R+S>-1 THEN 100
40
```

Programs 6–10

2.7 FLOWCHARTS

As we have said the principal task for a programmer is to find a suitable way of expressing the solution strategy to solve a particular problem. At this stage we must introduce you to what must be the ugliest word in computer jargon: algorithm. This word is used to mean a general solution strategy, and is defined as a series of instructions or procedural steps for the solution of a specific problem. You will notice that in this case the computer is not mentioned. Apart from that, the definition of program and algorithm are identical. A program then is an algorithm written for a computer.

There are three basic ways of stating an algorithm:

(i) a description
(ii) BASIC coding
(iii) a flowchart

Flowcharts are a bit like blueprints and appeal to those of us who like to see events displayed in pictorial, chart or cartoon form.

We display the different functions within an algorithm by using different shaped boxes.

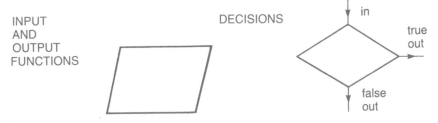

INPUT
AND
OUTPUT
FUNCTIONS

DECISIONS

in

true
out

false
out

45

ASSIGNMENTS   START/STOP

An ➤ shows the sequence of the algorithm, and the boxes contain appropriate scripts.

The first program from Unit 1 can be expressed in flowchart form as follows:

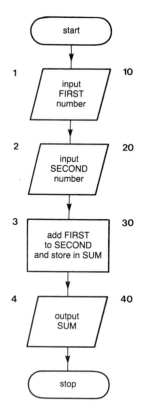

Figure 4   Flowchart of Program 1 from Unit 1

The descriptions of the functions in the boxes are in cryptic-English but could be followed by someone who has no knowledge of BASIC. In that respect we say that we try to keep these descriptions language independent. The numbers on the left-hand side of the boxes refer to the statements in the descriptive algorithm in Figure 4 of Unit 1, and the numbers on the right-hand side of the boxes refer to the statements in the BASIC program in Program 1 of Unit 1.

SAQ 6

Construct a flowchart for the percentage program (Program 1).

The decision box

You have seen how decisions are effected in BASIC using the IF . . . THEN . . . statement. The logic is:

IF assertion is true THEN go to line X

otherwise (assertion is false) carry on to the next line

The basic idea of branching to line X or carrying on to the next line is depicted in the flowchart by two exit lines from a decision box. The decision of line 40 of Program 4:

40 IF M = −9999 THEN 80

could be depicted in language independent form

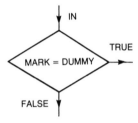

The assertion MARK = DUMMY may be expressed as a question

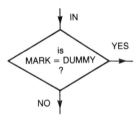

Flowchart style is up to you. The test of the effectiveness of a flowchart is whether or not you can follow the flowchart easily some time after its composition! Or, if you are trying to communicate your ideas to somebody else, whether they can follow your flowchart easily.

A flowchart for Program 4 is given below.

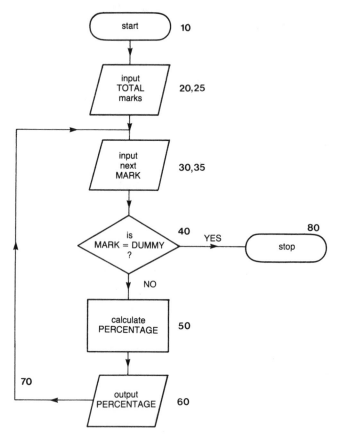

Figure 5 Flowchart for percentage program

The numbers on the right-hand side of the flowchart boxes refer to the statement numbers in the program. Statement 70 GOTO 30 is represented by a loop back to box 30.

SAQ 7
Write a flowchart for the program you wrote in answer to SAQ 3.

Now that we have introduced the idea of flowcharts, we can use them to help plan the structures of the programs that we are going to write.

2.8 Counting

As we have said, computers are good at carrying out lots of repetitive procedures. If however we wish to control these activities rather than just start and stop them, as we did in the last example, then we must use the computer to count the repetitions for us. If we carry out a specified number of repetitions of an activity, we start counting at the first activity, add one for each subsequent activity, until we reach a predetermined limit. We can depict this procedure in flowchart form.

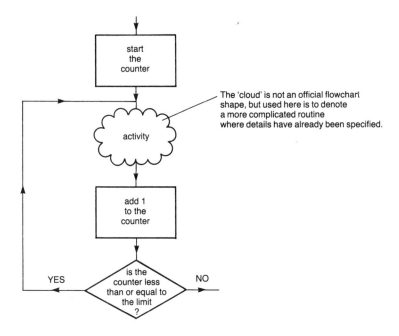

The 'cloud' is not an official flowchart shape, but used here is to denote a more complicated routine where details have already been specified.

Figure 6   A counter in a flowchart

Notice that there are three parts to the counter:
  (i)   the procedure that sets the counter to its initial value;
 (ii) the procedure for adding 1 to the counter each time the activity is completed;
(iii) the procedure for stopping the counter and leaving the activity when it has been executed the required number of times.

Great care must be taken to ensure that we exit from such a repetitive loop at exactly the point we wish to. As a warning, note that though this loop has counted up to 10, the value of the location COUNT on leaving the loop will be 11. This is a point which you would have to be very careful about if you wished to use the number in COUNT later on in the program.

SAQ 8
How many numbers will be inputted with the flowcharts?

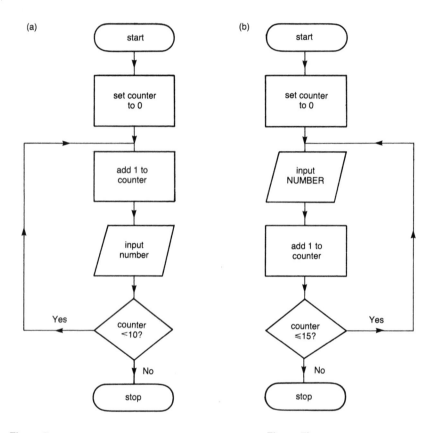

Figure 7a   **Figure 7b**

SAQ 9
Make the following program read 5 numbers by completing the IF ... THEN ... statement.

```
10  LET C=0
20  INPUT N
30  IF C=      THEN 60
40  LET C = C+1
50  GOTO 20
60  END
```

Program 11

Example 3
Write a BASIC program to calculate and output the percentage marks for a group of 5 pupils.

50

Solution

If we assume that the 'activity' in the cloud in the flowchart of Figure 6 was

> input the mark
>
> calculate the percentage
>
> output the percentage

then we can display the algorithm for this solution in flowchart form.

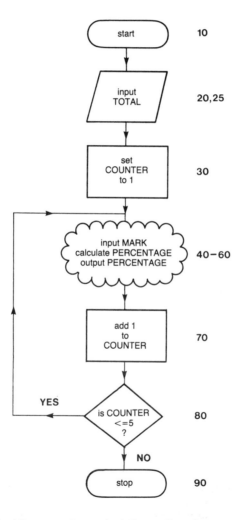

Figure 8   Flowchart for percentage calculation on 5 marks

This tells us the structure of the program that we need to write. The actual program can now be written by modifying Program 4 to incorporate the counter. So the required program is:

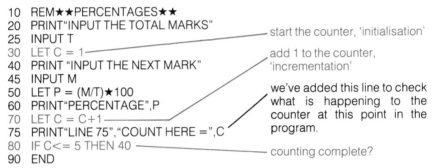

```
10  REM★★PERCENTAGES★★
20  PRINT"INPUT THE TOTAL MARKS"
25  INPUT T
30  LET C = 1 ─────────────────────── start the counter, 'initialisation'
40  PRINT "INPUT THE NEXT MARK"         add 1 to the counter,
45  INPUT M                             'incrementation'
50  LET P = (M/T)★100                   we've added this line to check
60  PRINT"PERCENTAGE",P                 what is happening to the
70  LET C = C+1 ──────────────────────  counter at this point in the
75  PRINT"LINE 75","COUNT HERE =",C      program.
80  IF C<= 5 THEN 40 ─────────────────── counting complete?
90  END
```

Program 12   Adding a counter to the percentage program

```
RUN
INPUT THE TOTAL MARKS
? 75
INPUT THE NEXT MARK
? 57
PERCENTAGE        76
LINE 75        COUNT HERE =    2
INPUT THE NEXT MARK
? 62
PERCENTAGE        82.6667
LINE 75        COUNT HERE =    3
INPUT THE NEXT MARK
? 43
PERCENTAGE        57.3333
LINE 75        COUNT HERE =    4
INPUT THE NEXT MARK
?39
PERCENTAGE 52
LINE 75        COUNT HERE =    5
INPUT THE NEXT MARK
? 70
PERCENTAGE        93.3333          ── Note: on emergence from the
LINE 75        COUNT HERE =    6 ──   loop the value of the counter
READY                                is 6.
```

Ⓚ Program 12.

Exercise 1

In question 2 of Assignment 1, you wrote a program to calculate the cost of double glazing a window. If you wanted to use the program to calculate the costs of several windows, you would have to run the program again and again. This exercise asks you to modify the program to cover more than one window.

Notice that the 'activity' for repetition will be:

```
input height and width of window

calculate cost of installation of
this window

output the cost
```

(a)   Draw a flowchart algorithm to calculate and output the cost of each of six windows.

(b)   Code the algorithm in BASIC. K your answer and try a run for six windows on your microcomputer.

(c)   Extend your program to cope with any chosen number of windows, to be specified at the beginning of the program.

Exercise 2

Extend the problem posed in question 1(b) of Assignment 1. The 'activity' for repetition will be:

```
calculate the yield

output the year and its yield

calculate the deposit for the next
year
```

(a)   Draw a flowchart algorithm to calculate and output the yield for each year up to six years. Check your answer.

(b)   Code this algorithm in BASIC in full detail. Check your answer. K

(c)   Extend the algorithm to calculate and output the yield for each year up to any chosen number of years, to be specified at the beginning of the program. Check your answer. K

2.9 Comparisons

We have seen how the BASIC language allows us to compare two numbers. We often wish to decide whether a particular value is larger or smaller than another. This is a process which is fundamental to sorting items of data. Throughout the course we will consider sorting methods in some detail, so let's start with the simplest case.

Example 4

Devise an algorithm in descriptive form to input two numbers and to output the larger of the two.

Comment

We have expressed our algorithms as flowcharts throughout most of this unit so this time we will use the decriptive method introduced in Unit 1.

Solution

1. Start.
2. Input first number.
3. Input second number.
4. If first number > second number then go to 7 otherwise carry on to 5.
5. Output second number.
6. Go to 8.
7. Output first number.
8. Stop.

This is not the neatest solution, but is close to the layman's 'first attempt' at the problem. We will seek neater solutions when we return to sorting methods in a later unit.

Assignment 2

1.   Devise a flowchart and write a BASIC program to input two numbers and output the smaller of the two. Modify the program so that it will process (a) five pairs of numbers, (b) any number of pairs of numbers.

2.   Extend the 'mark – percentage' algorithm on page 41, and express it in the form of flowchart and BASIC program:

(a)   to accommodate a class of any size;
(b)   to calculate the average percentage mark;
(c)   to pick out the highest mark.

Objectives of Unit 2

Now that you have completed this Unit, check that you are able to:

Combine literal printing and variable print in PRINT statements	☐
Use , to space PRINT statements	☐
Use GOTO to repeat the use of a program	☐
Use a dummy value to terminate a program	☐
Use IF . . . THEN . . .	☐
Find the logical state of assertions including >, <, =	☐
Construct flowcharts	☐
Insert counters in flowcharts and programs to control the repeated use of part of a program or flowchart	☐

Answers to SAQ's and Exercises

SAQ 1

(a)   AREA 48
(b)   LENGTH 8   WIDTH 6   AREA 48
(c)   LENGTH   WIDTH   AREA
      8   6   48
(d)   PRINT "LENGTH", B, "WIDTH", C
(e)   PRINT "LENGTH", B
      PRINT "WIDTH", C
      PRINT "AREA", A
(f)   PRINT "LENGTH", "WIDTH", " ¸ ", "AREA"

└── this prints a blank

SAQ 2

All you need to do is add
      35   GOTO 10

SAQ 3

```
10  INPUT N
15  IF N = −9999 THEN 40
20  LET S = N★N
30  PRINT S
35  GOTO 10
40  END
```

Program 13

(Note that this terminating value is not quite as satisfactory as using −9999 as a dummy mark. You can't have a mark of −9999, but you might perhaps want to square −9999; this program would refuse to do it.)

SAQ 4

Values		Assertion		
A	B	Expressions	Its value	Its logical state
3	7	A>B	3>7	F
5	3	A>B	5>3	T
−3	5	A>B	−3>5	F
8	5	A<B	8<5	F
3	9	A<B	3<9	T
8	−2	A<B	8<−2	F

If you got any of these wrong, look at them again on the number line

A   B   A to the left of B means A<B true

B   A   A to the right of B means A>B true

SAQ 5

(a)	40	(b)	100	(c)	40	
(d)	40	(e)	40			

Your computer could help solve this problem for you. The statements

    40 PRINT "40"
and 100 PRINT "100"

will cause the appropriate line to be output.

The following programs show how you could have solved (a) and (b) above.

Program to solve (a)
```
10  LET A = 7
20  LET B = −8
30  IF A−B< 0 THEN 100
40  PRINT "40"
50  GOTO 999
100 PRINT "100"
999 END
```

Program 14

Program to solve (b)
```
10  LET X = 3
20  LET Y = −3
30  IF X/Y=−1 THEN 100
40  PRINT "40"
50  GOTO 999
100 PRINT "100"
999 END
```

Program 15

Effect of running Program 14
```
RUN
40
READY
```

Effect of running Program 15
```
RUN
100
READY
```

SAQ 6   **SAQ 7**

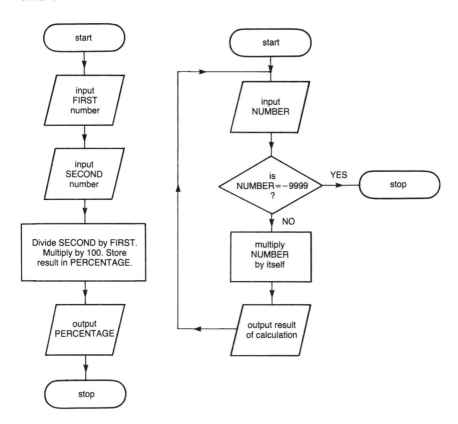

SAQ 8

(a)   10   (b)   16

SAQ 9

30   IF C = 4 THEN 60

Exercise 1

1(a)

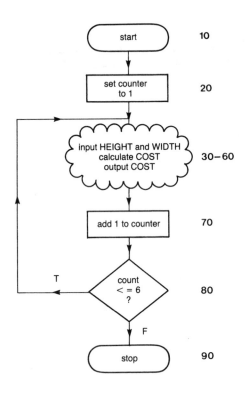

```
                          ( start )              10

                   ┌──────────────────┐
                   │   set counter    │          20
                   │      to 1        │
                   └──────────────────┘

              ╭─────────────────────────╮
              │ input HEIGHT and WIDTH  │
              │    calculate COST       │        30-60
              │     output COST         │
              ╰─────────────────────────╯

                   ┌──────────────────┐
                   │ add 1 to counter │          70
                   └──────────────────┘

                        ╱        ╲
                  T    ╱  count    ╲
              ◄───────╱   < = 6     ╲            80
                      ╲     ?      ╱
                       ╲        ╱
                          │ F

                        ( stop )               90
```

1(b)

```
10  REM★★COST OF DOUBLE GLAZING★★
20  LET C = 1
30  PRINT "ENTER HEIGHT IN METRES"
35  INPUT H
40  PRINT"ENTER WIDTH IN METRES"
45  INPUT W
50  LET K=14★(H+W)+40★(H★W)+50
60  PRINT"WINDOW",C,"COST",K
70  LET C = C+1
80  IF C<=6 THEN 30
90  END
```

Lines 20, 70 and 80 are
the counter

Program 16

```
RUN
ENTER HEIGHT IN METRES
? 1.5
ENTER WIDTH IN METRES
? 2
WINDOW        1        COST        219
ENTER HEIGHT IN METRES
? 1.5
ENTER WIDTH IN METRES
```

58

```
? 3
WINDOW        2      COST      293
ENTER HEIGHT IN METRES
? 1.5
ENTER WIDTH IN METRES
? 4
WINDOW        3      COST      367
ENTER HEIGHT IN METRES
? 2.5
ENTER WIDTH IN METRES
? 2
WINDOW        4      COST      313
etc:
```

1(c)

```
10  REM★★COST OF DOUBLE GLAZING★★
12  PRINT"ENTER NUMBER OF WINDOWS"
14  INPUT N
20  LET C = 1
30  PRINT"ENTER HEIGHT IN METRES"
35  INPUT H
40  PRINT"ENTER WIDTH IN METRES"
45  INPUT W
50  LET K = 14★(H+W)+40★(H★W)+50
60  PRINT"WINDOW",C,"COST",K
70  LET C = C+1
80  IF C <=N THEN 30
90  END
```

Program 17

Exercise 2

2(a)

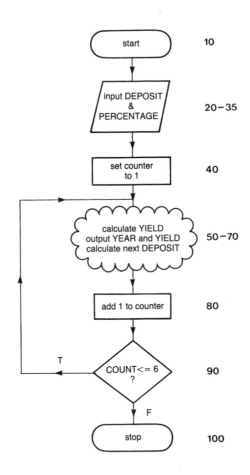

2 (b) Program

```
10  REM★★COMPOUND INTEREST★★
20  PRINT "ENTER DEPOSIT"
25  INPUT D
30  PRINT"ENTER PERCENTAGE INTEREST"
35  INPUT P
40  LET C = 1
50  LET Y = (P★D)/100
60  PRINT "YEAR ";C,"YIELD",Y
70  LET D = D+Y
80  LET C = C+1
90  IF C <= 6 THEN 50
100 END
```

Program 18

```
RUN
ENTER DEPOSIT
? 500
ENTER PERCENTAGE INTEREST
? 12.5
YEAR 1          YIELD          62.5
YEAR 2          YIELD          70.3125
YEAR 3          YIELD          79.1016
YEAR 4          YIELD          88.9893
YEAR 5          YIELD          100.113
YEAR 6          YIELD          112.627
READY
```

2(c)   Program

```
10   REM★★COMPOUND INTEREST★★
15   PRINT"ENTER NUMBER OF YEARS"
16   INPUT N
20   PRINT"ENTER DEPOSIT"
25   INPUT D
30   PRINT"ENTER PERCENTAGE INTEREST"
35   INPUT P
40   LET C = 1
50   LET Y = (P★D)/100
60   PRINT"YEAR ";C,"YIELD",Y
70   LET D = D+Y
80   LET C = C+1
90   IF C <= N THEN 50
100 END
```

Program 19

```
RUN
ENTER NUMBER OF YEARS
? 4
ENTER DEPOSIT
? 1000
ENTER PERCENTAGE INTEREST
? 13.75
YEAR 1          YIELD          137.5
YEAR 2          YIELD          156.406
YEAR 3          YIELD          177.912
YEAR 4          YIELD          202.375
READY
```

UNIT 3
Strings

3.1 What is a string?

The first two units were concerned with processing numbers. The layman often sees the computer as a 'number cruncher' but this is certainly not the main function of a computer, especially in a commercial environment. In this Unit we will see how a computer may be used to manipulate characters using the BASIC language.

By character we mean the alphabet in capitals, the ten digits 0–9, punctuation marks and some special characters as follows:

@, A, B, C, D, E, F, G, H, I, J, K, L, M, N, O, P, Q, R, S, T, U, V, W, X, Y, Z, [, \,], ↑, ←,

0, 1, 2, 3, 4, 5, 6, 7, 8, 9, :, ;, <, =, >, ?, Space, !, ,, #, $, %, &, ., (,), +, ★, −, /.

You have learnt to write programs using numbers (3, 57, −92, etc.) and variables (A, X, Z, etc.). BASIC also allows us to enter characters into the computer in groups.

These groups of characters are referred to as strings. Some examples of strings are:

CAT	(a word)
MARGARET THATCHER	(a name)
Z9)?27	(a mixture of characters)
ABC 123W	(a car registration number)

i.e. a string can be any mixture of characters – even a space is a very important character in a string!

As far as BASIC is concerned, a number is treated as a number when it is to be used to do some arithmetic, otherwise it is considered to be a string of numeric characters. When we look at a car or telephone number we see it as a group of numeric characters; we would not use this collection of digits to do any serious arithmetic.

Store locations for strings

How then can we signal to the computer that the group of characters which we are entering should be treated as numbers for arithmetic purposes, or as just a string of characters? The distinction is made in BASIC by how we label the storage locations into which we put the characters. If a store location name is followed by the symbol $ then the characters which are entered into that location are treated as strings of characters.

You saw in Unit 1 that the store locations for numbers in a minimal BASIC system are the 286 locations:

A, A0, . . . A9
B, B0, etc

The store locations for strings in a minimal BASIC are a further 286 locations:

A$, A0$, . . . A9$
etc
. . . Z7$, Z8$, Z9$

64

You read these out loud as follows:

A$ A string or A dollar
B9$ B nine string or B nine dollar

Thus you can now think of a microcomputer as having two areas for store locations: one for numbers and one for characters. This is illustrated in Figure 1.

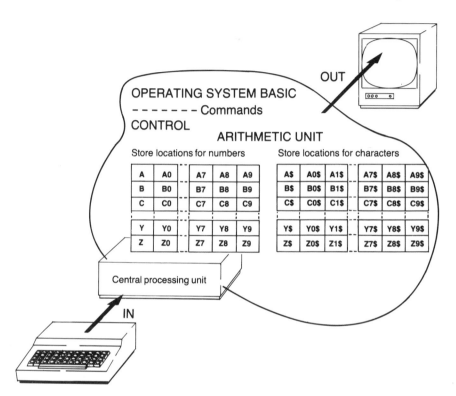

Figure 1   A summary of our system so far

" " with strings
Usually we have to show the computer that we want our string of characters to be treated as a string. To do this we put " " around the string. Thus we write

10   LET Q$ = "HELLO"
and
30   IF Q$ = "HELLO" THEN 80
and so on.

SAQ 1
Which of the following are valid store location names for strings:
(a) A$ (b) M8 (c) T7$ (d) B9 (e) C$3 (f) 8P$ (g) 2$ (h) 5$L

SAQ 2

Which of the following are correct BASIC statements:

(a) LET A = 87
(b) LET B$ = "FRED"
(c) LET M$ = 9583
(d) LET K8 = "JAM POT"
(e) LET L17 = 38

3.2. More about strings

'How long is a piece of string?' is a pertinent question here. In other words, how many characters can be input, stored or output as a single group? Once again this depends on the computer you are using. Initially in this course we will assume that a store location for strings will hold up to 40 characters, and that this restriction will apply to inputting and outputting strings. As most microcomputer screens are about 40 characters wide this is a convenient restriction. So you must now think of a string memory location, not just as a labelled pigeon-hole, but as a location with 40 sub-divisions, as shown in Figure 2.

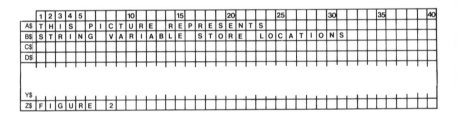

Figure 2   Size of string store locations

We have been discussing strings as if they were new but you have met them before in Unit 1. There we used the PRINT statement to output messages which were enclosed in quotation marks. We implied that the string enclosed in quotation marks was output literally character by character. Then we saw in Unit 2 how the commas between the elements of a PRINT statement caused the strings to be spaced out across the screen or printer.

3.3 PRINT . . .;. . .

From what we have covered so far you will realise that the layout of information on the screen is very important. This is just as true for strings as it is for numbers.

When handling textual information, ie strings of characters in the form of words or codes, we want the strings to be printed as in a sentence and not spaced out across the screen in print zones. The PRINT . . .;. . . statement achieves this effect for us. PRINT H$;T$ will take the characters in store location H$ and print them on

66

the left-hand side of the output device followed immediately by the characters from location T$.

In the next few pages we are going to simulate a data recording service of the not too distant future and use it to demonstrate the inputting and outputting of strings. Let's start by writing a program which simulates a telephone answering service.

CLEAR

Before using strings we have to declare that we intend to use some of our memory locations for storing strings. We tend to clear a generous section of memory for our needs in any program, thus CLEAR 100 at line 20 in the following program clears 100 character locations for use in the program.* The effect of CLEAR however is to set to zero all memory locations, so the statement must be placed at the head of a program, for we would not wish all our memory locations to be set to zero in the middle of a program run.

```
10   REM★★TELE ANSWER★★
20   CLEAR 100
30   PRINT "HELLO"
40   PRINT "PLEASE STATE YOUR TELEPHONE NUMBER"
50   INPUT T$
60   PRINT ─────────────────────────────── this prints a blank line
70   PRINT "HELLO", T$
80   PRINT
90   PRINT "HELLO"; T$
100  PRINT
110  PRINT "HELLO "; T$
120  PRINT
130  PRINT "HELLO"; " "; T$
140  END
```

Program 1   Printing strings

To help you analyse this program we have put below a 'trace' at the side of a typical run. The trace indicates which line in the program generates which line in the output.

	Trace
RUN	
HELLO	. . . 30
PLEASE STATE YOUR TELEPHONE NUMBER	. . . 40
? 58632	. . . 50
	. . . 60
HELLO 58632	. . . 70
	. . . 80
HELLO58632	. . . 90
	. . . 100
HELLO 58632	. . . 110
	. . . 120
HELLO 58632	. . . 130
>READY	

* You do not need to use CLEAR on the BBC Computer. When using these programs on a BBC Computer, omit all CLEAR lines.

Comments

Trace 50   INPUT T$ generated ? Our response was 58632 which the computer treats as a string and not as a number. (If we had written INPUT T, then 58632 would be treated as a number.)

Trace 70   The PRINT . . .,. . . on line 70 prints the 5 of the telephone number at the 15th print position across the output line, whereas

Trace 90   The PRINT . . .;. . . of line 90 prints the 5 immediately adjacent to the O of HELLO.

Neither way is satisfactory, but:

Trace 110   Lines 110 and 130 show alternative ways of introducing the required
Trace 130   spaces, either by printing HELLO▽(110) or by inserting the string ▽ in its own right into the output statement. (▽ indicates a space.)

K̲ Program 1.

SAQ 3
Study this program and work out what the print output will be. Write down the output in the grid below.

```
 10  PRINT "PRINT LAYOUT"
 20  LET B$ = "BASIC"
 30  LET C$ = "COURSE"
 40  PRINT
 50  PRINT B$, C$
 60  PRINT
 70  PRINT B$;C$
 80  PRINT
 90  PRINT B$; " "; C$
100  END
```

Program 2

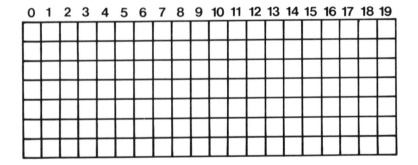

SAQ 4
Write a program which would print out the following:

68

0	1	2	3	4	5	6	7	8	9	10	11	12	13	14	15	16	17	18	19
B	A	S	I	C										B	A	S	!	C—	
B	A	S	I	C	B	A	S	I	C	B	A	S	I	C	B	A	S	I	C
B	A	S	I	C		B	A	S	I	C		B	A	S	I	C			

On BBC Computers make 'BASIC' starting at column 14 line 1 begin at the start of the 2nd print zone.

3.4 INPUT "... ";...

We have used the PRINT"..." as a prompt for an INPUT statement in several of our programs so far. Most BASIC's have a facility to allow us to combine these two into one statement. Thus in the above program, we could replace:

```
40  PRINT "PLEASE STATE YOUR TELEPHONE NUMBER"
50  INPUT T$
```

with

```
40  INPUT "PLEASE STATE YOUR TELEPHONE NUMBER";T$*
```

The INPUT statement will always generate a ? however, so in the next program we form the prompt into a direct question.

Also, in the last program we used the string "HELLO" several times. In the next program we will save a little typing by storing this string in location H$ at the start of the program.

```
10  REM★★TELE ANSWER★★
20  CLEAR 100                               BBC: 20 omit line
30  LET H$="HELLO"                          no question mark here
40  PRINT H$
50  INPUT "WHAT IS YOUR TELEPHONE NUMBER";T$
60  PRINT                                   BBC: 50 omit;
70  PRINT H$, T$
80  PRINT
90  PRINT H$; T$
100 PRINT
110 PRINT H$;" ";T$
120 END
```

Program 3   The computer asks the questions

```
RUN                                         computer response to line 50
HELLO
WHAT IS YOUR TELEPHONE NUMBER? 58632

HELLO              58632
```

*On BBC Computers leave out the semi colon. We shall remind you to do this throughout this Unit. After that you will, we hope remember to do so automatically.

HELLO58632

HELLO 58632

READY

K Program 3.

SAQ 5
What would appear on the screen when this program was run assuming your
name is John Smith and your age 45?

```
10   LET T$ = "THANK YOU"
20   INPUT "WHAT IS YOUR NAME"; N$                    BBC: 20 omit;
30   PRINT
40   INPUT "WHAT IS YOUR AGE"; A$                     BBC: 40 omit;
50   PRINT
60   PRINT T$, N$, A$
```

Program 4

3.5. Numbers and strings in print statements

We could have entered the telephone number of the previous program into a
numeric store location. We would of course soon run into problems if the number
were too long, or contained spaces (eg 01 693 4539). Let's compare how BASIC
would output this data from numeric and string store locations.

In this program note how we use the string of characters in S$ to print a scale
across the output page.

```
10    REM★★TELE ANSWER★★
20    CLEAR 100
30    LET H$="HELLO"
35    LET S$="123456789012345678901 2345"
40    PRINT H$
50    INPUT "WHAT IS YOUR TELEPHONE NUMBER";T$     BBC: 50 omit;
55    INPUT "WILL YOU REPEAT THAT PLEASE";T        BBC: 55 omit;
60    PRINT S$
70    PRINT H$, T$
75    PRINT H$,T
80    PRINT S$
90    PRINT H$;T$
95    PRINT H$;T
100   PRINT S$
110   PRINT H$;" ";T$
115   PRINT H$;" ";T
120   END
```

Program 5   Printing strings and numbers

70

```
RUN                                              Trace
HELLO
WHAT IS YOUR TELEPHONE NUMBER? 58632
WILL YOU REPEAT THAT PLEASE? 58632
1 2 3 4 5 6 7 8 9 0 1 2 3 4 5 6 7 8 9 0 1 2 3 4 5    60 S$  numbers  each  print
HELLO                        5 8 6 3 2                   position across the page.
HELLO                        5 8 6 3 2              75 note that the first digit 5 is
1 2 3 4 5 6 7 8 9 0 1 2 3 4 5 6 7 8 9 0 1 2 3 4 5       placed at the 16th position,
HELLO58632                                              the 15th is reserved for the
HELLO  5 8 6 3 2                                   95 sign of the number in T, but
1 2 3 4 5 6 7 8 9 0 1 2 3 4 5 6 7 8 9 0 1 2 3 4 5       if the sign is '+' it is not
HELLO  5 8 6 3 2                                        printed, but a space is left.
HELLO     5 8 6 3 2                               115 A  similar  effect  occurs  in
READY                                                   95 and 115.*

RUN
HELLO
WHAT IS YOUR TELEPHONE NUMBER?–58632
WILL YOU REPEAT THAT PLEASE?–58632
1 2 3 4 5 6 7 8 9 0 1 2 3 4 5 6 7 8 9 0 1 2 3 4 5
HELLO                       – 5 8 6 3 2
HELLO                       – 5 8 6 3 2              75
1 2 3 4 5 6 7 8 9 0 1 2 3 4 5 6 7 8 9 0 1 2 3 4 5
HELLO–5 8 6 3 2                                     note  the  effect  when  T$
HELLO–5 8 6 3 2                                     95 and T both hold –58632.*
1 2 3 4 5 6 7 8 9 0 1 2 3 4 5 6 7 8 9 0 1 2 3 4 5
HELLO  – 5 8 6 3 2
HELLO  – 5 8 6 3 2                                 115
READY
```

K Program 5.

SAQ 6

Write a program to input your name as a string and your age as a number and to output the message, 'My name is   and I am   years old' with the normal spacing.

Data recording service

The following is a further example of how print layout is achieved in BASIC. We can imagine that in the not too distant future our TV set, telephone and computer will be linked together as an 'intelligent' terminal. On seeing an attractive advertisement we may 'dial' a number and the following dialogue might ensue.

	Trace
HELLO	30
THIS IS A DATA–RECORDING SERVICE	40
	50
PLEASE ENTER THE DETAILS AS REQUESTED	60

*The BBC Computer produces a different effect – try it and see.

```
                                                                        70
YOUR NAME? C. A. SMITH                                                   80
YOUR TELEPHONE NUMBER? 23685                                            90
NUMBER OR NAME OF HOUSE? 77                                            100
ROAD? CHALMERS ROAD                                                    110
TOWN OR CITY? WORTHING                                                 120
YOUR POSTAL CODE? BR7 9QY                                              130
                                                                      140
                                                                      150
                                                                      160
THANK YOU FOR ENQUIRY                                                  170
                                                                      180
YOUR PERSONAL DETAILS HAVE BEEN RECORDED AS:                          190
NAME C. A. SMITH TELEPHONE NO. 23685                                  200
ADDRESS 77 CHALMERS ROAD                                              210
            WORTHING BR7 9QY                                          220
                                                                      230
DETAILS OF OUR SERVICES AND PRODUCTS                                  240
WILL BE SENT TO YOU                                                   250
YOUR PERSONAL DETAILS WILL REMAIN CONFIDENTIAL                        260
```

(Of course, instead of 'will be sent to you' it will eventually be 'will now be output to your terminal', and then the only details needed to be input would be a subscriber code.)

This simulated dialogue was achieved by the following program.

```
10   REM★★DATA–RECORD★★
20   CLEAR 100
30   PRINT "HELLO"
40   PRINT "THIS IS A DATA–RECORDING SERVICE"
50   PRINT
60   PRINT "PLEASE ENTER THE DETAILS AS REQUESTED"
70   PRINT
80   INPUT "YOUR NAME";N$
90   INPUT "YOUR TELEPHONE NUMBER";T$
100  INPUT "NUMBER OR NAME OF HOUSE";H$
110  INPUT "ROAD";R$
120  INPUT "TOWN OR CITY";C$
130  INPUT "YOUR POSTAL CODE";P$
140  PRINT
150  PRINT
160  PRINT
170  PRINT "THANK YOU FOR YOUR ENQUIRY"
180  PRINT
190  PRINT "YOUR PERSONAL DETAILS HAVE BEEN RECORDED AS:"
200  PRINT "NAME ";N$;" TELEPHONE NO. ";T$
210  PRINT "ADDRESS ";H$;" ";R$
220  PRINT "             ";C$;" ";P$
230  PRINT
240  PRINT "DETAILS OF OUR SERVICES AND PRODUCTS"
250  PRINT "WILL BE SENT TO YOU"
```

260 PRINT "YOUR PERSONAL DETAILS WILL REMAIN CONFIDENTIAL"

Program 6   Data recording service

K⃞   Program 6.   (BBC: omit; in 80, 90, 100, 110, 120, 130.)

3.6   Standard letters

A data recording service, such as we have just looked at, may be in the future, but standard personalised letters are with us now. Such a letter would be composed on a word-processor, but if your micro does not have word processing facilities available, you could achieve modest results using BASIC. Your own choice of letter will be left to you in Exercise 2.

Example 1
A bank recruiting office receives many enquiries about employment. Its policy is to interview suitable applicants initially at its local branch. A stereotyped letter is sent from the recruiting office to each applicant containing individual details of the proposed interview. Devise a BASIC program to write such a letter.

Solution
The following program would do this job.

```
10   REM★★LETTER WRITER★★
20   CLEAR 100
30   INPUT A$ ──────────────────────── applicant's name
40   INPUT B$ ──────────────────────── date of letter of application
50   INPUT C$ ──────────────────────── name of interviewer
60   INPUT D$ ──────────────────────── time of interview
70   INPUT E$ ──────────────────────── date of interview
80   INPUT F$ ──────────────────────── location of interview
90   INPUT G$ ──────────────────────── name of employee replying
100  PRINT
110  PRINT
120  PRINT"DEAR  ";A$;","
130  PRINT
140  PRINT "THANK YOU FOR YOUR LETTER OF  ";B$;"."
150  PRINT "WE INVITE YOU TO ATTEND FOR INTERVIEW WITH"
160  PRINT C$;" AT ";D$;" ON ";E$
170  PRINT "AT OUR  ";F$;" BRANCH."
180  PRINT
190  PRINT "YOURS SINCERELY,"
200  PRINT
210  PRINT
220  PRINT
230  PRINT G$
240  PRINT
250  PRINT
260  END
```

Program 7   Bank interview letter

73

This would result in the following run:

```
RUN
? MISS JONES                                        30
? 13TH OCTOBER                                      40
? MR FELLOWS                                        50
? 10.00 AM                                          60
? 20TH OCTOBER                                      70
? HIGH ST. SIDCUP                                   80
? C. A. SIDWELL                                     90
                                                   100
                                                   110
DEAR MISS JONES,                                   120
                                                   130
THANK YOU FOR YOUR LETTER OF 13TH OCTOBER.         140
WE INVITE YOU TO ATTEND FOR INTERVIEW WITH         150
MR FELLOWS AT 10.00 AM ON 20TH OCTOBER             160
AT OUR HIGH ST. SIDCUP BRANCH.                     170
                                                   180
YOURS SINCERELY,                                   190
                                                   200
                                                   210
                                                   220
C.A. SIDWELL                                       230
```

The user of the program might find it difficult to use since all he gets is a series of prompts ?. He might, therefore, make a skeletal aide-memoire to remind him of the structure of the letter:

```
? A$
? B$
? C$
? D$
? E$
? F$
? G$


DEAR A$,

THANK YOU FOR YOUR LETTER OF B$.
WE INVITE YOU TO ATTEND FOR INTERVIEW WITH
C$ AT D$ ON E$
AT OUR F$ BRANCH.

YOURS SINCERELY,


G$
```

Ⓚ Program 7

Exercise 1
An estate agent periodically sends out a letter to check whether clients on his

books are still looking for a property, and that his details of their requirements (eg type of property, price range, etc) are correct. Devise a BASIC program to write such a letter.

Exercise 2
We all write letters requesting things, eg details of a product, a service, a holiday, a job, etc. Devise a BASIC program to write a letter which will cover as wide a range of applications as possible, leaving you to fill in only the particular details of each enquiry.

3.7   Patterns, files, READ with DATA

READ with DATA
So far in this course we have entered data at the keyboard during the execution of a program as a response to an INPUT statement. Another way of introducing data into a program is to store it in DATA statements within the program itself and then to READ the items into the program from the DATA statements as required. Usually, data is stored at the end of a program, or program segment.

Every time the computer comes to a READ statement it takes the next item of data from the DATA queue and places it in the location specified in the READ statement. For a READ statement to be executed there must be a corresponding item of DATA available in the DATA queue.

Thus in this program the following happens.

```
10   READ A$
20   READ B$
30   READ C$
100  DATA TOM, DICK
110  DATA HARRY
```

Some computers require "   " around strings in DATA statements eg 100 DATA "TOM", "DICK"

Program 8

At 10, READ tells the computer to take the first item of DATA and put it in location A$. The first DATA item occurs in line 100 and is TOM so TOM goes in location A$. At the next READ statement (20), the computer takes the next DATA item which is DICK and so on. You can check that this has happened by putting:

```
40   PRINTA$
50   PRINT B$
60   PRINT C$
```

into the program.

SAQ 7
What is wrong with this program segment?

```
10   READ A$
20   READ B
30   READ C
40   READ D$
50   DATA PAUL, MARY, 63
```

Program 9

75

A more complex example is shown by this program segment:

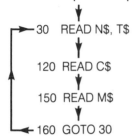

```
  30  READ N$, T$

 120  READ C$

 150  READ M$

 160  GOTO 30
```

```
200 DATA   BENNY, COPPER, DRAPER
210 DATA   EDDIE, GWYNNE
220 DATA   HETTIE
230 DATA   MORLEY, PROSSER, SMYTHE, WEEKS
240 DATA   WILSON, WRIGHT
```

Here is what happens:

First time round loop

N$	reads	BENNY
T$	reads	COPPER
C$	reads	DRAPER
M$	reads	EDDIE

Stores at end of first time round

N$	BENNY
T$	COPPER
C$	DRAPER
M$	EDDIE

Second time round loop

N$	reads	GWYNNE
T$	reads	HETTIE
C$	reads	MORLEY
M$	reads	PROSSER

(i.e. next unread item of DATA)

Stores at end of second time round

N$	GWYNNE
T$	HETTIE
C$	MORLEY
M$	PROSSER

SAQ 8

What will the final state of the stores be when all the data has been read?

SAQ 9

What would the contents of locations A$, B$ and C$ be after this program segment has read all the DATA items?

```
10  READ A$
20  READ B$
30  READ C$
40  GOTO 20
50  DATA TINKER, TAILOR, SOLDIER
60  DATA SAILOR, RICH MAN
```

Program 10

Files and records

Quite often we want to record data which is of one kind, i.e. it makes up a file of information. A telephone directory is a good example of what in data processing is called a file, that is a collection of similar records. Each record has the form

Name	Address	Telephone number

and is said to consist of a number of fields – in this case three: name, address and telephone number. A record is then a collection of fields and a file is a collection of records. A telephone directory is arranged in alphabetical order of surnames which gives it a simple structure.

Comparing strings

We may wish to compare strings. Suppose, for example, we have a personal telephone directory in our microcomputer and we wish to find out whether SMITH is in our record. The computer will have to compare the string "SMITH" against all the strings in the name field of our directory. It can do this very easily because each letter is represented inside the computer by a binary code. Thus

A is 100 0001

B is 100 0010

and so on. (See the Appendix to this unit for a full list of binary codes.) So words placed in alphabetical order on paper will be represented in the computer by codes in numerical order.

Thus if

A$ = CAT
B$ = DOG
C$ = CAT
D$ = FISH
E$ = CATS

A$ = C$

But   B$ > A$ (it is further on in the alphabet)
and   E$ > A$ (the extra S on CAT puts it after CAT in alphabetical order.)

We shall now use this facility in our examples.

Example 2

Set up a data file of names and associated telephone numbers. Write a BASIC program to search through the file to find a particular name, and if found then output the associated telephone number.

Solution

We could attempt a descriptive algorithm as follows:

1. Start.
2. Input query name.
3. Read next record of the data file (i.e. name and number).
4. If the end of the file has been reached (data name = "ZZZZ") then output message 'not found in file' and go to 7 otherwise carry on to 5.
5. If query name = data name then output name and number and go to 7 otherwise carry on to 6.
6. Return to 3 for next record.
7. Stop.

However, BASIC does not generally allow statements as complicated as 4 and 5, and so we have to split up these statements as shown in the next algorithm:

1. Start.
2. Input query name.
3. Read next record from data file.
4. If the end of file has been reached then go to 7 otherwise carry on to 5.
5. If query name = data name then go to 9 otherwise carry on to 6.
6. Return to 3 for next record.
7. Output message 'not in file'.
8. Stop.
9. Output name and number.
10. Stop.

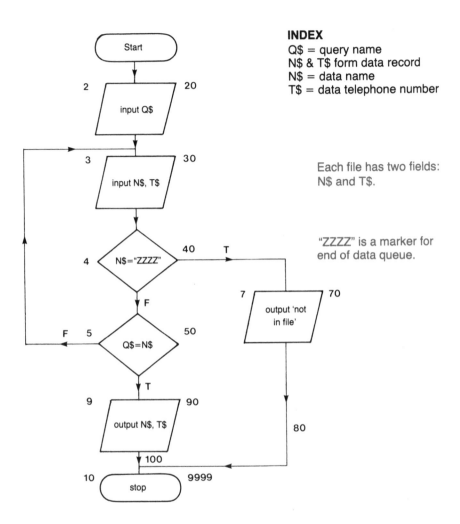

INDEX
Q$ = query name
N$ & T$ form data record
N$ = data name
T$ = data telephone number

Each file has two fields:
N$ and T$.

"ZZZZ" is a marker for
end of data queue.

Figure 3   Searching a telephone directory

Now each record contains two fields on this occasion: name and number.

Field 1	Field 2
Name N$	Telephone Number T$
BENNY	1234

e.g.

so each DATA item must contain information for each field. Thus the READ line will be:

READ N$, T$

and the DATA lines are of the form:

DATA BENNY, 1234

Notice that the end-of-file number is a DATA item (line 310) so it has to have data to fill T$ as well as N$. Without this an error message (out of data) would appear on the screen. So we write

DATA ZZZZ, END OF FILE

and not just

DATA ZZZZ

This is an open string because it contains spaces. Some BASIC's would require this string to be enclosed in quotation marks.

```
10   REM★★TELEPHONE DIRECTORY★★
15   CLEAR 100
20   INPUT "SURNAME OF PERSON SOUGHT";Q$
30   READ N$, T$                    ]——————————————READ
40   IF N$="ZZZZ" THEN 70
50   IF Q$=N$ THEN 90
60   GOTO 30
70   PRINT Q$;" IS NOT IN THE FILE"
80   GOTO 9999
90   PRINT Q$;"'S NUMBER IS ";T$
100  GOTO 9999
200  DATA BENNY, 1234
210  DATA COPPER, 9823
220  DATA DRAPER, 1850
230  DATA EDDIE, 7294
240  DATA GWYNNE, 5821
250  DATA HETTIE, 4539                                    ——————DATA
260  DATA MORLEY, 7830
270  DATA PROSSER, 1383
280  DATA SMYTHE, 1147
290  DATA WEEKS, 5529
300  DATA WILSON, 9936
310  DATA ZZZZ, END OF FILE
9999 END
```

Program 11   Telephone directory

Typical run

```
RUN
SURNAME OF PERSON SOUGHT? EDDIE
EDDIE'S NUMBER IS 7294

>READY
RUN
SURNAME OF PERSON SOUGHT? BROWNE
BROWNE IS NOT IN THE FILE

>READY
```

```
RUN
SURNAME OF PERSON SOUGHT? WEEKS
WEEKS'S NUMBER IS 5529

>READY
RUN
SURNAME OF PERSON SOUGHT? WEEK
WEEK IS NOT IN THE FILE
```

In the fourth run we entered the name "WEEK" whereas the name "WEEKS" was actually in the file. The computer compares these patterns of characters and finds them unequal. If we were looking through a telephone directory we might realise that we were really looking for WEEKS rather than WEEK. We could of course, re-run the program with a variety of spellings of a name, if we were in doubt.

K   Program 11. (BBC: omit ; in 20.)

SAQ 10
What changes would you have to make to Program 11 to input a person's telephone number and output the subscriber's name or 'is not in list'.

3.8 Sorting

You will have noticed that the telephone directory data in Example 2 was in alphabetical order as you would expect. It would be difficult for the user in normal practice if this were not so. However, our solution to this searching problem did not use this information; we just searched through the data file record by record until we found the name, or reached the end of the file. Our algorithm would have worked equally well had the data not been in alphabetical order. We shall spend some time later in the course sorting and searching data, at which point you will realise the advantages of sorting data into alphabetical order.

Let's make a modest start with this problem.

Example 3
Write a BASIC program to enter two names into the computer and output that name which would come first in alphabetical order.

Solution
Descriptive algorithm

1. Start.
2. Input first name.
3. Input second name.
4. If first name < second name then 7 otherwise carry on to 5.
5. Output second name.
6. Go to 8.
7. Output first name.
8. Stop.

An outline flowchart for the solution of this problem is shown in Figure 4.

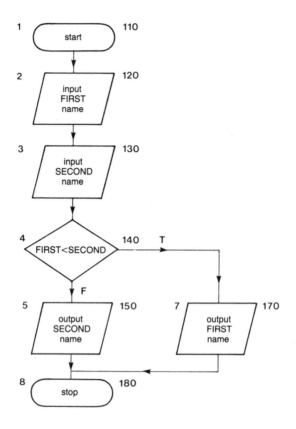

Figure 4 Finding the first of two in alphabetical order

```
100 CLEAR 100
110 REM★★FIRST IN ALPHA-ORDER★★
120 INPUT"FIRST NAME";A$
130 INPUT"SECOND NAME";B$
140 IFA$<B$ THEN 170
150 PRINT"FIRST IN ALPHA-ORDER IS ";B$
160 GOTO180
170 PRINT"FIRST IN ALPHA-ORDER IS ";A$
180 END
```

Program 12

Typical run

```
RUN                                 >READY
FIRST NAME? BROWN                   RUN
SECOND NAME? SMITH                  FIRST NAME? SMITH
FIRST IN ALPHA-ORDER IS BROWN       SECOND NAME? BROWN
                                    FIRST IN ALPHA-ORDER IS BROWN
```

K Program 12. (BBC: omit; in 120 and 130.)

82

The 3 card trick

Suppose now that we wanted to input three names and output the name that comes first in alphabetical order. A standard solution to this would be to follow the approach in Figure 5.

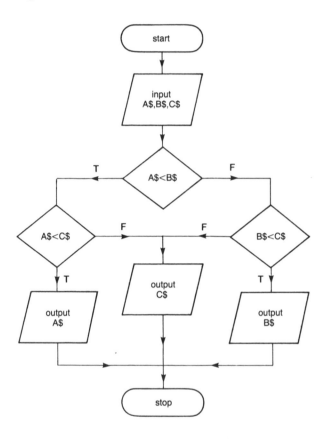

Figure 5   Finding the first of three in alphabetical order

When asked to solve this problem most students present an answer similar to the algorithm in Figure 5. It is a perfectly good solution, but it bodes ill for the future. Future trouble stems from the fact that we have had to utilise 3 decision and 3 output functions. This method would overtax our patience and ingenuity if we tried to repeat it for 4, 5 . . . let alone 10 names. The fundamental problem is allowing each variable to retain its own individual storage location, and how we are best able to label that location.

A simpler method of solving this problem is to input the names one by one and to store lowest-so-far in A$. The program retains only lowest-so-far, destroying all the other discarded data. In the next Exercise we suggest you try this approach to solving the problem.

Exercise 3
Write a BASIC program to input three names and output that name which would come first in alphabetical order using the method discussed in the last few lines.

Exercise 4
A data file of European countries and their capital cities is suggested below. Write a BASIC program to use this file as the basis of a quiz with the user, presenting him with the country and asking him to name the capital city. Respond to his input by telling him whether he is correct or not, and in the latter case giving him the correct answer.

```
140  DATA FRANCE, PARIS
150  DATA WEST GERMANY, BONN
160  DATA THE NETHERLANDS, THE HAGUE
170  DATA POLAND, WARSAW
180  DATA ITALY, ROME
190  DATA SPAIN, MADRID
200  DATA PORTUGAL, LISBON
210  DATA HUNGARY, BUDAPEST
220  DATA DENMARK, COPENHAGEN
230  DATA NORWAY, OSLO
240  DATA ZZZZ, END OF FILE.
```

Assignment 3

1. Compose a descriptive algorithm and draw a flowchart to accompany the BASIC program in program 15.

2. Modify your program for Exercise 4 to count the numbers of correct and incorrect responses, and to give a summary of the marks at the end of the quiz.

3. Devise an algorithm and write a BASIC program to do the following task. Store several words as individual letters in DATA statements, e.g. the words 'algorithm' and 'flowchart' could be stored:

```
900 DATA A,L,G,O,R,I,T,H,M
910 DATA F,L,O,W,C,H,A,R,T
```

Count the number of vowels and consonants contained in the words, and output the totals of these counts together with the ratio total number of vowels/total number of consonants.

Objectives of Unit 3

Now that you have completed this Unit, check that you are able to use the following in simple programs:

String storage locations ☐
CLEAR ☐
PRINT . . .;. . . ☐

INPUT "...";...
READ
DATA (one field only)
IF A$ = B$ THEN ...
DATA (more than one field)
Simple sorting procedure

□
□
□
□
□
□

Answers to SAQ's and Exercises

SAQ 1
Valid string locations: A$, T7$.
Of the others, M8 and B9 are number store locations.
The rest are neither number nor string store locations.

SAQ 2
(a), (b) and (e) are correct but (e) is not acceptable in minimal BASIC.
(c) is incorrect: M$ is a string location so you need "9583"
(d) is incorrect: K8 is a number store location so the string "JAM POT" cannot be
    assigned to it.

SAQ 3

P	R	I	N	T		L	A	Y	O	U	T								
B	A	S	I	C										C	O	U	R	S	E
B	A	S	I	C	C	O	U	R	S	E									
B	A	S	I	C		C	O	U	R	S	E								

(Answer shown for standard print zones.)

SAQ 4
```
10   LET B$ = "BASIC"
20   PRINT B$, B$
30   PRINT B$; B$; B$; B$
40   PRINT B$; " "; B$; " "; B$
50   END
```

Program 13

SAQ 5
WHAT IS YOUR NAME? JOHN SMITH
WHAT IS YOUR AGE? 45
THANK YOU   JOHN SMITH   45

SAQ 6
```
10   INPUT "WHAT IS YOUR NAME"; N$
20   INPUT "WHAT IS YOUR AGE"; A
```

```
30   PRINT "MY NAME IS ";N$;" AND I AM ";A." YEARS OLD"
40   END
```

Exercise 1
Exercises 1 and 2 are very similar in nature and an answer for Exercise 1 has not
been included.

Exercise 2
(BBC: omit; in INPUT lines.)

```
10   REM★★ENQUIRY LETTER★★
20   CLEAR 500
30   PRINT "DETAILS OF ADDRESSEE"
40   PRINT
50   INPUT "NAME . . .";N$
60   INPUT"STREET . . .";S$
70   INPUT"TOWN . . .";T$
80   PRINT
90   INPUT "DATE FOR THIS LETTER";D$
100  PRINT
110  PRINT"DETAILS OF PRODUCT/SERVICE"
120  PRINT
130  PRINT"ITEM OF INTEREST"
140  INPUT I$
150  PRINT"SOURCE OF INFORMATION"
160  INPUT A$
170  INPUT "DATE OF SOURCE";E$
180  PRINT
190  PRINT
200  PRINT
210  PRINT
220  PRINT N$
230  PRINT S$
240  PRINT T$
250  PRINT
260  PRINT
270  PRINT D$
280  PRINT
290  PRINT
300  PRINT"DEAR SIR,"
310  PRINT
320  PRINT"WILL YOU KINDLY SEND ME DETAILS OF"
330  PRINT I$;","
340  PRINT "AS ITEMISED IN THE"
350  PRINT A$
360  PRINT"DATED  ";E$;"."
370  PRINT
380  PRINT
390  PRINT"YOURS FAITHFULLY,"
400  PRINT
410  PRINT
```

Program 14

```
420  PRINT
430  PRINT"O.L. SEYMOUR"
```

Typical run

```
RUN
DETAILS OF ADDRESSEE

NAME. . .? E P SOFTWARE LTD
STREET. . .? EDGWARE ROAD
TOWN . . .? LONDON

DATE FOR THIS LETTER? 12TH OCTOBER 1980

DETAILS OF PRODUCT/SERVICE

ITEM OF INTEREST
? BUSINESS SOFTWARE PACKAGES
SOURCE OF INFORMATION
? MAGAZINE "MODERN COMPUTING"
DATE OF SOURCE? 10TH OCTOBER


E P SOFTWARE LTD
EDGWARE ROAD
LONDON

12TH OCTOBER 1980

DEAR SIR,

WILL YOU KINDLY SEND ME DETAILS OF
BUSINESS SOFTWARE PACKAGES,
AS ITEMISED IN THE
MAGAZINE "MODERN COMPUTING"
DATED 10TH OCTOBER.

YOURS FAITHFULLY,


O.L. SEYMOUR
```

SAQ 7

Line 20 will try to read the second DATA item which is MARY, which is a string, but the location in line 20 is a number location. The computer would stop and indicate a syntax error. To read "MARY", line 20 must be 20 READ B$

Line 40 calls for a fourth DATA item but there are only three items in line 50.

SAQ 8

N$	SMYTHE
T$	WEEKS
C$	WILSON
M$	WRIGHT

SAQ 9

A$	TINKER
B$	SAILOR
C$	RICH MAN

Notice that "RICH MAN" is read as one item since there is no comma between the two words. If you run this program you will get a message such as 'out of data at line 20'. Why?

SAQ 10
Calling the number A$, changes are needed to lines 20, 50, 70 and 90 as follows:

```
20   INPUT "NUMBER OF PERSON SOUGHT"; A$
50   IF A$= T$ THEN 90
70   PRINT "SUBSCRIBER NUMBER"; A$; "IS NOT IN FILE"
90   PRINT "SUBSCRIBER NUMBER"; A$; "IS"; N$
```

Exercise 3
A simple method of solving this problem is shown in the Program 15. The names are input one by one, and the 'lowest so far' always stored in A$. The program, however, only retains this one item of information, all other data is lost.

```
10   REM★★FIRST IN ALPHA-ORDER★★
15   CLEAR 100
20   INPUT"FIRST NAME";A$              (BBC: omit; in INPUT lines)
30   INPUT "NEXT NAME";B$
40   IF B$="ZZZZ" THEN 90
50   IF A$<B$ THEN 70
60   LET A$=B$
70   PRINT"FIRST IN ALPHA-ORDER SO FAR IS  ";A$
80   GOTO 30
90   PRINTA$;"  WAS OVERALL FIRST"
100  END
```

Program 15

```
RUN
FIRST NAME? TOM
NEXT NAME? SID
FIRST IN ALPHA-ORDER SO FAR IS SID
NEXT NAME? JOE
FIRST IN ALPHA-ORDER SO FAR IS JOE
NEXT NAME? PETE
FIRST IN ALPHA-ORDER SO FAR IS JOE
```

NEXT NAME? FRED
FIRST IN ALPHA-ORDER SO FAR IS FRED
NEXT NAME? BILL
FIRST IN ALPHA-ORDER SO FAR IS BILL
NEXT NAME? RON
FIRST IN ALPHA-ORDER SO FAR IS BILL
NEXT NAME? ALAN
FIRST IN ALPHA-ORDER SO FAR IS ALAN
NEXT NAME? ZZZZ
ALAN WAS OVERALL FIRST

>READY

Exercise 4
```
10   REM★★EUROPEAN CAPITALS QUIZ★★
20   CLEAR 500
30   READ C$,T$
40   IF C$="ZZZZ"THEN 130
50   PRINT"WHAT IS THE CAPITAL OF  ";C$
60   INPUT A$
70   IF A$=T$ THEN 110
80   PRINT"NO SORRY! THE CAPITAL OF"
90   PRINT C$;" IS ";T$
100  GOTO 30
110  PRINT"YES THAT'S RIGHT"
120  GOTO 30
130  PRINT"THAT'S THE END OF THE QUIZ"
135  END
140  DATA FRANCE, PARIS
150  DATA WEST GERMANY, BONN
160  DATA THE NETHERLANDS, THE HAGUE
170  DATA POLAND, WARSAW
180  DATA ITALY, ROME
190  DATA SPAIN, MADRID
200  DATA PORTUGAL, LISBON
210  DATA HUNGARY, BUDAPEST
220  DATA DENMARK, COPENHAGEN
230  DATA NORWAY, OSLO
240  DATA ZZZZ, END OF FILE
```

Program 16

RUN
WHAT IS THE CAPITAL OF FRANCE
? PARIS
YES THAT'S RIGHT
WHAT IS THE CAPITAL OF WEST GERMANY
? BERLIN
NO SORRY! THE CAPITAL OF
WEST GERMANY IS BONN
WHAT IS THE CAPITAL OF THE NETHERLANDS
? HAGUE
NO SORRY! THE CAPITAL OF

THE NETHERLANDS IS THE HAGUE
WHAT IS THE CAPITAL OF POLAND
? WARSAW
YES THAT'S RIGHT
WHAT IS THE CAPITAL OF ITALY
? ROME
YES THAT'S RIGHT
WHAT IS THE CAPITAL OF SPAIN
? MADRID
YES THAT'S RIGHT
WHAT IS THE CAPITAL OF PORTUGAL
? LISBON
YES THAT'S RIGHT
WHAT IS THE CAPITAL OF HUNGARY
?PRAGUE
NO SORRY! THE CAPITAL OF
HUNGARY IS BUDAPEST
WHAT IS THE CAPITAL OF DENMARK
? COPANHEEN
NO SORRY! THE CAPITAL OF
DENMARK IS COPENHAGEN
WHAT IS THE CAPITAL OF NORWAY
? OSLO
YES THAT'S RIGHT
THAT'S THE END OF THE QUIZ

>READY

Appendix

American Standard Code for Information Interchange or ASCII Code
That part of the code which concerns us here is shown below.

	32	1	49
!	33	2	50
"	34	3	51
£	35	4	52
$	36	5	53
%	37	6	54
&	38	7	55
'	39	8	56
(	40	9	57
)	41	:	58
*	42	;	59
+	43	<	60
,	44	=	61
−	45	>	62
.	46	?	63
/	47	@	64
0	48	A	65

B	66	R	82
C	67	S	83
D	68	T	84
E	69	U	85
F	70	V	86
G	71	W	87
H	72	X	88
I	73	Y	89
J	74	Z	90
K	75	[	91
L	76	/	92
M	77	]	93
N	78	ˆ	94
O	79	—	95
P	80	£	96
Q	81		

UNIT 4
Lists

4.1 Variables

We have already seen how a memory location may store several different values during the course of a program's execution. Thus the value in a store location may vary during a run, and so we often refer to the location names as variables in a program. Thus the 286 store labels:

A, A0, A1, . . . A9, B, B0, . . . Z8, Z9

are called numeric variables, and their counterparts:

A$, A0$, A1$, . . . A9$, B$, B0$, . . . Z8$, Z9$

are called string variables. The store labels are used in expressions in program statements just as mathematicians use variables in equations.

4.2 Lists

Lists and supermarkets seem inextricably linked. We go in with a list of items which we wish to buy, and emerge with the items and a list of prices in the form of a receipt. The list of prices results from the process of transferring the items from the basket to the counter. This is a fairly random process but we could have given the list a more meaningful order in a variety of ways. With a lot of effort we could have taken the items out of the basket in order of price, i.e. the cheapest first, the next cheapest next, and so on with the most expensive last, so that the till roll of prices would be in order of cost. Similarly, we could have taken them out of the basket in order of weight, the lightest first through to the heaviest last; and by so doing impose a completely different order on the receipt list. Being able to relate the position in the list in some way to the value of the item, is the most useful feature of lists, as we shall see by the end of this Unit.

4.3 List variables

Most of the data that we have considered so far can be classified into sets. We have considered sets of test marks, sets of names and associated telephone numbers, sets of countries and their capital cities. Most data can be classified in some way. If we are collecting data for some purpose, this very purpose gives the set of values common characteristics. There are obvious advantages to naming the storage locations for items in a set of data in a way which emphasises that all the items belong to one set. Even better, it would be useful if the storage location names identified the position of an item within the set.

For example, storage, or variable, notation which emphasises that the values are in some way associated with each other, and allocates a position within the set. This is achieved in the following way.

Consider a set of marks in a teacher's mark book. They form a natural list and in our minimal BASIC could be allocated storage locations symbolised in the following way:

Item	Storage location symbol
The first member of the M-list is 42	M(1) = 42
The second member of the M-list is 67	M(2) = 67
The third member of the M-list is 90	M(3) = 90
etc . . .	

M(1), M(2), M(3) are like separate memory locations. You can take any of the 572 store locations and put numbers in brackets after them to make list store locations, e.g.

List name	List store locations in that list
M(I)	M(1), M(2), M(3) . . .
A0(I)	A0(1), A0(2), A0(3) . . .
C$(I)	C$(1), C$(2), C$(3) . . .
Q6$(I)	Q6$(1), Q6$(2), Q6$(3) . . .

The number in the brackets (here shown as I) is called the index of the list, and may be any positive integer up to a limit set by your computer. We called it the M-list, the M standing for 'mark', but if your version of BASIC provides for longer variable names then we would advise you to express it as the MARK-list, and the list variables become MARK(1), MARK(2), MARK(3) . . . and generally MARK(I).

String lists
As you can see from the table above, lists can be string lists as well as numeric lists. Thus if you name a list M(I), it is clearly a list of numbers but M$(I) would be a list of strings, e.g. a list of names could be stored:

Index	Item	Variable name
1	Jones	N$(1), or NAME$(1)
2	Alan	N$(2), or NAME$(2)
3	Smith	N$(3), or NAME$(3)
etc	etc	etc

Figure 1 String list names

Lists and arrays
A table of data, like that shown in Figure 1, is often referred to as an array of data. With the data displayed in rows and columns in this way (indexed by item), a table is often referred to as a two-dimensional array. A list (i.e. just one column of data) is similarly called a one-dimensional array. We will see how BASIC provides for two-dimensional arrays in a later Unit.

DIM or how long is a list?
As long as you choose! We said that the index may be any reasonable positive integer, and within the overall memory limitations of a particular computer, we can choose a list to be of any desired length, provided that we warn the system first. On some microcomputers you do not need to warn the computer of lists of 10 or fewer items but the BBC Computer requires advance warning of all lists. To do this you use a DIMENSION statement:

line number DIM A (length of list)

which must appear in the program before you use the array A. So in this unit we include DIM statements (printed in colour). Even if your computer does not need DIM statements for small arrays, it is alright to leave the DIM statements in your programs.

Items and index numbers

The following paper and pencil exercises should reinforce your understanding of what is meant by the terms item and index, and their often only fleeting relationship. They also prepare the ground for the interchange-sort procedure which we will consider in detail later in this Unit.

Example 1

Transfer the item of lowest value in the following list to position 1, by comparing in turn each of the values in the remainder of the list with the current value at position 1. Interchange the items if the one in the remainder of the list is lower than that at position 1. (It is easier to do than to describe!)

List: 3, 42, −8, 9, −11

Start		Compare & interchange stages			
position or index	item	1st run c	2nd run c&i	3rd run c	4th run c&i
1	3	3	−8	−8	−11
2	42	42	42	42	42
3	−8	−8	3	3	3
4	9	9	9	9	9
5	−11	−11	−11	−11	−8

Figure 2   Sort to place lowest number first

SAQ 1

Carry out the procedure shown in Example 1 for the following list of numbers:

6,8,4,7,3,9,1.

4.4   List input and output

Before we can manipulate the items in a list we have to get the list of items into the computer, and after processing usually get another list out.

Example 2

Write a BASIC program to input three numbers into a list and output the elements of the list in reverse order.

Solution

We will call the list A(I). The required program is then:

```
10   REM★★EXAMPLE 2★★
15   DIM A (3)
20   INPUTA(1)
```

```
30  INPUTA(2)
40  INPUTA(3)
50  PRINT
60  PRINT
70  PRINTA(3),A(2),A(1)
80  END
```

Program 1   Reversing the order of a list

Typical run

```
RUN
? 29
? 32
? −17

−17   32   29

>READY
```

K̲ Program 1.

We have done as requested in the question, but have not made a significant advance in programming technique since we could have done the job with the techniques of earlier units simply by calling the variables P, Q and R and outputting them as R, Q and P. To do the job better we need to count the list as it is inputted so that we can use the counter in reverse order when we output the list. The next example adds this refinement.

Counting a list
Example 3
Write a program to input five numbers into a list, to display the items of the list and its index in the form of a table, and then output the elements of the list in reverse order.

Solution
As listed in the question, there are three main parts to the solution and we can display these in flowchart form as in Figure 3.

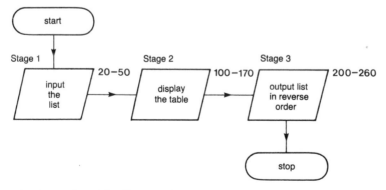

Figure 3   Stages in solving Example 3

97

Stage 1   We use the variable C to count the elements of the list on input, and to act as an index for the L-list.

```
10  REM★★INPUT A LIST★★
15  DIM L(5)
20  LET C=1
30  INPUT"ENTER THE NEXT NUMBER";L(C)
40  LET C=C+1
50  IF C<=5 THEN 30
```

Program 2   Counting a list on entry

Stage 2   The table will have the form you met in the answer to SAQ 1. A simple PRINT . . .,. . . will suffice to display the table.

```
100  REM★★DISPLAY THE TABLE★★
110  PRINT
120  PRINT
130  PRINT"INDEX","ITEM"
140  LET C=1
150  PRINT C,L(C)                          ─── prints the table
160  LET C=C+1
170  IF C<=5 THEN 150
```

Program 3   Printing the list in input order

Stage 3   Now we make C count from 5 down to 1 in order to print the list in reverse order.

```
200  REM★★OUTPUT LIST IN REVERSE★★
210  PRINT
220  PRINT
230  LET C=5
240  PRINT L(C)                            ─── prints list in reverse order
250  LET C=C−1
260  IF C>=1 THEN 240
```

Program 4   Printing in reverse order

We have shown the three program modules that provide the solution. All we have to do now is put them together as follows. The few changes (which don't affect what the program does) are explained in the comments.

Changes

```
10  REM★★INPUT A LIST★★
15  DIM L(5)
20  LET C=1
30  INPUT"ENTER THE NEXT NUMBER";L(C)
40  LET C=C+1
50  IF C<=5 THEN 30
60  REM ┐                        REM statements to help
70  REM ┘                        reader see the divisions in
                                 the program.
100 REM★★DISPLAY THE TABLE★★
110 PRINT
120 PRINT
130 PRINT"INDEX","ITEM"
```

98

```
140 LET D=1
150 PRINT D,L(D)
160 LET D=D+1
170 IF D<=5 THEN 150
180 REM
190 REM
200 REM★★OUTPUT LIST IN REVERSE★★
210 PRINT
220 PRINT
230 LET E=5
240 PRINT L(E)
250 LET E=E-1
260 IF E>=1 THEN 240
270 END
```

We've used D as an index to remind you that its name doesn't matter – only its value.

More REM's

150 BBC PRINT;D,L(D)

And we've used E here.

END added.

Program 5   The full reverse list program

```
RUN
ENTER THE NEXT NUMBER? -8
ENTER THE NEXT NUMBER? 15
ENTER THE NEXT NUMBER? 23
ENTER THE NEXT NUMBER? -4
ENTER THE NEXT NUMBER? 19

INDEX        ITEM
1            -8
2            15
3            23
4            -4
5            19

19
-4
23
15
-8
READY
```

K   Program 5.

To solve the problem in Example 3 we've done quite a bit of programming but the program only works for a list of five numbers. A small reward for a great effort! But if we change statements 20–50 which counted the five items, we can make the program accept any number of items so long as we know the number before inputting.

But we need to make DIM M$ depend on the number of items we are inputting. Because the counter C will go up to N+1 (watch line 50), DIM M$ needs to be N+1.

```
10   REM★★INPUT A LIST OF N ITEMS★★
20   INPUT"HOW MANY ITEMS IN THE LIST";N
25   DIM M$(N+1)
30   LET C=1
40   INPUT "ENTER THE NEXT ITEM";M$(C)
```

— any number of items can now be entered into the list M$(C)

```
50   LET C=C+1
60   IF C<=N THEN 40
```

Program 6

To be able to input any number of items of data into individual store locations with just half a dozen statements represents a significant improvement in programming technique. But, of course, we are never satisfied! Why should we bother to count the items, especially if the list is long, when we can get the computer to do it for us? The next exercise asks you to do this.

Exercise 1
Write a BASIC program to (a) input a list of numbers of unknown length; terminate the list with the dummy '−9999'. Call the list P(C) and assume that the list will be 30 or less items. So DIM P (31) will declare the list. Check your answer.
(b) Now modify your program to output those items whose index is odd.

4.5   The FOR . . . NEXT . . . loop

As we have said (repeatedly!) a computer is good at lots of repetitive operations. In order to control these operations we usually have to count them. Since we introduced the idea of counting in Unit 2, we have used the following sequence of statements several times.

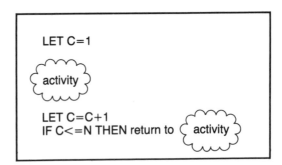

Program 7

These repetitive operations are so important in programming that special provision is made for them. In BASIC this is done by means of the FOR . . . NEXT . . . facility.

The sequence in Program 7 has three elements:

LET C = 1   which starts the count

LET C=C+1   which defines the incremental step (1 in this case; 2 in line 270 of the answer to Exercise 1)

C<=N   which stops the counting process

The same features occur in the FOR . . . NEXT . . . loop where the above sequence becomes:

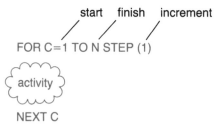

start   finish   increment

FOR C=1 TO N STEP (1)

activity

NEXT C

Program 8

Notice that NEXT C returns control to the line FOR C=1 TO N STEP (1) without you having to put the line number of FOR C . . . in the NEXT C statement.

Arrays and FOR. . . NEXT loops were made for each other. Together they form possibly the most potent facility of the BASIC language. Let's look in detail at how these loops work, and then repeat some of our earlier routines with lists using this new facility.

Examples of FOR. . . NEXT loops in action

(a)
```
10   FOR I=4 TO 10 STEP (2)
20   PRINT I
30   NEXT I
RUN
4
6
8
10
READY
```

(c)
```
10   FOR J=−3 TO 10 STEP(3)
20   PRINT J
30   NEXT J
RUN
−3
0
3
6
9
READY
```

(b)
```
10   FOR K=11 TO 4 STEP(−2)
20   PRINT K
30   NEXT K
RUN
11
9
7
5
READY
```

(d)
```
10   FOR L=4 TO −5 STEP(−2)
20   PRINT L
30   NEXT L
RUN
4
2
0
−2
−4
READY
```

Programs 9–12

SAQ 2
Write out the lists of numbers printed out by the following loops.

(a)
```
10   FOR E=1 TO 9 STEP(2)
20   PRINT E
30   NEXT E
```

(b)
```
10   FOR F=−30 TO −18 STEP(3)
20   PRINT F
30   NEXT F
```

101

(c)	(d)
10 FOR G=8 TO −4 STEP(−5)	10 FOR H=−2 TO −11 STEP(−4)
20 PRINT G	20 PRINT H
30 NEXT G	30 NEXT H

Programs 13–16

FOR. . . NEXT. . . with STEP (1)

The above examples and SAQ's had steps of 2, 3, −2, −4, and −5. Quite often, however, we simply want to use a step of 1. When that is the case, you can omit STEP(1) from the statement. Thus

FOR C=1 TO N

NEXT C

Program 17

is taken by the computer to mean a step of 1.

Input/output routines with FOR. . . NEXT

Routines are made easier by the FOR. . . NEXT facility. For example we can rewrite Program 5 using these loops. Notice that at lines 20 and 150 we require a step of 1 so STEP(1) has been omitted.

Comparison with Program 5

```
10  REM★★INPUT A LIST OF 5 NAMES★★
15  DIM L$(5)
20  FOR C=1 TO 5
30  INPUT "ENTER THE NEXT NAME";L$(C)          Replaces lines 20–50
40  NEXT C
50  REM
60  REM
100 REM★★DISPLAY THE TABLE★★
110 PRINT
120 PRINT
130 PRINT"INDEX","NAME"
140 PRINT
150 FOR D=1 TO 5
160 PRINT D, L$(D)                             Replaces lines 140–170
170 NEXT D
180 REM
190 REM
200 REM★★OUTPUT LIST IN REVERSE ORDER★★
210 PRINT
220 PRINT
230 FOR E=5 TO 1 STEP(−1)
240 PRINT E,L$(E)                              Replaces lines 230–260
250 NEXT E
280 END
```

Program 18 Using FOR. . . NEXT. . . to reverse a list

```
RUN
ENTER THE NEXT NAME? DICKENS
ENTER THE NEXT NAME? HARDY
ENTER THE NEXT NAME? SNOW
ENTER THE NEXT NAME? AUSTEN
ENTER THE NEXT NAME? ORWELL

INDEX          NAME

1              DICKENS
2              HARDY
3              SNOW
4              AUSTEN
5              ORWELL

5              ORWELL
4              AUSTEN
3              SNOW
2              HARDY
1              DICKENS
READY
```

K Program 18.

General FOR. . . NEXT loop

The FOR. . . NEXT loop can be expressed in quite general terms as

FOR I = S TO F STEP (J)

activity

NEXT I

providing that S, F and J are given 'reasonable' values before the loop is executed. Unreasonable values would be something like

S=2, F=10, and STEP(−3)

since you can't get from 2 to 10 in steps of −3, in the normal course of events.

Exercise 2
In Exercise 2 of Unit 2 you wrote a program (Program 19) to calculate the yield on an investment for a period of years to be specified. Re-write lines 40–90 of the program using a FOR. . . NEXT loop.

Exercise 3
If you are mathematically inquisitive you might like to try the following which demonstrates the potential of the FOR. . . NEXT loop. Write a program to tabulate the squares and cubes of the odd integers from 1 to 21 inclusive.

Output display
We always aim at a clear presentation of output data on the screen or printer. The FOR. . . NEXT facility is used widely in presenting output routines.

Use to skip lines. As you saw in the layout of letters in Unit 3 it is useful to 'print' blank lines. The following routine does this for you.

```
10  REM★★FOR....NEXT★★
20  REM★★TO SKIP LINES IN A PRINT ROUTINE★★
30  PRINT "HELLO"
40  FOR H=1 TO 10   ┐
50  PRINT            ├─────────── instruction to print 10 blank lines
60  NEXT H          ┘
70  PRINT"HELLO FROM 11 LINES BELOW"
80  END
```

Program 19

```
RUN
HELLO
```


HELLO FROM 11 LINES BELOW

K Program 19.

Drawing a line.   We may wish to print lines across the screen or page, e.g. to separate blocks of data or just to underline. The following routine does this.

```
10  REM★★FOR....NEXT★★
20  REM★★TO DRAW LINES★★
30  FOR M=1 TO 40   ┐
40  PRINT'★';        ├────────────instruction to print ★ 40 times
50  NEXT M          ┘
60  PRINT
90  END
```

Program 20

```
RUN
```

★★

> READY

SAQ 3
Why does line 40 in Program 20 have ; at the end of the line? What happens if line 40 is 40 PRINT "★"?

K Program 20.

Loops in flowcharts
Loops are so important that they have a special flowchart symbol of their own:

104

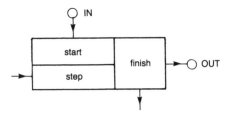

Figure 4a   Flowchart symbol for a FOR. . . NEXT. . . loop

The floating ends are the connections to the activity:

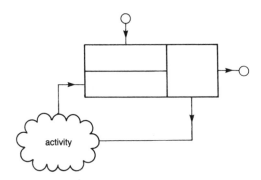

Figure 4b   Flowchart symbol's relationship to activity

4.6   Nested loops

Program 20 drew a line of 40 asterisks. We can re-write the program so that we can specify in line 30 a number of asterisks and so vary the length of the line. So with the program:

```
10   REM★★LINES OF DIFFERENT LENGTH★★
20   LET N=1                                        number to go in line 30
30   FOR M=1 TO N
40   PRINT "★";
50   NEXT M
60   PRINT
70   END
```

Program 21

we get

```
RUN
★
READY
```

To vary the line length we simply key in

20 LET N= required length

and key run:

20 LET N=2

RUN
★★
READY

20 LET N=3

RUN
★★★
READY

20 LET N=4

RUN
★★★★
READY

20 LET N=8

RUN
★★★★★★★★
READY

20 LET N=16

RUN
★★★★★★★★★★★★★★★★
READY

20 LET N=32

RUN
★★★★★★★★★★★★★★★★★★★★★★★★★★★★★★★★
READY

K̲ Program 21.

Nested FOR. . . NEXT loops
You have seen in Program 21 how you can control the effect of the FOR. . . NEXT
loop of lines 30–50 by changing the value of N. We hope by now that the 'obvious'
question springs to your mind: 'Why not control the value of N by using another
FOR. . . NEXT loop?' The following program does just that. The M-loop of lines
30–50 is itself controlled by the N-loop of lines 20–70. The M-loop is said to be
'nested' within the N-loop.

```
10  REM★★NESTED FOR. . . NEXT LOOPS★★
20  FOR N=1 TO 16
30  FOR M=1 TO N                          Inner loop: controls number
40  PRINT"★";                             of ★ in each row
50  NEXT M
60  PRINT                                 Outer loop: controls the
70  NEXT N                                rows
80  END
```

Program 22 Nested loops

```
RUN
★
★★
★★★
★★★★
★★★★★
★★★★★★
★★★★★★★
★★★★★★★★
★★★★★★★★★
★★★★★★★★★★
★★★★★★★★★★★
★★★★★★★★★★★★
★★★★★★★★★★★★★
★★★★★★★★★★★★★★
★★★★★★★★★★★★★★★
★★★★★★★★★★★★★★★★
READY
```

It is important that you understand how this works. For example, when the computer has just finished printing the 9th row of asterisks N will be 9. It leaves the inner loop (line 50) and control goes to the outer loop (line 60). A blank line is printed and N then increases to its next value of 10. Control reverts to the inner loop at line 30. The computer then goes around the inner loop (lines 30–50) ten times before exiting again to line 60.

K Program 22.

More print patterns from loops
If generating print patterns with loops appeals to you, here is another one plus two Exercises.

```
10  REM★★NESTED FOR. . . NEXT LOOPS★★
15  LET P=1
20  FOR N=1 TO 5
25  LET P=2★P                             Multiplies current value of
30  FOR M=1 TO P                          P by 2 for each pass
40  PRINT"★";                             around loop.
50  NEXT M
60  PRINT
70  NEXT N
80  END
```

Program 23

```
RUN
★★                                                                    P= 2
★★★★                                                                  P= 4
★★★★★★★★                                                              P= 8
★★★★★★★★★★★★★★★★                                                      P=16
★★★★★★★★★★★★★★★★★★★★★★★★★★★★★★★★                                      P=32

READY
```

K Program 23.

Exercise 4
Write a program using nested loops to print out the 7, 8 and 9 multiplication tables.

Exercise 5
Write a program using nested loops to print out rectangles of asterisks of dimensions to be chosen by the user.

4.7 Interchanging

We considered the problem of finding the smaller of 2 numbers in Unit 2, and the smallest of 3 in Unit 3. In this Unit we have done exercises on interchanging items of a list, in preparation for writing an interchange program.

We have been comparing the items of a list with that at position 1, and interchanging if the item in the list is smaller than that at position 1. When you did this in SAQ 1, you did it manually and we have not yet looked at the problems of writing a program to perform the interchange. We can't just say

Copy A into B and then B into A

since the first transaction 'copy A into B' overwrites and destroys what's in B, giving us copies of A in A and in B. Instead we have to put the contents of B away in some safe temporary store before we overwrite B with A. We can show the process diagrammatically:

```
               TEMP←B
               B←A
               A←TEMP
```

Where ← means place the number in the right hand store into the left hand store.

Suppose, for example, you want to sort a list of names N$-list and you want to interchange the first name, N$(1) with some other name N$(K) at position K. This can be done using a temporary store location T$:

```
               T$←N$(K)
               N$(K)←N$(1)
               N$(1)←T$
```

108

Remember that it is the contents of N$(1) and N$(K) that are being swapped. Suppose N$(1)=FRED and N$(K)=JIM then this is what is happening:

	Store locations		
	N$(1)	N$(K)	T$
start	FRED	JIM	
next stage	FRED	JIM	JIM
next stage	FRED	FRED	JIM
end	JIM	FRED	JIM

(The fact that T$ still has JIM in it doesn't matter: we have achieved the object which is to swap the locations of FRED and JIM).

Flowchart for name sort
In the number sort (SAQ 1) we wanted to put the lowest number at the top of the list. So we test each name in turn against the one currently at the top of the list and interchange only if the name under test comes before the one at the top of the list. A flowchart for this is:

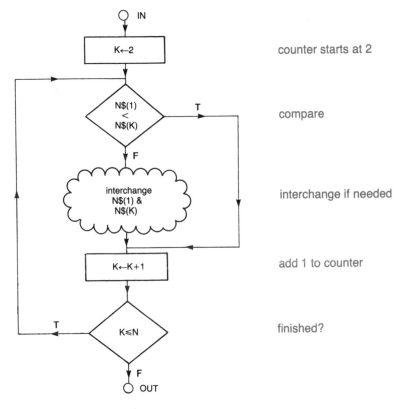

counter starts at 2

compare

interchange if needed

add 1 to counter

finished?

Figure 5a Flowchart for interchange

109

Or, if we want to use the special flowchart symbol for FOR. . . NEXT. . . , it would look like:

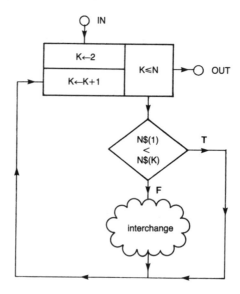

Figure 5b   Flowchart for interchange with FOR. . . NEXT. . . symbol

This new routine can now be used to construct a program.

Example 4
Write a program to enter a list of names of unknown length into an array, print out this list with index in input order. By means of the interchange routine place the name of lowest alphabetic value in position 1 in the list, and output the new list.

Solution

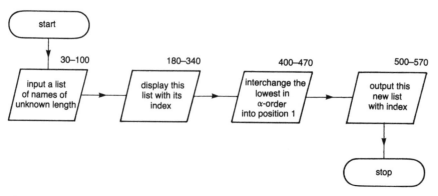

Figure 6   Flowchart for Example 4

110

Interchange program

```
10   REM★★FIRST IN ALPHA-ORDER★★
20   CLEAR 100
25   DIM N$(30)
30   PRINT"ENTER A LIST OF NAMES ONE BY ONE"
40   PRINT"END THE LIST WITH ZZZZ"
50   PRINT
60   LET I=1
70   INPUT"NEXT NAME";N$(I)
80   IF N$(I)="ZZZZ" THEN 200         ├─────────── inputting list
90   LET I=I+1
100  GOTO 70
180  REM★★★★★★★★★★★★★★
190  REM★★WE DON'T WANT ZZZZ IN OUR LIST, SO★★  ┐ finding number
200  LET N=I−1                                   ├─ of names
210  REM★★★★★★★★★★★★★★                           ┘ entered
300  PRINT
310  PRINT"INDEX","ITEM"
320  FOR J=1 TO N
330  PRINT J, N$(J)              ├─────────── print list
340  NEXT J
400  REM★★★★★★★★★★★★
410  REM★★INTERCHANGE ROUTINE★★
420  FOR K=2 TO N
430  IF N$(1)<N$(K) THEN 470
440  LET T$=N$(K)
450  LET N$(K)=N$(1)             ├─────────── interchange
460  LET N$(1)=T$
470  NEXT K
500  REM★★★★★★★★★★★★
510  PRINT
520  PRINT"LIST AFTER INTERCHANGE"
530  PRINT
540  PRINT"INDEX","ITEM"
550  FOR L=1 TO N
560  PRINT L,N$(L)               ├─────────── print interchanged order
570  NEXT L
580  END
```

Program 24 Finding the first item in alphabetical order

Interchange program runs

```
RUN
ENTER A LIST OF NAMES ONE BY ONE
END THE LIST WITH ZZZZ

NEXT NAME? JONES
NEXT NAME? PRICE
NEXT NAME? DAVIES
NEXT NAME? EVANS
NEXT NAME? ZZZZ
```

INDEX	ITEM
1	JONES
2	PRICE
3	DAVIES
4	EVANS

LIST AFTER INTERCHANGE

INDEX	ITEM
1	DAVIES
2	PRICE
3	JONES
4	EVANS

READY

If a print routine is inserted into the interchange procedure as below (lines 470–478), then we can look at the effect of each pass round the loop.

```
400  REM★★★★★★★★★★★★★★★★★★★★★★★★★★★★★★★★★★★★★★★★★★
410  REM★★INTERCHANGE ROUTINE★★
420  FOR K=2 TO N
430  IF N$(1)<N$(K) THEN 470
440  LET T$=N$(K)
450  LET N$(K)=N$(1)
460  LET N$(1)=T$
470  PRINT
472  FOR L=1 TO N
474  PRINT N$(L);" ";
476  NEXT L
478  PRINT
480  NEXT K
500  REM★★★★★★★★★★★★★★★★★★★★★★★★★★★★★★★★★★★★★★★★★★
```

lines 472–478: print routine to observe pass round the loop

K̄ Program 24 with lines 400 to 500 as above.

Assignment 4

1. It will probably have occurred to you by now that, having placed the item of lowest value into position 1, we could repeat the procedure by placing the item of lowest value in the remainder of the list into position 2, and so on for the rest of the list. The sort of the complete list in this way demands nested FOR. . . NEXT. . . loops.

Modify Program 24 to sort a complete list into alphabetical order.

2. Input a file of names and associated telephone numbers into two lists N$(I) and T$(I) respectively. Use the index I to search through the file to find a particular name, and if found then to output the associated telephone number.

Objectives of Unit 4

Now that you have completed this Unit, check that you are able to write simple programs using:

List store location names
 to input lists ☐
 to print lists ☐

Counters to count the number of items in a list. ☐

FOR. . . NEXT. . . loops
 to print a list ☐
 to input a list ☐
 to print ★ layouts ☐

Nested loops
 to print ★ layouts ☐

Interchange routine ☐

Answers to SAQ's and Exercises

SAQ 1
The six stages of the procedure are shown here in the following program run:

```
RUN
ENTER A LIST OF NAMES ONE BY ONE
END THE LIST WITH ZZZZ

NEXT NAME? 6
NEXT NAME? 8
NEXT NAME? 4
NEXT NAME? 7
NEXT NAME? 3
NEXT NAME? 9
NEXT NAME? 1
NEXT NAME? ZZZZ
```

INDEX	ITEM
1	6
2	8
3	4
4	7
5	3
6	9
7	1

```
6  8  4  7  3  9  1

4  8  6  7  3  9  1

4  8  6  7  3  9  1

3  8  6  7  4  9  1

3  8  6  7  4  9  1

1  8  6  7  4  9  3
```

LIST AFTER INTERCHANGE

INDEX	ITEM
1	1
2	8
3	6
4	7
5	4
6	9
7	3

READY

Exercise 1

Notice that we've used lots of REM statements to tell you how the program works.

```
5    DIM P(31)
10   REM★★A LIST OF NUMBERS OF UNKNOWN LENGTH★★
20   PRINT"ENTER THE ELEMENTS OF THE LIST"
22   PRINT"ITEM BY ITEM AS REQUESTED"
24   PRINT"END THE LIST WITH THE DUMMY '−9999'"
26   PRINT
30   LET C=1
40   INPUT"ENTER THE NEXT NUMBER";P(C)
50   IF P(C)=−9999 THEN 100                          ───────── Input sequence
60   LET C=C+1
70   GOTO 40
80   REM★★★★★★★★★★★★★★
90   REM★★REMEMBER 'C' COUNTED −9999 AS AN ITEM★    Taking correct
100  LET N=C−1   ]───────────────────────────────────  total from counter
110  REM★★★★★★★★★★★★★★
120  REM
130  REM
200  REM★★OUTPUT THE ITEMS WHOSE INDEX IS ODD★★
210  REM★★3=1+2..5=3+2..7=5+2..ETC. . . . . . . . . .★★
220  LET C=1
230  PRINT
240  PRINT
250  PRINT"ODD INDEX","ITEM"                         ───────── Output sequence
260  PRINT C,P(C)
270  LET C=C+2
```

114

```
280  IF C<=N THEN 260
290  END
```

Program 25

```
RUN
ENTER THE ELEMENTS OF THE LIST
ITEM BY ITEM AS REQUESTED
END THE LIST WITH THE DUMMY '−9999'

ENTER THE NEXT NUMBER? 42
ENTER THE NEXT NUMBER? −12
ENTER THE NEXT NUMBER? 37
ENTER THE NEXT NUMBER? 92
ENTER THE NEXT NUMBER? 11
ENTER THE NEXT NUMBER? −3
ENTER THE NEXT NUMBER? −9999

ODD INDEX     ITEM
1             42
3             37
5             11
READY
```

SAQ 2

(a) 1, 3, 5, 7, 9.   (c) 8, 3, −2.
(b) −30, −27, −24, −21, −18. (d) −2, −6, −10.

Exercise 2

```
10   REM★★COMPOUND INTEREST★★
20   PRINT"ENTER YEARS, DEPOSIT AND %INTEREST"
30   INPUT N,D,P
35   REM★★★★★★★★★★★★★★
40   FOR C=1 TO N
50   LET Y=(P★D)/100
60   PRINT "YEAR ";C,"YIELD ";Y                  The FOR NEXT . . . loop
70   LET D=D+Y
80   NEXT C
90   REM★★★★★★★★★★★★★★
100  END
```

Program 26

```
RUN
ENTER YEARS, DEPOSIT AND %INTEREST
? 5,500,11.25
YEAR      1          YIELD     56.25
YEAR      2          YIELD     62.5781
YEAR      3          YIELD     69.6182
YEAR      4          YIELD     77.4502
YEAR      5          YIELD     86.1634
READY
```

Exercise 3

```
10  REM★★SQUARES AND CUBES★★
20  PRINT"NUMBER","SQUARE","CUBE"
30  FOR I=1 TO 21 STEP(2)
40  LET S=I★I
50  LET C=I★I★I
60  PRINT I,S,C
70  NEXT I
80  END
```
Program 27

```
RUN
NUMBER          SQUARE          CUBE
1               1               1
3               9               27
5               25              125
7               49              343
9               81              729
11              121             1331
13              169             2197
15              225             3375
17              289             4913
19              361             6859
21              441             9261
READY
```

SAQ 3

; suppresses the print return so that the print head stops after printing ★. Thus the next ★ will be printed on the same line. Without ; the asterisks would be printed in a column 40 print lines deep.

Exercise 4

```
10   REM★★MULTIPLICATION TABLES★★
40   FOR T=7 TO 9
50   FOR K=1 TO 12
60   LET P=K★T
70   PRINT K;" TIMES ";T;"=";P
80   NEXT K
90   PRINT
100  NEXT T
110  END
```
Program 28

```
RUN
1 TIMES 7 = 7
2 TIMES 7 = 14
3 TIMES 7 = 21
4 TIMES 7 = 28
5 TIMES 7 = 35
6 TIMES 7 = 42
7 TIMES 7 = 49
8 TIMES 7 = 56
9 TIMES 7 = 63
```

```
10 TIMES 7 = 70
11 TIMES 7 = 77
12 TIMES 7 = 84

1 TIMES 8 = 8
2 TIMES 8 = 16
3 TIMES 8 = 24
4 TIMES 8 = 32
5 TIMES 8 = 40
6 TIMES 8 = 48
7 TIMES 8 = 56
8 TIMES 8 = 64
9 TIMES 8 = 72
10 TIMES 8 = 80
11 TIMES 8 = 88          we still have a lot to learn about 'tabulation'.
12 TIMES 8 = 96

1 TIMES 9 = 9
2 TIMES 9 = 18
3 TIMES 9 = 27
4 TIMES 9 = 36
5 TIMES 9 = 45
6 TIMES 9 = 54
7 TIMES 9 = 63
8 TIMES 9 = 72
9 TIMES 9 = 81
10 TIMES 9 = 90
11 TIMES 9 = 99
12 TIMES 9 = 108

READY
```

Exercise 5

```
10   INPUT "LENGTH OF RECTANGLE"; L
20   INPUT "WIDTH OF RECTANGLE"; W          BBC: omit; in 10 and 20
30   FOR I=1 TO W
40   FOR J = 1 TO L
50   PRINT "★";
60   NEXT J
70   PRINT
80   NEXT I
```

UNIT 5
An end to strings and PRINT

5.1 Introduction

The earlier units were concerned with introducing topics; new ideas came thick and fast. This Unit is mainly concerned with strings, but you will meet the TAB statement which is an important addition to your printing repertoire. The title of this Unit is a slight exaggeration, but by the end of this Unit you will have met most of the main string and print functions of the BASIC language.

5.2 Length of a string of characters

We asked the question 'How long is a piece of string?' in Unit 3. At the time it may have seemed a rather facetious question, but the number of characters contained in a particular string storage location is often a vital piece of information. This is especially so if we are trying to use the memory allocation of a particular computer as efficiently as possible.

In BASIC the operation LEN(A$) gives the length of A$ as a number of characters. Thus:

If A$="FRED" then LEN (A$) = 4
If B$="I" LEN (B$) = 1

SAQ 1
What are the values of the following:

(a) LEN (C$) where C$= "ANN"   (c) LEN (E$) where E$ = "72"
(b) LEN (D$) where D$ = "A"   (d) LEN (F$) where F$ = "CAT 123"

Example 1
Write a BASIC program to input a list of words, ending with ZZZZ, and to print out the length of each word.

Solution
We have arranged the program to read in the words from a DATA statement in order to reduce the inputting time needed. Each word read from DATA is held in W$ (line 100) and its length stored in L (line 120). Then the result is printed out at line 140.

```
10  REM★★LENGTH OF A WORD★★
20  REM★★★★★★★★★★★★
30  REM★★READ WORDS FROM A DATA LIST ONE BY ONE★★
40  REM★★AND OUTPUT THEIR LENGTHS★★
90  REM★★★★★★★★★★★★
100 READ W$
110 IF W$="ZZZZ" THEN 200
120 LET L=LEN(W$)                          READ, LEN, PRINT cycle
130 PRINT
140 PRINT W$;" HAS ";L;" LETTERS"
150 GOTO 100
200 END
900 DATA DEVISE, AN, ALGORITHM, AND, WRITE, A, BASIC, PROGRAM
910 DATA ZZZZ
```

Program 1   Measuring word lengths

```
RUN
DEVISE HAS 6 LETTERS

AN HAS 2 LETTERS

ALGORITHM HAS 9 LETTERS

AND HAS 3 LETTERS

WRITE HAS 5 LETTERS

A HAS 1 LETTERS

BASIC HAS 5 LETTERS

PROGRAM HAS 7 LETTERS
```
K͟ Program 1.

5.3 Frequency tables

Measuring the frequency with which something occurs is commonly needed in
handling numerical information. For example, a knowledge of the frequency with
which certain letters occur in normal language usage is an important factor in
code-breaking activities. In order to measure frequencies it is useful to be able to
use the simple technique used in statistical analysis of tally marks. This first paper
and pencil example introduces this.

Tally marks
Example 2
Find the frequency with which each vowel occurs in the words in the following
DATA statements.

```
900  DATA THE, HORSE, STOOD, STILL, TILL, HE, HAD, FINISHED, THE, HYMN
910  DATA WHICH, JUDE, REPEATED, UNDER, THE, SWAY, OF, A,
     POLYTHEISTIC
920  DATA FANCY, THAT, HE, WOULD, NEVER, HAVE, THOUGHT, OF,
     HUMOURING
930  DATA IN, BROAD, DAYLIGHT, ZZZZ
```

Solution
There are two ways to approach the problem.
(a) Go through crossing out and counting up all the A's, and then through again
     counting the number of E's, etc. This would involve 5 passes through the data
     for fairly sparse information (i.e. for a low hit-rate);
(b) Draw up a table as below and take each vowel in sequence:

THÉ: put a tally mark in the E row;

HÓRSÉ: put a mark in the O row, followed by another in the E row;

STÓÓD: put two more marks in the O row.

121

Vowel	Count				Total count or frequency
A	卌	1111			9
E	卌	卌	卌	1	16
I	卌	卌			10
O	卌	卌			10
U	卌	1			6

900 DATA THÉ, HÓRSÉ, STÓÓD, STÍLL, TÍLL, HÉ, HÁD, FÍNÍSHÉD, THÉ, HYMN
910 DATA WHÍCH, JÚDÉ, RÉPÉÁTÉD, ÚNDÉR, THÉ, SWÁY, ÓF, Á, PÓLYTHÉÍSTÍC
920 DATA FÁNCY, THÁT, HÉ, WÓÚLD, NÉVÉR, HÁVÉ, THÓÚGHT, ÓF, HÚMÓÚRÍNG
930 DATA ÍN, BRÓÁD, DÁYLÍGHT, ZZZZ

Figure 1 Completed tally count

SAQ 2
Use the tally method to draw up a frequency table of the lengths of words for the data in Example 2.

Getting the computer to count
Having found a paper and pencil method of counting frequencies, we now need a method of getting the computer to do the counting of a list. The power of lists is derived from an apt use of the index. In question 2 of Assignment 4 we saw how the items of two lists of data (name and telephone number lists) were linked by a common index. The 3rd member of the number-list was the telephone number for the 3rd name in the name-list, etc. Generally the I-th member of the name-list is linked to the I-th member of number-list.

Suppose we want to count the number of times the digits 0, 1, 2, . . . 9 occur in a sequence. We can use 10 counters:

C(0), C(1), C(2) . . .   C(9)

each of which will be zero at the start. To count the digits in 473808 we take the first digit in the sequence: 4. 1 is added to C(4) and so on:

Digits entered	Counters after entry									
	C(0)	C(1)	C(2)	C(3)	C(4)	C(5)	C(6)	C(7)	C(8)	C(9)
start	0	0	0	0	0	0	0	0	0	0
4	0	0	0	0	1	0	0	0	0	0
7	0	0	0	0	1	0	0	1	0	0
3	0	0	0	1	1	0	0	1	0	0
8	0	0	0	1	1	0	0	1	1	0
0	1	0	0	1	1	0	0	1	1	0
8	1	0	0	1	1	0	0	1	2	0

So the idea is that when I is entered at the key-board, increment C(I) by 1. This can be achieved in just two BASIC statements.

```
120 INPUT I
140 LET C(I)=C(I)+1
```
———————————————— A list counter

SAQ 3

The sequence

```
10  INPUT N
20  LET C(N)=C(N)+1
```

is used to count the number of 0's, 1's, 2's, etc. in the following input data: 3, 1, 0, 5, 9, 9, 6, 6, 6, 0, 4, 4, 2, 4, 1, 2, 1, 3, 0, 2, 1, 3. What are the values of the following:

(a)   C(3) after 3 numbers have been inputted.
(b)   C(9) after 12 numbers have been inputted.
(c)   C(1) after all the numbers have been inputted.
(d)   C(0) after all the numbers have been inputted.

We will now use this method of counting a list in an example.

Example 3

Write a program to input a sequence of single digits and to output the frequency with which each digit occurs.

Solution

A digit is one of the set of 10 numbers 0, 1, 2, 3 . . . 9. We will enter these one by one, with the sequence being terminated by −9999. So far, very routine!

The counting list will have 10 counters:

C(0), C(1), C(2) . . .   C(9)

The program to solve the complete problem has two parts. (i) The input and increment routine incorporates the two statements 120 and 140 discussed above. (ii) The output routine is driven by a FOR. . . NEXT loop, with index J running from 0 to 9.

```
10   REM★★COUNT THE NUMBER OF TIMES EACH DIGIT IS ENTERED★★
20   REM★★AND STORE IN A COUNT-LIST C(I)★★
30   REM★★★★★★★★★★★★★★★★★★★★★★
40   DIM C(10)
100  PRINT"ENTER A SERIES OF INDIVIDUAL DIGITS"
110  PRINT"ENDING THE LIST WITH −9999"
120  INPUT"NEXT DIGIT";I
130  IF I=−9999 THEN 200
140  LET C(I)=C(I)+1
150  GOTO 120
190  REM★★★★★★★★★★★★★★★★★★
200  PRINT
210  PRINT"DIGIT","COUNT"
220  PRINT
230  FOR J=0 TO 9
240  PRINT J, C(J)
250  NEXT J
260  END
```

(statements 120–150) — input and counting routine
(statements 230–250) — printing table

Program 2   Counting with a list counter C(I)

Typical output

(After entering 3, 7, 6, 4, 9, 1, 4, 9, 2, 7, 8, 0, 1, 5, 2, 7, −9999.)

DIGIT	COUNT
0	1
1	2
2	2
3	1
4	2
5	1
6	1
7	3
8	1
9	2

K Program 2.

Frequency table for string lengths

We have written two programs so far in this Unit: the first to find the lengths of strings, and the second to build up a frequency table.

In the following exercise we want you to combine these two ideas to build up a frequency table of lengths of words. If you wish you can use the words in the DATA statements already used in Example 2. Assume that the words will not be longer than 15 characters, so the length-list will have elements:

L(1), L(2), L(3) . . .   L(15).

Exercise 1

Write a program to read in a set of words and to display a frequency table of their lengths.

5.4 Frequency diagrams

Frequency diagram for number of vowels

The picture of tally marks in Figure 1 makes a more immediate impact on us and somehow gives us more information about the distribution of frequencies of the vowels than just the column of figures. So why not get the computer to print a picture for us? You saw how to print rows of asterisks in Unit 4 by driving the print head across the page (or screen) with a FOR. . . NEXT loop of variable range.

SAQ 4

What will appear on the screen as a result of the following program?

```
10  READ A
20  FOR I=1 TO A
30  PRINT "★";
40  NEXT I
```

```
45   PRINT
50   GOTO 10
100  DATA 2, 5, 7, 8, 3, 1
```

Program 3

We can do the same thing using the frequencies from Figure 1 to determine the range and thus the number of asterisks printed across the page. This will generate a picture of the distribution.

Example 4
Write a program to print out a frequency diagram for the distribution of vowels given in Example 2.

Solution
Notice that this program draws the diagram from the frequencies we have already calculated. We have stored these frequencies in the DATA statement in line 900.

We read the frequencies (lines 50 to 80) with a counter F(K) where F(1) is the number of a's, F(2) the number of e's, etc.

Then we print asterisks across the page according to the value of F(K) (lines 220 to 250).

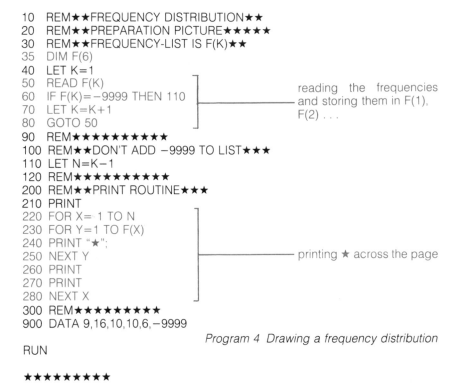

```
10   REM★★FREQUENCY DISTRIBUTION★★
20   REM★★PREPARATION PICTURE★★★★★
30   REM★★FREQUENCY-LIST IS F(K)★★
35   DIM F(6)
40   LET K=1
50   READ F(K)                              ⎤
60   IF F(K)=−9999 THEN 110                  ⎥   reading the frequencies
70   LET K=K+1                               ⎥   and storing them in F(1),
80   GOTO 50                                 ⎦   F(2) . . .
90   REM★★★★★★★★★★
100  REM★★DON'T ADD −9999 TO LIST★★★
110  LET N=K−1
120  REM★★★★★★★★★★
200  REM★★PRINT ROUTINE★★★
210  PRINT
220  FOR X= 1 TO N                          ⎤
230  FOR Y=1 TO F(X)                        ⎥
240  PRINT "★";                             ⎥
250  NEXT Y                                 ⎥   printing ★ across the page
260  PRINT                                  ⎥
270  PRINT                                  ⎥
280  NEXT X                                 ⎦
300  REM★★★★★★★★★★
900  DATA 9,16,10,10,6,−9999
```

Program 4 Drawing a frequency distribution

```
RUN
```

★★★★★★★★★

★★★★★★★★★★★★★★★★

★★★★★★★★★★

★★★★★★★★★★

★★★★★★

K̲ Program 4.

Frequency diagram for length of words

If we want to draw a diagram of the frequencies with which the word lengths occurred in SAQ 1, we need to modify Program 4. Two modifications are necessary:

First the frequency list contains more items. There are 15 frequencies (1 to 15) plus −9999, so that's 16 items and we add 35 DIM F(16) to Program 4.

Second the print routine at line 220 will run into problems when the frequency is zero. We can't drive the FOR. . . NEXT loop from 1 to 0! So we must prevent the program going into the FOR. . . NEXT loop when the frequency is zero. To do this we add 225 IF F(X)=0 THEN 260.

So the program is

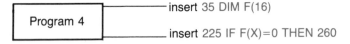

And of course, line 900 is now:

900 DATA 1, 5, 4, 6, 9, 0, 1, 3, 1, 0, 0, 1, 0, 0, 0, −9999.

A run of the modified Program 4 produces:

```
★
★★★★★
★★★★
★★★★★★
★★★★★★★★★

★
★★★
★

★
```
―――――――――――→―――――print out ends about here!

Figure 2   Frequency diagram of modified Program 4

K̲ Program 4 (modified).

5.5 Tabulation

We've got the essential ingredients of a picture, but it is still far from being a meaningful diagram. It will help if we have the facility to move the print head across the page or screen to any pre-determined position. In typing this is called tabulation (to arrange in tabular or table-form). In BASIC the TAB function does this for us.

We take the same approach as we did in Unit 3, namely to write a snippet of program which explains itself – an approach well worth cultivating!

First, look at what happens if you number print positions across the screen:

```
50  PRINT"1234567890123456789012345678901234567890"
60  PRINT"A";TAB(5);"E";TAB(7);"I";TAB(19);"O";TAB(31);"U"

RUN
1234567890123456789012345678901234567890
A   E I           O           U
READY
```
Program 5

You can see that TAB(5) printed E at the sixth position. Why? Because the machine counts print positions from position 0. This is demonstrated by Program 6 where the scale across the screen goes from 0:

```
50  PRINT"0123456789012345678901234567890123456789"
60  PRINT"A";TAB(5);"E";TAB(7);"I";TAB(19);"O";TAB(31);"U"

RUN
0123456789012345678901234567890123456789
A    E I           O           U
READY
```
Program 6

Now TAB(5) goes to the position labelled 5 but it is still in the sixth position across the screen.

SAQ 5
Write a program to print COL 1, COL 2, COL 3 across the screen with COL 1 starting at position 0, COL 2 at position 10 and COL 3 at position 20.

Variable TAB and its effects
We can drive line 60 of the vowel print with a FOR. . . NEXT loop to produce an actual table.

```
50  FOR I=1 TO 7
60  PRINT"A";TAB(5);"E";TAB(7);"I";TAB(19);"O";TAB(31);"U"
70  NEXT I
```
Program 7

```
RUN
A    E  I          O              U
A    E  I          O              U
A    E  I          O              U
A    E  I          O              U
A    E  I          O              U
A    E  I          O              U
A    E  I          O              U
READY
```

Here is another example which shows how we can drive TAB with a variable. If we use TAB(V) where V is a variable, we can drive the print head to different positions across the screen. The program

```
30   FOR A=1 TO 10
40   PRINT TAB(A);"HELLO"
50   NEXT A
60   END
```

Value of A in TAB(A) is determined by the loop variable A.

Program 8

produces:

```
RUN
HELLO
 HELLO
  HELLO
   HELLO
    HELLO
     HELLO
      HELLO
       HELLO
        HELLO
         HELLO
>READY
```

We can go one step further and combine these two effects in one program:

```
50   FOR I=1 TO 7
60   PRINT TAB(0+I);"A";TAB(5+I);"E";TAB(7+I);"I";
65   PRINT TAB(19+I);"O";TAB(31+I);"U"
70   NEXT I
80   END
```

Program 9

```
RUN
A    E  I        O          U
 A    E  I        O          U
  A    E  I        O          U
   A    E  I        O          U
    A    E  I        O          U
     A    E  I        O          U
      A    E  I        O          U
```

SAQ 6
Write a program segment to input three numbers of the user's choice which will

128

place the string "HEADING" at three different positions across the same output line.

TAB and the frequency diagram

We are now in a position to set out the frequency diagram of figure 2 in a more attractive manner.

The print routine of the modified Program 4 (lines 200 to 300) was:

```
200  REM★★PRINT ROUTINE★★★★★★★★★★★★★
210  PRINT
220  FOR X=1 TO N
225  IF F(X)=0 THEN 260
230  FOR Y=1 TO F(X)
240  PRINT "★";
250  NEXT Y
260  PRINT
270  PRINT
280  NEXT X
300  REM ★★★
```

Program 4 (modified)

We add:

line 212 to print column headings.

line 214 to print a rule across the screen.

line 216 to start the column divides (the rest of the divides we printed by the following loop).

line 222 (in the loop) prints X and F(X) across the page plus the column divides. This line ends in ";" which makes the next PRINT instruction (line 240) appear on the same line.

You will probably have to study this carefully to see all the detail in it:

10 to 120 see Program 4.

```
200  REM★★PRINT ROUTINE★★★★★★★★★★★★★★
210  PRINT
212  PRINT"LENGTH";TAB(8);"FREQ";TAB(18);"TALLY"
214  PRINT"— — — — — — — — — — — — — — — — — — — "
216  PRINT TAB(7);"I";TAB(12);"I"
220  FOR X= 1 TO N
222  PRINT TAB(2);X;TAB(7);"I";TAB(9);F(X);TAB(12);"I";TAB(14);
225  IF F(X)=0 THEN 260
230  FOR Y=1 TO F(X)
240  PRINT"★";
250  NEXT Y
260  PRINT
280  NEXT X
300  REM★★★★★★★★★★★★★★★★★★★★★★★★★★★★★★★★★★★★★
900  DATA 1,5,4,6,9,0,1,3,1,0,0,1,0,0,0,−9999
```

Program 10

RUN

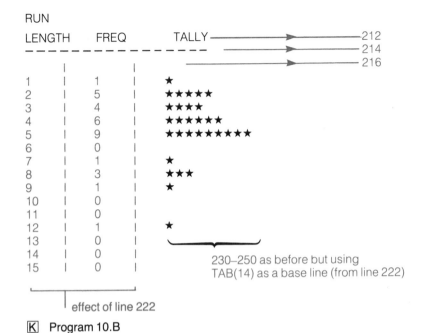

LENGTH	FREQ	TALLY
1	1	★
2	5	★★★★★
3	4	★★★★
4	6	★★★★★★
5	9	★★★★★★★★★
6	0	
7	1	★
8	3	★★★
9	1	★
10	0	
11	0	
12	1	★
13	0	
14	0	
15	0	

→ 212
→ 214
→ 216

230–250 as before but using
TAB(14) as a base line (from line 222)

effect of line 222

K̲ Program 10.B

Exercise 2
Modify Program 4 to give a print-out similar to that developed for Program 10 and to include the following points:
(a) an appropriate change of headings;
(b) a print-out of the letters A, E, I, O and U as appropriate in the left-hand column;
(c) an appropriate scale at the base of the diagram.

5.6 Cutting up strings

Let's now look at a string which, though being an entity in its own right, contains more than one item of information. For example, 23 June 1971 is a single date but there are occasions when we only want to look at part of it, e.g. the month.

Filing dates
How many times have you been faced with a box on a form like this?

If we look at D D M M Y Y the presentation has problems. Compare

23rd June 1971, or 230671

and 14th Sept 1973, and 140973.

The later date has the smaller number. Whereas with

4 July 1933, or 040733

15 Jan 1967, and 150167

the later date has the larger number. Clearly then D D M M Y Y is not very useful for filing dates.

The solution is to put the dates in the form Y Y M M D D. This makes the four dates above:

330704, 670115, 710623, and 730914

giving date and number consistency.

Dates are usually stored as numbers in the machine for use in calculations but are entered as strings to allow checking procedures to occur before they are stored.

If we are interested in a salary increment, then the year and month parts of the number would be important. If we are a music centre and send out reminders to our clients every three months to have their pianos tuned, then only the month may be important. The whole data-string is important in its own right, but we can see that there may be valid reasons for cutting it up.

LEFT$(X$,I) and RIGHT$(X$,I)
If we want to consider part of a string, then we need a statement that will do this for us. We will start with two such statements.

LEFT$(X$,I) gives the left-most I characters of the string X$.

e.g. if X$ = "CUTTING"
then LEFT$(X$,3) = CUT

RIGHT$(X$,I) gives the right-most I characters of X$.

e.g. RIGHT$(X$,4) = TING

Let's get the machine to tell us its own story. We enter a 6-character string and use the index I of the FOR. . . NEXT loop to peel off sub-strings of lengths 1 to 6. The scale (line 30) helps you to identify what's happening.

```
10  REM★★STRING TEST★★
20  INPUT "ENTER A 6-CHARACTER STRING";X$
30  PRINT TAB(10);"1234567890"
40  FOR I=1 TO 6
50  LET A$=LEFT$(X$,I)
60  PRINT I;TAB(10);A$
70  NEXT I
```

60 BBC: PRINT;I;TAB(10);A$

Program 11

Left string run

```
RUN
ENTER A 6-CHARACTER STRING? 123456
        1234567890
1       1
2       12
3       123
4       1234
5       12345
6       123456
READY
```

Now if we change line 50 of Program 11 to

50 LET A$=RIGHT$(X$,I)

and enter the string ABCDEF the result is:

Right string run

```
RUN
ENTER A 6-CHARACTER STRING? ABCDEF
        1234567890
1       F
2       EF
3       DEF
4       CDEF
5       BCDEF
6       ABCDEF
READY
```

K Program 11. Then change line 50 for RIGHT$.

SAQ 7

If A$ = 1A2B3C4D, what are the following:

(a) LEFT$ (A$,1)   (c) RIGHT$ (A$,3)
(b) LEFT$ (A$,4)   (d) RIGHT$(A$,4)

Cutting up strings of variable length

Program 11 is a bit awkward because we had to specify (in line 40) how long the string was to be: 6 characters. But we might want to input strings of any length. This is easily done by modifying Program 11 so that the computer measures the length of the string we input and runs that length to control the FOR. . . NEXT loop. The modifications required are:

```
20   INPUT"ENTER A STRING";X$
40   FOR I=1 TO LEN(X$)  ⎤
50   LET A$=LEFT$(X$,I)  ⎬──── LEN(X$) acts as the upper limit of the loop.
60   PRINT A$            ⎦
70   NEXT I
80   END
```

Program 12

132

```
RUN
ENTER A STRING? HAMSTRING
          1234567890
1         H
2         HA
3         HAM
4         HAMS
5         HAMST
6         HAMSTR
7         HAMSTRI
8         HAMSTRIN
9         HAMSTRING
READY
```

K Program 12.

Exercise 3
Write a program to output those words in the DATA statements of the answer to Exercise 1 which began with a vowel.

Exercise 4
Write a program to change the output of the RIGHT$ run of Program 11 to:

```
        F
       EF
      DEF
     CDEF
    BCDEF
   ABCDEF
```

MID$(X$,I,J)
We have used LEFT$ and RIGHT$ to cut sections off either end of a string, but we might want a section in the middle of a string, e.g. M M in Y Y M M D D. There is another BASIC statement that will give us a section of this type:

MID$(X$,I,J)

This will cut a sub-string of length J, starting from position I:

MID$(X$,I,J)
         │ │ └────── length of sub-string from position I
         │ └─────── position in the string

e.g., if X$ = POSITION

MID$(X$,5,2) = TI

and MID$(X$,2,4) = OSIT

We will use the computer again to demonstrate MID$ at work by a further modification to Program 11. We have already adapted Program 11 to allow us to input a string of any length. This gave us:

133

```
10  REM★★STRING TEST★★
20  INPUT "ENTER A STRING";X$
30  PRINT TAB(10);"1234567890"
40  FOR I=1 TO LEN(X$)
50  LET A$=LEFT$(X$,I)
60  PRINT I;TAB(10);A$
70  NEXT I
```

BBC: 60 PRINT;I;TAB(10);A$

Program 13

If we now change line 50 to

50 LET A$=MID$(X$,I,1)

and input SHOESTRING we get:

```
RUN
ENTER A STRING? SHOESTRING
          1 2 3 4 5 6 7 8 9 0
1         S
2         H
3         O
4         E
5         S
6         T
7         R
8         I
9         N
10        G
READY
```

Here MID$ is looking at all possible sub-strings of length 1.
If we now use

50 LET A$=MID$(X$,I,2)

and input STRINGENT we get:

```
RUN
ENTER A STRING? STRINGENT
          1 2 3 4 5 6 7 8 9 0
1         S T
2         T R
3         R I
4         I N
5         N G
6         G E
7         E N
8         N T
9         T──────────────────────────────────'null' string
READY
```

K Program 13.

The last sub-string caused problems. We can't get a sub-string 2 characters long from a string of 9 characters starting at the 9th character. In trying to do so we enter a default state, and are given a null-string as a reward. There must always be

134

enough characters left of the original string to take out the sub-string.

Generally, if we wish to take out J characters we will not be able to start this sub-string beyond the (LEN(X$)−J+1)th position.

Yes, +1.

e.g., if LEN(X$)=10 and J=3, then LEN(X$)−J=7;

but we can get a string of length 3 from a string of length 10 if we start at 8, i.e. character positions 8, 9 10 of the original string.

SAQ 8
Write a program to accept as input London telephone numbers in the form 01 XXX XXXX and output the exchange codes only. (Remember that the spaces are characters just as much as the digits.)

Mid-string program
As you have probably spotted, MID$ can cut left sub-strings and right sub-strings if we want it to. In other words, it can give us every possible sub-string. Here is a program that makes it do that for us. First it prints out all sub-strings of length 1, then all of length 2 and so on until it prints the whole word which is the only sub-string of the same length as the word itself!

```
10   REM★★STRING TEST★★
20   INPUT"ENTER A STRING";X$
30   PRINT"  J";TAB(5);"  I";TAB(10);"1234567890"
35   FOR J=1 TO LEN(X$)
40     FOR I=1 TO (LEN(X$)−J+1)
50     LET A$=MID$(X$, I,J)
60     PRINTJ;TAB(5);I;TAB(10);A$
70     NEXT I
72   PRINT" "
75   NEXT J
80   END
```

BBC: 60 PRINT ; etc

J is the length of the sub-string, starting at I.

Program 14

RUN
ENTER A STRING? STRING

Note headings and scale

J	I	1234567890
1	1	S
1	2	T
1	3	R
1	4	I
1	5	N
1	6	G
2	1	S T
2	2	T R
2	3	R I
2	4	I N
2	5	N G

135

```
3    1    S T R
3    2    T R I
3    3    R I N
3    4    I NG

4    1    S T R I
4    2    T R I  N
4    3    R I  NG

5    1    S T R I  N
5    2    T R I  NG

6    1    S T R I  NG
```

READY

K Program 14.

5.7 VAL

Having found a method of cutting up strings, we now need a method of examining what we have got. One such method is to use VAL(A$) which looks at the numeric value of A$.

VAL(A$) gives us the numerical value of the string A$ provided A$ starts with +, − or a digit. In all other cases, VAL(A$) = 0.

Program to demonstrate VAL
In the following program we input seven strings (123456, 12345A, ... ABCDEF) and look at VAL for the string, VAL for the left-string of 2 characters and VAL of the mid-string of 2 characters starting from the third character.

You will see that if the left-most character of the string (or sub-strings) is a digit, then a value will be given, even if the rest of the string contains non-numeric characters.

```
10   REM★★THE VAL FUNCTION★★
20   INPUT "NEXT STRING";N$
25   IF N$="ZZZZ" THEN 999
30   LET N=VAL(N$)
40   LET P=VAL(LEFT$(N$,2))
50   LET Q=VAL(MID$(N$,3,2))
60   PRINT" "
70   PRINT N,P,Q
80   PRINT" "
90   GOTO 20
999  END
```

Program 15

```
RUN
NEXT  STRING?   123456

 123456          12        34
```

```
NEXT  STRING?  1 2 3 4 5 A
 1 2 3 4 5              1 2      3 4
NEXT  STRING?  1 2 3 4 A B
 1 2 3 4               1 2      3 4
NEXT  STRING?  1 2 3 A B C
 1 2 3                1 2      3
NEXT  STRING?  1 2 A B C D
 1 2                  1 2      0
NEXT  STRING?  1 A B C D E
 1                    1        0
NEXT  STRING?  A B C D E F
 0                    0        0
```

VAL still gives the value of the left-most digits, even though the string contains AB–non-numeric characters.

A is now at position 3, so VAL (A$)=0

K Program 15.

SAQ 9
What are the values of the following?

(a) VAL (A$) where A$=54
(b) VAL(B$) where B$=76XY
(c) VAL(C$) where C$=A3
(d) VAL (D$) where D$ = −132
(e) VAL(LEFT$(E$,2)) where E$=593

(f) VAL (LEFT$(F$,1)) where F$=8AM
(g) VAL(LEFT$(G$,2)) where G$=Z35
(h) VAL(RIGHT$(H$,1)) where H$=593
(i) VAL(RIGHT$(I$,2)) where I$=8AM
(j) VAL(RIGHT$(J$,2)) where J$=Z35

Date string check
We are now in a position to see how VAL can be put to practical use, in this case to check the accuracy of dates keyed into a computer. This is typical of what happens in computers all the time. We know errors will frequently happen when data is keyed in so, wherever possible, we try to use the computer to detect the errors.

Example 5
Write a program to carry out data checks on the 3 fields of a 6-digit date-string.

Solution
The date-string D$ has three fields in the form:

We are going to consider the years 1980 and 1981 only; so:

VAL(LEFT$(D$,2)) should have a range of 80–81,
VAL(MID$(D$,3,2)) should have a range of 1–12,
VAL(RIGHT$(D$,2)) should have a range of 1–31.

This is a fairly complex process as we first need to decide on the steps involved. These are given in the following flowchart (Figure 3).

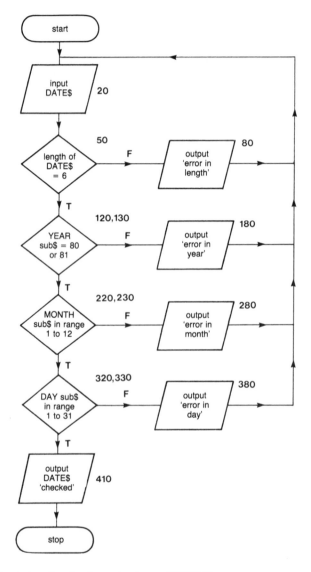

Figure 3   Flowchart showing the four checks on YYMMDD

The program is fairly straightforward as it goes through each of the four checks. If any check fails, the program prints an error message and returns control to line 20. If there are no errors it runs through to line 410 where the correct entry is confirmed.

```
10  REM★★DATE CHECK★★
20  INPUT"NEXT DATE";D$                              ── length check
30  IF D$="ZZZZ" THEN 900
50  IF LEN(D$)=6 THEN 110
80  PRINT"!!!!!!ERROR IN DATE LENGTH!!!!!!"          included here, for demon-
90  GOTO 20                                          stration purposes; would
100 REM★★★★★★★                                       not appear in a checking
110 PRINT"STRING LENGTH CORRECT"                     routine normally.
120 IF VAL(LEFT$(D$,2))=80 THEN 210   ⎤── year check
130 IF VAL(LEFT$(D$,2))=81 THEN 210   ⎦
180 PRINT"!!!!!!ERROR IN YEAR FIELD!!!!!!"
190 GOTO 20
200 REM★★★★★★★
210 PRINT"YEAR FIELD CORRECT"──────────── demonstration only
220 IF VAL(MID$(D$,3,2))<1 THEN 280    ⎤── month check
230 IF VAL(MID$(D$,3,2))<=12 THEN 310  ⎦
280 PRINT"!!!!!!ERROR IN MONTH FIELD!!!!!!"
290 GOTO 20
300 REM★★★★★★★
310 PRINT"MONTH FIELD CORRECT"──────────── demonstration only
320 IF VAL(RIGHT$(D$,2))<1 THEN 380    ⎤── day check
330 IF VAL(RIGHT$(D$,2))<=31 THEN 410  ⎦
380 PRINT"!!!!!!ERROR IN DAY FIELD!!!!!!"
390 GOTO 20
400 REM★★★★★★★★
410 PRINT"DATE STRING WITHIN CHECK LIMITS"
490 GOTO 20
900 PRINT"END OF DATE CHECK"
```

Program 16

Typical run

```
READY
RUN
NEXT DATE? 1234567
!!!!!!ERROR IN DATE LENGTH!!!!!!
NEXT DATE? 123456
STRING LENGTH CORRECT
!!!!!!ERROR IN YEAR FIELD!!!!!!
NEXT DATE? 803456
STRING LENGTH CORRECT
YEAR FIELD CORRECT
!!!!!!ERROR IN MONTH FIELD!!!!!!
NEXT DATE? 801256
STRING LENGTH CORRECT
YEAR FIELD CORRECT
MONTH FIELD CORRECT
!!!!!!ERROR IN DAY FIELD!!!!!!
```

NEXT DATE? 800131
STRING LENGTH CORRECT
YEAR FIELD CORRECT
MONTH FIELD CORRECT
DATE STRING WITHIN CHECK LIMITS
NEXT DATE? ZZZZ
END OF DATE CHECK
READY

K̲ Program 16.

Assignment 5

1. Write a program to find the frequency with which each vowel occurs in the words in the JUDE data of Example 2, giving also a summary of the total number of vowels and consonants which occur in these words.

2. Write a program to input a string of characters and to output this string in reverse order.

Objectives of Unit 5

Check that you are now able to write simple programs:

Using LEN(A$)   ☐

Using LETC(I)=C(I)+1 to count frequencies   ☐

To print a frequency diagram   ☐

Using TAB to print in columns   ☐

Using TAB to print a frequency table with headings and scale   ☐

Using LEFT$(X$,I)   ☐
     and RIGHT$(X$,I)   ☐

Using MID$(X$,I,J)   ☐

Using VAL(A$)   ☐

Answers to SAQ's and Exercises

SAQ 1
(a) 3; (b) 1; (c) 2 (not 72 – LEN counts the number of characters); (d) 7 (LEN counts the characters regardless of whether they are numbers, letters or spaces).

SAQ 2
Your answer should be:

Word length	Count	Total
1	1	1
2	~~1111~~	5
3	1111	4
4	~~1111~~ 1	6
5	~~1111~~ 1111	9
6		0
7	1	1
8	111	3
9	1	1
10		0
11		0
12	1	1
13		0
14		0
15		0

SAQ 3
(a) C(3)=1 (Not 3! C(3) has counted the number of 3's inputted.)
(b) C(9)=2
(c) C(1)=4
(d) C(0)=3

Exercise 1
The solution appears in the following text.

SAQ 4

★★
★★★★★
★★★★★★★
★★★★★★★★
★★★
★

SAQ 5

10 PRINT"COL1";TAB(9);"COL2";TAB(19);"COL3"

SAQ 6

10 INPUT A,B,C
20 PRINT TAB(A);"HEADING";TAB(B);"HEADING";TAB(C);"HEADING"

Program 17

Exercise 2

10 REM★★FREQUENCY DISTRIBUTION★★
15 REM★★PREPARATION PICTURE★★★★★
20 REM★★FREQUENCY-LIST IS F(K)★★
25 DIM V$(5)

```
 30  DIM F(6)
 32  FOR I=1 TO 5                  ⎤              reads in the vowels from
 34  READ V$(I)                    ⎬────────────  800 into a vowel list
 36  NEXT I                        ⎦
 40  LET K=1                       ⎤
 50  READ F(K)                     ⎪
 60  IF F(K)=−9999 THEN 110        ⎬────────────  reads in the frequencies
 70  LET K=K+1                     ⎪              from 900
 80  GOTO 50                       ⎦
 90  REM★★★★★★★★
100  REM★★DON'T ADD −9999 TO LIST★★★
110  LET N=K−1
120  REM★★★★★★★★
200  REM★★PRINT ROUTINE★★★★★★★★★★★★★★★
210  PRINT
212  PRINT"VOWEL";TAB(8);"FREQ";TAB(18);"TALLY"
214  PRINT"========================="
220  FOR X= 1 TO N
222  PRINT TAB(2);V$(X);TAB(7);"I";TAB(10);F(X);TAB(14);"I";TAB(16);
230  FOR Y=1 TO F(X)              ⎤────────────  prints out from word list
240  PRINT "★";                   ⎦
250  NEXT Y
260  PRINT
280  NEXT X
290  PRINT"....SCALE....";TAB(15);"0....5....0....5....0"
300  REM★★★★★★★★
800  DATA A,E,I,O,U
900  DATA 9,16,10,10,6,−9999
```

Program 18

```
VOWEL    FREQ           TALLY
=============================
  A    I    9   I   ★★★★★★★★★
  E    I   16   I   ★★★★★★★★★★★★★★★★
  I    I   10   I   ★★★★★★★★★★
  O    I   10   I   ★★★★★★★★★★
  U    I    6   I   ★★★★★★
 ····SCALE····  0 ···· 5 ···· 0 ···· 5 ···· 0
```

K   Program 18.

SAQ 7

(a) 1;   (b) 1A2B;   (c) C4D;   (d) 3C4D.

Notice that LEFT$ and RIGHT$ treat all characters in a string in the same way. It doesn't matter whether they are numbers or letters, they still get counted.

Exercise 3

```
10  REM★★IS LEFT-MOST CHARACTER A VOWEL?★★
20  READ W$
30  IF W$="ZZZZ" THEN 9999
```

```
40   LET L$=LEFT$(W$,1)
50   IF L$="A" THEN 200
60   IF L$="E" THEN 200
70   IF L$="I" THEN 200
80   IF L$="O" THEN 200
90   IF L$="U" THEN 200
100  GOTO 20
190  REM★★★★★★★★★
200  PRINT
210  PRINT L$, W$
220  GOTO 20
230  REM★★★★★★★★★
900  DATA THE, HORSE, STOOD, STILL, TILL, HE, HAD, FINISHED, THE, HYMN
910  DATA  WHICH,  JUDE,  REPEATED,  UNDER,  THE,  SWAY,  OF,  A,
POLYTHEISTIC
920  DATA FANCY, THAT, HE, WOULD, NEVER, HAVE, THOUGHT, OF,
HUMOURING
930  DATA IN, BROAD, DAYLIGHT, ZZZZ
9999 END
```
Program 19

```
RUN

U          UNDER

O          OF

A          A

O          OF

I          IN
```
K Program 19.

Exercise 4
```
10   REM★★STRING TEST★★
20   INPUT"ENTER 6-CHARACTER STRING";X$
30   PRINT TAB(10);"1234567890"
40   FOR I=1 TO 6
50   LET A$=RIGHT$(X$,I)
60   PRINT I;TAB(16−I);A$                    60 BBC: PRINT;I etc
70   NEXT I
```
Program 20

```
RUN
ENTER 6-CHARACTER STRING? ABCDEF
              1234567890
1
2                    F
3                    EF
4                    DEF
5                    CDEF
6                    BCDEF
                     ABCDEF
```
K Program 20.

SAQ 8

```
10   INPUT"NEXT TELEPHONE NUMBER";N$
20   LET A$=MID$ (N$,4,3)
30   PRINT A$
40   GOTO 10
```

Program 21

K̲ Program 21.

SAQ 9

(a) 54;   (b) 76 (stops at letters);   (c) 0 (starts with a letter. Therefore 0);   (d) −132;   (e) 59;   (f) 8;   (g) 0 (starts with a letter);   (h) 3;   (i) 0 (starts at A which is a letter);   (j) 35.

UNIT 6
Mainly about dice and games

6.1 Random numbers

The programming function which allows us to inject a sense of fun into a program is the one which generates random numbers. This function is at the heart of many of the game-playing and simulation programs which are now available for microcomputers.

You will have met random numbers when playing games; games which involve tossing a coin or throwing a dice, or drawing numbers out of a hat. These domestic games have become institutionalised in casinos, bingo clubs, the ritualistic draw for the FA Cup competition, and, of course, on a larger scale, the monthly draw for premium bonds. Although we all have an intuitive idea of what we mean by a sequence of random numbers, it is quite difficult to define the idea clearly. Let's have a look at some number sequences to try and clarify this idea.

Here are three 'thought experiments' each of which involves throwing a six-sided die fifteen times. Imagine that in the first experiment the uppermost values of the dice had those values shown in sequence A shown in Figure 1. The second experiment generated the numbers shown in sequence B and the third experiment gave us the numbers shown in sequence C.

Sequence A
5,1,2,4,6,3,2,1,6,3,5,4,3,4,2
Sequence B
6,6,6,6,6,6,6,6,6,6,6,6,6,6,6
Sequence C
1,2,3,4,5,6,1,2,3,4,5,6,1,2,3

Figure 1   Random sequences?

Most of us would be quite happy that sequence A represented a typical sequence of numbers generated by throwing a die fifteen times. This number sequence shows no definable patterns or repetitions and each number occurrence would seem to be 'equally likely'. We are not surprised at the appearance of any of the sub-sequences in this main sequence. By contrast, however, sequence B is quite unreasonable. We would certainly not expect to have thrown fifteen sixes with fifteen consecutive throws of the die. We would be highly suspicious had this happened and we would blame a weighted die. Intuitively, we would be prepared to accept that sequence A had occurred 'by chance' but would not be prepared to accept that this was so for sequence B.

Another feature about random number sequences which we learn by experience is that, in long sequences, localised 'unfair' occurrences iron themselves out. What we mean by this is that after, say, a hundred throws, we would expect on average about sixteen ones, about sixteen twos, sixteen threes and so on. In other words, over a longer sequence we expect the 'laws of chance' to apply. If we now consider sequence C with its emerging pattern ' ...6,1,2,3,4,5,6,1 ... ' continued for a hundred throws then this long term averaging-out effect would be satisfied. But once again this sequence would not be intuitively acceptable to us as random because we would not expect this sequential pattern to persist over a hundred throws by chance alone.

These concepts of 'statistical averaging' over a sequence of throws, and of the 'reasonableness' of the patterning of the numbers in sequence are intuitively acquired from games of chance. There are statistical techniques to test these two features of a random number sequence but we will not be concerned with those techniques here.

A computer is a very determinate machine. You will therefore not be surprised to learn that quite special features have to be programmed into the machine to achieve a sequence of random numbers. For our uses, however, we will assume that a table of random numbers has been stored in the machine's memory. The sequence of numbers is very long and generation would have to occur for a long time before the sequence repetition became apparent. To achieve a different random number sequence from one program execution to another, all that a machine has to do is to start reading this table of random numbers from a different point. This starting point is often referred to as the 'seed' and we talk about random number sequences as starting from different seeds. Because the computer has to 'contrive' random number sequences, the numbers produced are usually referred to as pseudo-random numbers

6.2 The RND function

If you are using the BBC computer, you can omit this section and move straight on to 6.3 RND on the BBC Computer. The BBC RND function is very much easier to use than the method described in 6.2.

To get random numbers on a microcomputer you use the function RND. RND varies widely on different microcomputers as the previous paragraph testifies. But most microcomputers use something like the system described in this section. You will have to check the exact details of the system for your microcomputer in its manual.

RND is a function that requires an argument. That is a number in brackets after it:

$$RND(A)$$
$$\underline{\qquad} \text{ the argument of RND}$$

'A' might be negative, zero or positive and the following program explores the effects of different values for A.

```
10   REM★★THE RND FUNCTION★★
20   INPUT"NEXT ARGUMENT FOR RND";A
30   FOR I=1 TO 10
40   LET B=RND(A)
50   PRINT B
60   NEXT I
70   END
```

Program 1   Effect of A on RND

```
RUN
NEXT ARGUMENT FOR RND?−1
 .308601
 .308601
 .308601
 .308601
 .308601
```

Negative A seems to fix the random number

.308601
.308601
.308601
.308601
.308601

RUN
NEXT ARGUMENT FOR RND? 0
.811635
.811635
.811635
.811635
.811635
.811635
.811635
.811635
.811635
.811635

Zero A also seems to fix the random number

RUN
NEXT ARGUMENT FOR RND? 1
.245121
.305003
.311866
.515163
.0583136
.788891
.497102
.363751
.984546
.901591

These look more like a sequence of random numbers

RUN
NEXT ARGUMENT FOR RND? 2
.245121
.305003
.311866
.515163
.0583136
.788891
.497102
.363751
.984546
.901591

And so do these but they are the same as those with RND(1)

K Program 1 to see the effect of A on your microcomputer.

The RANDOMIZE function

As far as generating useful random numbers is concerned, we will ignore arguments other than 1. But the RND(1) function returns the same sequence of random numbers each time the program is run. (This may seem a little strange, but it is a very useful feature if, when testing a program, we wish to re-run it using the same sequence of random numbers.) To change the 'seed', i.e. to start the generator at a random point in the sequence we use the RANDOMIZE command. The effect of this command is shown in the next example.

```
10  REM★★RANDOMIZE★★
20  RANDOMIZE
30  FOR I=1 TO 10
40  LET B=RND(1)
50  PRINT B
60  NEXT I
70  END
```

Program 2 RANDOMISE to vary the sequence

```
RUN
 .58041
 .128928
 .928324
 .901162
 .532818
 .499882
 .286114
 .608704
 .342298
 .163376
RUN
 .0438479
 .891465
 .801263
 .656113
 .16401
 .835579
 .238398
 .0730044
 .581113
 .0987764
RUN
 .88598
 .484668
 .586328
 .119426
 .709225
 .988602
 .730404
 .752963
 .352425
 .878404
```

K Program 2.   (Your microcomputer may not need RANDOMIZE.)

RND(1)

What the above investigation demonstrates is that

RND(1)

will give random numbers within the range 0–1.

Changing the argument (A) doesn't seem to extend the range so how can we get other random numbers? Quite simply by multiplying RND(1) by another number. So:

RND (1) gives a random number in the range 0–1;
6★RND(1) gives a random number in the range 0–6;
and 52★RND(1) gives a random number in the range 0–52;
etc.

You can think of RND(1) as a 'conversion factor' which changes at will. The following program tries out this idea.

```
10  REM★★RND AS A CONVERSION FACTOR★★
20  RANDOMIZE
30  PRINT " I","RND(1)","6★RND(1)","52★RND(1)"
40  PRINT"– – –","– – – – – –","– – – – – –","– – – – – –"
50  FOR I=1 TO 10
60  LET B=RND(1)
70  LET C=6★B
80  LET D=52★B
90  PRINT I,B,C,D
100 NEXT I
110 END
```

Program 3 RND(1) as a conversion factor

RUN

I	RND(1)	6★RND(1)	52★RND(1)
1	.58041	3.48246	30.1813
2	.128928	.773567	6.70424
3	.928324	5.56994	48.2728
4	.901162	5.40697	46.8604
5	.532818	3.19691	27.7065
6	.499882	2.99929	25.9939
7	.286114	1.71669	14.8779
8	.608704	3.65223	31.6526
9	.342298	2.05379	17.7995
10	.163376	.980258	8.49557

RUN

I	RND(1)	6★RND(1)	52★RND(1)
1	.0438479	.263087	2.28009
2	.891465	5.34879	46.3562
3	.801263	4.80758	41.6657
4	.656113	3.93668	34.1179
5	.16401	.984057	8.52849
6	.835579	5.01347	43.4501

7	.238398	1.43039	12.3967
8	.0730044	.438026	3.79623
9	.581113	3.48668	30.2179
10	.0987764	.592658	5.13637

K Program 3. (If the print out overruns your screen, adjust line 90 using TAB e.g. 90 PRINT I; TAB(4);B; TAB(18);C;D and then lines 30 and 40 to match. BBC: use 90 PRINT;I,B,C,D.)

SAQ 1
Write a program to print out 6 random numbers in the range 0 to 5.999999.

The RND+1 function
If you look again at the output of Program 3 on the run with 6★RND(1), the numbers were:

3.48246
.773567
5.56994
5.40697
3.19619
2.99929
1.71669
3.65223
2.05379
.980258

Look now at the numbers before the decimal point (picked out in colour). They are:

3,0,5,5,3,2,1,3,2,0

i.e. members of the set

(0,1,2,3,4,5)

But, if we were throwing dice we would generate members of the set (1,2,3,4,5,6). All we have to do then, is to add 1 to each member of the first set to get the second.

Now in games we frequently want to throw a dice (outcomes 1,2,3,4,5,6) or use a pack of cards (52 outcomes) so we are particularly interested in the functions:

6★RND(1)+1 and 52★RND(1)+1

The following program allows us to explore these.

```
10  REM★★RND+1 AS A CONVERSION FACTOR★★
20  RANDOMIZE
30  PRINT" I","RND(1)","6★RND(1)+1","52★RND(1)+1"
40  PRINT"– – –","– – – – – – –","– – – – – – –","– – – – – –"
50  FOR I=1 TO 10
60  LET B=RND(1)
70  LET C=6★B+1
80  LET D=52★B+1
90  PRINT I,B,C,D
100 NEXT I
110 END
```
Note +1 in each line.

Program 4   6★RND(1)+1 and 52★RND(1)+1

```
RUN
I          RND(1)        6★RND(1)+1    52★RND(1)+1
___        _____         _____       _____
1          .58041        4.48246       31.1813
2          .128928       1.77357       7.70424
3          .928324       6.56994       49.2728
4          .901162       6.40697       47.8604
5          .532818       4.19691       28.7065
6          .499882       3.99929       26.9939
7          .286114       2.71669       15.8779
8          .608704       4.65223       32.6526
9          .342298       3.05379       18.7995
10         .163376       1.98026       9.49557


RUN
I          RND(1)        6★RND(1)+1    52★RND(1)+1
___        _____         _____       _____
1          .0438479      1.26309       3.28009
2          .891465       6.34879       47.3562
3          .801263       5.80758       42.6657
4          .656113       4.93668       35.1179
5          .16401        1.98406       9.52849
6          .835579       6.01347       44.4501
7          .238398       2.43039       13.3967
8          .0730044      1.43803       4.79623
9          .581113       4.48668       31.2179
10         .0987764      1.59266       6.13637
```

Ⓚ Program 4. (You may have to adjust the print pattern to fit your screen.)

The INT function

If you now look at the columns in the runs of Program 4 picked out in colour you will now see that we have generated the random numbers we needed. Column 3 has numbers from 1 to 6 and column 4 has numbers from 1 to 52.

But what about all the garbage to the right of the decimal point? Well, we have a function to get rid of that: the INT function.

The effect of INT(X) is to give the whole number (or integer part) of the number X, i.e. the largest integer which is not larger than X. The effect of INT is to 'chop' down to the next highest whole number:

INT(5.6) = 5
INT(3.9) = 3
INT(−3.2) = −4
INT(2) = 2

If INT(−3.2) = −4 surprises you, look at the number line and remember that INT always chops down to the next whole number. It doesn't 'round' numbers.

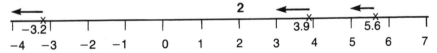

152

SAQ 2

What are the values of the following:
- (a) INT(4.5)
- (b) INT(9.1)
- (c) INT(−2.5)
- (d) INT(−0.99)
- (e) INT(1.01)

Now, with INT, we can at last generate the whole numbers from 1 to 6 and from 1 to 52 to use as dice or cards. All we need is

INT(6★RND(1)+1)
and INT(52★RND(1)+1)

The following program prints out the values of these two functions:

```
10   REM★★THE INT FUNCTION★★
20   RANDOMIZE
30   PRINT" I","RND(1)","INT(6★...+1)","INT(52★...+1)"
40   PRINT"−−−","−−−−−−−","−−−−−−−","−−−−−−−"
50   FOR I=1 TO 10
60   LET B=RND(1)
70   LET C=INT(6★B+1)
80   LET D=INT (52★B+1)
90   PRINT I,B,C,D
100  NEXT I
110  END
```

Program 5   INT to give whole numbers

RUN

I	RND(1)	INT(6★...+1)	INT(52★...+1)
1	.58041	4	31
2	.128928	1	7
3	.928324	6	49
4	.901162	6	47
5	.532818	4	28
6	.499882	3	26
7	.286114	2	15
8	.608704	4	32
9	.342298	3	18
10	.163376	1	9

RUN

I	RND(1)	INT(6★...+1)	INT(52★...+1)
1	.0438479	1	3
2	.891465	6	47
3	.801263	5	42
4	.656113	4	35
5	.16401	1	9
6	.835579	6	44

7	.238398	2	13
8	.0730044	1	4
9	.581113	4	31
10	.0987764	1	6

K Program 5.

6.3 RND on the BBC Computer

RND(1)

RND(1) on the BBC Computer gives you random numbers between 0 and
.99999999. Thus:

```
10   FOR I=1 TO 10
20   PRINT RND(1)
30   NEXT I
```

Program 6   RND(1) on BBC Computer

produced this run:

```
>RUN
0.971556531
4.82183245E−2      (=0.0482183245)      (The E notation is explained in Unit 7.)
0.649963649
0.403599263
0.481712491
0.783543998
0.784222102
0.439000082
0.815422113
0.138072818
>
```

If, however, you want random numbers over a bigger range, you simply multiply
RND(1) by the top limit of your range, e.g. if you want random numbers in the
range 0 to 100 you use

```
100*RND(1)
```

in line 20.

RND(n)

But for dice and card games we want whole numbers (integers). On the BBC
Computer you get these quite simply:

RND(6)   gives random whole numbers in the range 1 to 6, i.e. it simulates
throwing a die.

RND(52) gives random whole numbers in the range 1 to 52, i.e. it simulates
drawing a card from a pack of 52.

and so on. Thus

```
10   REM**RND(n)−BBC**
```

```
20   PRINT"I","RND(6)","RND(52)"
30   FOR I=1 TO 10
40   LET A = RND(6)
50   LET B= RND(52)
60   PRINT I,A,B
70   NEXT I
```

Program 7   RND(n)–BBC

produced:

RUN

I	RND(6)	RND(52)
1	6	1
2	5	36
3	6	33
4	1	36
5	5	22
6	3	48
7	1	42
8	2	16
9	6	31
10	2	47
	Die throw	Card draw

K   Program 7.

In the programs that follow you will sometimes see the word RANDOMIZE in lines such as

20   RANDOMIZE

If you are using the BBC Computer, omit these lines from your program.

6.4   Random number postscript

The following program simulates the tossing of a die 100 times.

```
10   REM★★100 TOSSES OF A DIE★★
20   RANDOMIZE                         BBC: omit 20
30   FOR I=1 TO 10
40   FOR J=1 TO 10
50   LET X=INT(6★RND(1)+1)             BBC: use 50 LETX=RND(6)
60   PRINT X;                          BBC: use 60 PRINT;X;" ";
70   NEXT J
80   PRINT
90   NEXT I
100  END
```

Program 8   Die toss

155

```
RUN
4  1  6  6  4  3  2  4  3  1
6  6  2  2  5  3  6  5  2  2
3  3  6  3  4  2  6  1  2  6
6  1  4  3  5  2  2  2  1  6
6  3  1  1  6  3  4  5  2  5
6  1  4  2  2  4  5  1  2  4
6  6  5  4  3  4  5  5  1  5
3  5  4  3  5  3  6  6  6  6
1  5  3  4  3  1  1  4  2  1
6  3  6  1  6  1  6  5  3  1
```

Ⓚ Program 8.

Just to make sure that you understand the INT function, try the following questions. (Not applicable to BBC Computer.)

SAQ 3
The program:

```
10  REM★★SAQ★★
20  FOR X=−3.8 TO −1.8 STEP(.2)
30  LET Y=INT(X)
40  PRINT X,Y
50  NEXT X
60  END
```

Program 9

prints out 10 pairs of numbers. What are they?

SAQ 4
The program:

```
10  REM★★SAQ★★
20  FOR X=1.6 TO 3.4 STEP(.2)
30  LET Y=INT(X)
40  PRINT X,Y
50  NEXT X
60  END
```

Program 10

prints out 9 pairs of numbers. What are they?

6.5 Two examples

This section is made up of two lengthy examples. We suggest that you try and treat them as exercises first and then compare your solution with ours.

Example 1
Write a program to simulate tossing a coin 100 times. Count and output the number of times the coin falls heads and tails.

Solution
The heart of the solution is a random number generator which produces a 1 or a 2.

We will use a 1 to represent a tail and 2 to represent a head. Using this approach, a descriptive algorithm for the solution to the problem is:

1. Start.
2. Set heads total and tails total to zero.
3. Start loop counter.
4. Generate the two values 1 and 2 randomly.
5. If random number equals 2 then go to statement 8 otherwise go on to statement 6.
6. Add 1 to tails total.
7. Go to statement 9.
8. Add 1 to heads total.
9. Add 1 to loop counter.
10. If loop counter <=100 then go to statement 4 otherwise go on to statement 11.
11. Output total heads and total tails.
12. Stop.

Figure 2 Descriptive solution to coin toss

Alternatively you may prefer a flowchart description to the solution:

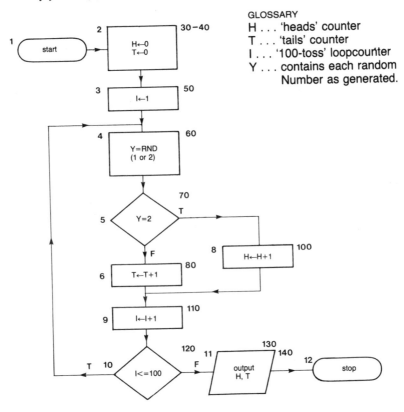

GLOSSARY
H . . . 'heads' counter
T . . . 'tails' counter
I . . . '100-toss' loopcounter
Y . . . contains each random Number as generated.

Figure 3 Flowchart for coin toss

And, finally, the program:

```
10  REM★★TOSS 1 COIN 100 TIMES★★
20  RANDOMIZE                          BBC: omit 20
30  LET H=0
40  LET T=0
50  LET I=1
60  LET Y=INT(2★RND(1)+1)              BBC: 60 LET Y=RND(2)
70  IF Y=2 THEN 100
80  LET T=T+1
90  GOTO 110
100 LET H=H+1
110 LET I=I+1
120 IF I<=100 THEN 60
130 PRINT"HEADS","TAILS"
140 PRINT H,T                          BBC: 140 PRINT; H,;T
150 END
```

```
RUN
HEADS           TAILS
51              49
RUN
HEADS           TAILS
57              43
RUN
HEADS           TAILS
55              45
```

Program 11   Coin toss

K̲ Program 11.

Example 2

Write a program to simulate tossing 2 coins 100 times. Count and output the number of times that the outcome of this imaginary experiment is: head-head (HH), tail-tail (TT), and head-tail or tail-head (HT or TH).

Solution

We use the same scoring rules: 1 for a tail and 2 for a head but we are now tossing 2 coins. We store the score from the first coin in C1 and the score from the second coin in C2. Then we add C1 and C2 to give the total score for that throw:

$S=C1+C2$

S can be 2, 3 or 4:

outcome	score
TT	$1+1=2$
TH or HT	$1+2=2+1=3$
HH	$2+2=4$

Then we count how many 2's we get, how many 3's and how many 4's.

Counter for 2's   T2
Counter for 3's   M1 (M for Mix of H's and T's)
Counter for 4's   H2

The flowchart of the solution is:

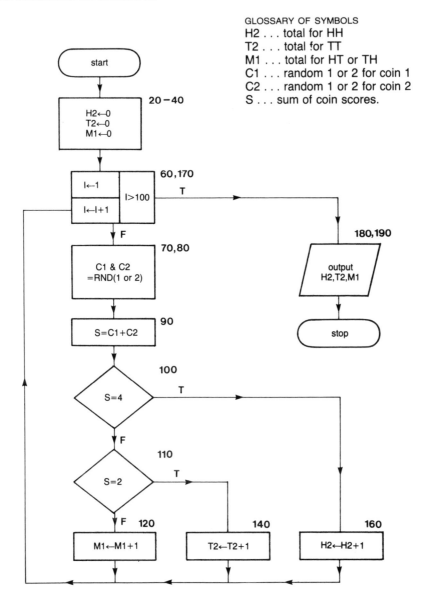

GLOSSARY OF SYMBOLS
H2 . . . total for HH
T2 . . . total for TT
M1 . . . total for HT or TH
C1 . . . random 1 or 2 for coin 1
C2 . . . random 1 or 2 for coin 2
S . . . sum of coin scores.

Figure 4   Flowchart for two coin toss

159

And the program is:

```
10   REM★★TOSS 2 COINS 100 TIMES★★
20   LET H2=0
30   LET T2=0
40   LET M1=0
50   RANDOMIZE                    BBC: omit 50
60   FOR I=1 TO 100
70   LET C1=INT(2★RND(1)+1)       BBC: 70 LET C1=RND(2)
80   LET C2=INT(2★RND(1)+1)       BBC: 80 LET C2=RND(2)
90   LET S=C1+C2
100  IF S=4 THEN 160
110  IF S=2 THEN 140
120  LET M1=M1+1
130  GOTO 170
140  LET T2=T2+1
150  GOTO 170
160  LET H2=H2+1
170  NEXT I
180  PRINT"TT","HT","HH"
190  PRINT T2,M1,H2
200  END
```

Program 12   Two coin toss

```
RUN
TT      HT      HH
21      54      25

READY:
RUN
TT      HT      HH
26      48      26

READY:
RUN
TT      HT      HH
26      48      26

READY:
RUN
TT      HT      HH
24      55      21
```

K   Program 12.

6.6   Keeping scores

You may have noticed that we have used some ungainly variable names, such as
T2, H2 and M1. Perhaps you have been thinking, 'What about lists? Couldn't they
be as useful here as they were with frequency tables?' Indeed they·could so let's
try a score list S(I) for the coin tossing. So we say:

If the score is 2, add 1 to the number in S(2)
If the score is 3, add 1 to the number in S(3)
If the score is 4, add 1 to the number in S(4)
generally
If the score is S add 1 to the number in S(S)

Application to tossing two coins
If we go back to Example 2, we can re-use lines 10 to 90 and then put in our new scoring system:

100 LET S(S)=S(S)+1

The program then becomes:

```
10   REM★★TOSS 2 COINS 100 TIMES★★
15   DIM S(4)                              Note the addition of 15 DIM S(4)
20   LET S(4)=0
30   LET S(3)=0
40   LET S(2)=0
50   RANDOMIZE                             50   BBC: omit line
60   FOR I=1 TO 100                        70   BBC: LET C1=RND(2)
70   LET C1=INT(2★RND(1)+1)                80   BBC: LET C2=RND(2)
80   LET C2=INT(2★RND(1)+1)
90   LET S=C1+C2
100  LET S(S)=S(S)+1
110  NEXT I
120  PRINT "TT","HT","HH"
130  PRINT S(2),S(3),S(4)
140  END
```

Program 13

```
RUN
TT            HT            HH
21            58            21

READY:
RUN
TT            HT            HH
27            47            26

READY:
RUN
TT            HT            HH
31            52            17

READY:
RUN
TT            HT            HH
19            55            26
```

K Program 13.

Score lists for dice
The score-list for throwing one die would be:

S(1), S(2), S(3) . . . S(6);

161

and for throwing two dice:

S(2), S(3), S(4) . . . S(12).

Exercise 1
Write a program to simulate throwing a die 100 times. Count and output the number of times each score occurs.

Exercise 2
Modify the program written for Exercise 1 to simulate the throwing of two dice 100 times.

Exercise 3
Write a program to display the data obtained from the program in Exercise 2, in the form of a frequency diagram.

6.7 Short cuts in program writing

Our programs are becoming quite long and the longer they are, the longer they take to key in on the computer. There are short cuts which help to speed up keying. We have deliberately avoided short cuts up to this point, feeling that intelligibility of coding is more important than speed. We will abbreviate some of our coding at times to show you what can be achieved, but will generally continue our policy of clarity of interpretation. If you are sending assignments to a tutor for marking, then please use short cuts sparingly.

The principal short cuts are:

1. The word LET may be omitted from assignment statements. Thus:

20 LET A=B can be written 20 A=B

2. More than one statement per line is allowed; the statements must be separated by :
    Thus:

10 LET A=7
20 LET B=8
30 PRINT A+B

can be written:

10 LET A=7: LET B=8: PRINT A+B

or, using the first short cut as well:

10 A=7: B=8: PRINT A+B

(This short cut speeds up program execution as well as keying time. Computers take up time interpreting each line number, so the fewer the line numbers, the quicker will be the execution.)

3. The word PRINT may be replaced by ? on some microcomputers. (Use P. on the BBC Computer). However, when you ask the computer to list your program you find that ? (or P.) is replaced by the full word PRINT.

E.g. if you key in

10   A=7: B=8: ?A+B   (BBC: P.A+B)

and then ask for LIST you get

10   A=7: B=8: PRINT A+B

4.   You can include expressions in PRINT statements. These expressions will be executed. We've already done this above where we said PRINT A+B

But, be careful

- Don't cram statements on a line just for the sake of doing so.

- Be very careful with transfer of control statements. E.g. GOTO... , IF... THEN... , and later on GO SUB... Remember, the lines referred to must exist and program control goes to the beginning of the line in the GOTO statement.

- Most programs spend 80% of their time in 20% of their coding. So, concentrate on abbreviating (and therefore speeding up) those statements which work the hardest, e.g. lines 70–120 in the solution to Exercise 3.

- The line number associated with a REM statement takes up run time so it is useful to tack a :REM... on to the end of other statements. We do so in programs later in this Unit. They don't all look as tidy as they ought to, though.

- Take care to distinguish clearly between : and ; in the listings of programs: yours, ours and especially those in computer magazines. The pairs (, < and), > are often barely distinguishable in some listings.

Some examples of short cuts

First Program 3 which was 6 lines can be written in 3 lines:

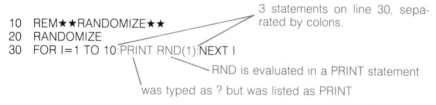

3 statements on line 30, separated by colons.

10   REM★★RANDOMIZE★★
20   RANDOMIZE
30   FOR I=1 TO 10:PRINT RND(1):NEXT I

RND is evaluated in a PRINT statement

was typed as ? but was listed as PRINT

Program 14

Second, Program 13 which was 14 lines can be written in 10:

10   REM★★TOSS 2 COINS 100 TIMES★★
20   DIM S(4):S(4)=0:S(3)=0:S(2)=0 ————— 3 assignment statements without LET
50   RANDOMIZE
60   FOR I=1 TO 100
70   C1=INT(2★RND(1)+1):C2=INT(2★RND(1)+1) this is where the work is
90   S=C1+C2:S(S)=S(S)+1 being done, 70 to 90 are
110 NEXT I executed 100 times
120 PRINT"TT","HT","HH" ⎤
130 PRINT S(2),S(3),S(4) ⎦ ———— not worth condensing, because it is executed only
140 END once per run

Program 15

SAQ 5

Try using the short cuts on Program 23.

6.8   Concatenation

Having gone to a lot of trouble in Unit 5 to cut up strings, we will now spend some time putting them back together. This second ugliest word in the computing repertoire means to chain or link together. Program 16 shows us what is happening.

```
20   INPUT A$
30   INPUT B$
40   PRINT A$+B$
50   END
```

Program 16   Concatenation

```
RUN
?GET
?TOGETHER
GETTOGETHER
```

```
RUN
?CONCATE
?NATION
CONCATENATION
```

SAQ 6

Write a program to input a word and output its plural assuming that all words only need s adding to make their plurals.

Program 17 shows how we can use concatenation to build up a string from a list of symbols. We have stored the letters in line 40 (DATA) and in the loop 110–140 we add a new letter to the string on each pass around the loop.

```
10   REM★★CONCATENATION★★
20   REM★★SET UP DIRECTORY★★
25   DIM A$(10)
30   FOR I=1 TO 10: READ A$(I):NEXT I
40   DATA A,B,C,D,E,F,G,H,I,J
50   REM★★★★★★★★★★★★★★★★★★★★★★★★
100  C$="":REM★★EMPTY C$★★
110  FOR J=1 TO 10
120  C$=C$+A$(J)
130  PRINT J,C$                         BBC: 130 PRINT;J,C$
140  NEXT J
150  END
```

Program 17

164

```
RUN
1          A
2          AB
3          ABC
4          ABCD
5          ABCDE
6          ABCDEF
7          ABCDEFG
8          ABCDEFGH
9          ABCDEFGHI
10         ABCDEFGHIJ
```

K̲ Program 17.

This process is of great value in textual analysis, but we will use it for codes and games.

6.9 STR$

This function has the reverse effect to the VAL-function. The VAL-function gives the numerical value of a string, and the STR$-function turns a number into just a string of characters.

STR$(X) gives the string representation of the value of X.

Printing STR$
STR$(N) looks very much like N itself as the following program shows:

```
10   REM★★THE STR$-FUNCTION★★
20   INPUT"NEXT NUMBER";N              20 BBC: omit ;
25   PRINT"01234567890123456789 0"
30   PRINT N, STR$(N)                  30 BBC: use PRINT;N,STR$(N)
40   END
```
Program 18

```
RUN
NEXT  NUMBER?  17
0 1 2 3 4 5 6 7 8 9 0 1 2 3 4 5 6 7 8 9 0
  1 7                          1 7
RUN
NEXT  NUMBER?−17
0 1 2 3 4 5 6 7 8 9 0 1 2 3 4 5 6 7 8 9 0
− 1 7                        − 1 7
RUN
NEXT  NUMBER?  99 . 34
0 1 2 3 4 5 6 7 8 9 0 1 2 3 4 5 6 7 8 9 0
  99 . 34                      99 . 34
RUN
NEXT  NUMBER?−99 . 34
0 1 2 3 4 5 6 7 8 9 0 1 2 3 4 5 6 7 8 9 0
−99 . 34                     −99 . 34
```

K̲ Program 18.

However, in each run the second figure (coloured) is treated as a string. This is very clearly shown on the BBC Computer if you add

35 PRINT; N,N

Now both numbers are treated as numbers.

In the next program (Program 19) we make use of the fact that STR$(8) treats 8, say, as a string so that we add the character 8 (as opposed to its value) onto the end of a string.

```
50  REM★★★★★★★★★★★★★★★★★★★★★★★★
100 C$="":REM★★EMPTY C$★★
110 FOR J=1 TO 10
120 C$=C$+STR$(J)
130 PRINT J,C$                       BBC: 130 PRINT;J,C$
140 NEXT J
150 END
```
Program 19

Output on some microcomputers:

```
RUN
1           1
2           1 2
3           1 2 3
4           1 2 3 4
5           1 2 3 4 5
6           1 2 3 4 5 6
7           1 2 3 4 5 6 7
8           1 2 3 4 5 6 7 8
9           1 2 3 4 5 6 7 8 9
10          1 2 3 4 5 6 7 8 9 10
```

Output on BBC Computer:

```
>RUN
1           1
2           12
3           123
4           1234
5           12345
6           123456
7           1234567
8           12345678
9           123456789
10          12345678910
```

Thus, except on the BBC Computer, we still cannot link the characters in adjacent positions because of the space allocated for the sign of the number.

K Program 19.

Exercise 4
Write a program to input a word from the keyboard, to code each letter as a number and output the code as sequence of numbers.

Guidance if required: set up a directory-list as in Program 17 but for the whole alphabet. Remember the DIM statement. Take each letter of the word and compare it with the items of the directory-list. When found in the directory, add that index, in string form, to the code string.

Exercise 5
Write a program to generate 20 random 3-letter words. (It's interesting to see how many times you have to run this program until you generate a bona fide word.)

Assignment 6

1. Write a program to deal a hand of cards, the size of which is left to you. Print out the hand in the form 1D, KC, 8H, 6S. . . , where D=diamonds, C=clubs, etc. 1=ace, T, J, Q. and K stand for ten, jack, queen and king. Remember that when a card has been dealt it cannot be dealt again.

   Guidance if required: write the program in sections:
   • set up the deck (we have previously called it a directory);
   • deal (using the RND generator 1–52 is easiest);
   • output.

   When a card has been dealt, put a marker (e.g. an ★) in that position to signal that it cannot be used again.

2. Write a program to simulate a game of snakes and ladders using a 4×4 board and one die.

   Guidance if required: though the board is square it can be represented in memory by a list B(I):
   i.e. B(1), B(2), B(3) . . . B(16)
   B(3)=+4 could be a ladder going up 4 places.
   B(9)=−7 could be a snake going down 7 places, etc.

   Don't forget that your last throw has to give the right number to complete the board at exactly 16.

   Suggestions (not part of the Assignment for your tutor): play the game a few times and estimate the average number of throws needed to run the board. Change the layout of the board and try some more runs. Design a bigger board, etc.

Objectives of Unit 6

When you have finished this unit, check that you are able to:

Use RND to generate random numbers between 0 and 1. □

Use INT and RND (or RND alone on some computers) to generate integer random numbers between 0 and a given integer N. □

Simulate the tosses of a coin. □

Simulate the tosses of two coins. ☐

Simulate the throw of a die. ☐

Simulate the throws of two dice. ☐

Use score lists. ☐

Abbreviate programs with ? (or P.) and multiple statement lines. ☐

Concatenate strings. ☐

Use STR$(X). ☐

Answers to SAQ's and Exercises

SAQ 1

```
10   RANDOMIZE
20   FOR I=1 TO 6
30   LET N=6★RND(1)
40   PRINT N
50   END
```

Program 20

SAQ 2

(a) 4;   (b) 9;   (c) −3;   (d) −1;   (e) 1.

SAQ 3

```
RUN
−3.8        −4
−3.6        −4
−3.4        −4
−3.2        −4
−3          −3
−2.8        −3
−2.6        −3
−2.4        −3
−2.2        −3
−2          −2
```

SAQ 4

```
RUN
1.6         1
1.8         1
2           2
2.2         2
2.4         2
2.6         2
2.8         2
3           3
3.2         3
```

Exercise 1

Descriptive algorithm for 1 die toss
1. Start.
2. Set the 6 total store locations to zero.
3. Start the 100-throws loop.
4. Generate a random score from the set (1,2,3,4,5,6).
5. Increment the total linked with this score.
6. If loop counter <=100 then go to statement 4 otherwise go on to statement 7.
7. Output score and total for each score value.
8. Stop.

```
10   REM★★THROW 1 DIE 100 TIMES★★
15   DIM S(6)
20   FOR J=1 TO 6
30   LET S(J)=0
40   NEXT J
50   RANDOMIZE                        BBC: 50 omit line
60   FOR I=1 TO 100                   BBC: 70 LET S=RND(6)
70   LET S=INT(6★RND(1)+1)
80   LET S(S)=S(S)+1
90   NEXT I
100  PRINT
110  PRINT"SCORE","FREQUENCY"
120  FOR K=1 TO 6
130  PRINT K,S(K)                     BBC: 130 PRINT;K,S(K)
140  NEXT K
150  END
```

Program 21

```
RUN
SCORE                    FREQUENCY
1                        12
2                        20
3                        16
4                        18
5                        16
6                        18


READY:
RUN

SCORE                    FREQUENCY
1                        9
2                        20
3                        19
4                        18
5                        14
6                        20
```

```
READY:
RUN
```

SCORE	FREQUENCY
1	14
2	28
3	17
4	18
5	15
6	8

```
READY:
RUN
```

SCORE	FREQUENCY
1	15
2	19
3	18
4	17
5	17
6	14

K̲ Program 21.

Exercise 2

```
10   REM★★THROW 2 DICE 100 TIMES★★
20   DIM S(15)
30   FOR J=2 TO 12
40   LET S(J)=0
50   NEXT J
60   RANDOMIZE                          BBC: 60 omit line
70   FOR I=1 TO 100
80   LET S1=INT(6★RND(1)+1)             BBC: 80 LET S1=RND(6)
90   LET S2=INT(6★RND(1)+1)             BBC: 90 LET S2=RND(6)
100  LET S=S1+S2
110  LET S(S)=S(S)+1
120  NEXT I
130  PRINT
140  PRINT"SCORE","FREQUENCY"
150  FOR K=2 TO 12
160  PRINT K,S(K)
170  NEXT K
180  END
```

Program 22

```
RUN
```

SCORE	FREQUENCY
2	1
3	5
4	10
5	13
6	11
7	19

8	16
9	5
10	10
11	5
12	5

K   Program 22.

How about 1000 throws? Well, just change 70 to 70 FOR I=1 TO 1000 (forget what the REM line says!) and you will get a run such as:

RUN

SCORE	FREQUENCY
2	31
3	59
4	74
5	118
6	151
7	173
8	118
9	100
10	89
11	61
12	26

READY:

Suggestions for further programs
1. How will you cope with printing a frequency diagram for this data, as 151 and 173 . . . would 'want to print' off the end of the line?
2. We need a general 'scaling' routine which adjusts to differing line widths, but makes best use of the full width of the page or screen.

Exercise 3
```
10   REM★★FREQUENCY DIAGRAM★★
20   DIM S(15)
30   FOR J=2 TO 12
40   LET S(J)=0
50   NEXT J
60   RANDOMIZE
70   FOR I=1 TO 100
80   LET S1=INT(6★RND(1)+1)
90   LET S2=INT(6★RND(1)+1)
100  LET S=S1+S2
110  LET S(S)=S(S)+1
120  NEXT I
130  PRINT
140  PRINT"FREQUENCY DIAGRAM"
150  PRINT
160  FOR K=2 TO 12
170  PRINT K;TAB(5);S(K);TAB(10);
175  IF S(K)=0 THEN 210
```

```
180 FOR L=1 TO S(K)
190 PRINT"★";
200 NEXT L
210 PRINT
220 NEXT K
230 END
```

Program 23.

```
RUN

FREQUENCY DIAGRAM
```

2	4	★★★★
3	6	★★★★★★
4	6	★★★★★★
5	8	★★★★★★★★
6	19	★★★★★★★★★★★★★★★★★★★
7	21	★★★★★★★★★★★★★★★★★★★★★
8	10	★★★★★★★★★★
9	11	★★★★★★★★★★★
10	8	★★★★★★★★
11	4	★★★★
12	3	★★★

K Program 23.

SAQ 5
The following solution is just one of many possible ways of shortening the program.

```
10   REM★★FREQUENCY DIAGRAM★★
20   DIM S(15)
30   FOR J=2 TO 12:S(J)=0:NEXT J
60   RANDOMIZE
70   FOR I=1 TO 100
80   S1=INT(6★RND(1)+1):S2=INT(6★RND(1)+1)
100  S=S1+S2:S(S)=S(S)+1
120  NEXT I
130  ?:?"FREQUENCY DIAGRAM":?
160  FOR K=2 TO 12
170  ?K;TAB(5);S(K);TAB(10);
175  IF S(K)=0 THEN 210
180  FOR L=1 TO S(K):?"★";:NEXT L
210  ?
220  NEXT K
230  END
```

Program 24

```
RUN

FREQUENCY DIAGRAM
```

2	4	★★★★
3	3	★★★
4	3	★★★
5	18	★★★★★★★★★★★★★★★★★★
6	11	★★★★★★★★★★★

7	13	★★★★★★★★★★★★★
8	11	★★★★★★★★★★★
9	13	★★★★★★★★★★★★★
10	9	★★★★★★★★★
11	11	★★★★★★★★★★★
12	4	★★★★

SAQ 6

```
10  REM★★PLURALS★★
20  LET A$="S"
30  INPUT B$
40  PRINT B$+A$
50  END
```

Exercise 4

```
10   REM★★SIMPLE CODE★★
20   CLEAR 500
30   DIM A$(26)
40   FOR I=1 TO 26
50   READ A$(I)
60   NEXT I
70   DATA A,B,C,D,E,F,G,H,I,J,K,L,M,N,O,P
80   DATA Q,R,S,T,U,V,W,X,Y,Z
100  INPUT"NEXT WORD FOR CODING";W$
110  L=LEN(W$)
120  FOR J=1 TO L
130  I=1
140  IF MID$(W$,J,1)=A$(I) THEN 200
150  I=I+1
160  GOTO 140
200  C$=C$+STR$(I)+" "
210  NEXT J
220  ?:?C$
230  END
```

— set up the directory

BBC: 100 omit;

— compare each letter of the word (W$) with each letter in the directory

— until found,

— then add the index in string form to the code-string

Program 25

```
RUN
NEXT WORD FOR CODING? COMPUTING

 3  15  13  16  21  20  9  14  7

READY:
RUN
NEXT WORD FOR CODING? PARLIAMENT

 16  1  18  12  9  1  13  5  14  20

READY:
RUN
NEXT WORD FOR CODING? PROFESSIONALS

 16  18  15  6  5  19  19  9  15  14  1  12  19

READY:
```

K Program 25.

Exercise 5

BBC: Watch line 20. When you delete CLEAR(100), you mustn't lose DIM A$(26)

```
10   REM★★RANDOM 3-LETTER WORDS★★
20   CLEAR (100):DIM A$(26)
30   FOR I=1 TO 26:REM★★FORM ALPHA-LIST★★
40   READ A$(I): NEXT I
50   DATA A,B,C,D,E,F,G,H,I,J,K,L,M,N,O,P
60   DATA Q,R,S,T,U,V,W,X,Y,Z
70   RANDOMIZE
80   INPUT"ANOTHER LIST";R$
90   IF R$<>"YES" THEN 190
100  FOR K=1 TO 20:REM★★ 20 WORDS★★
110  W$="":REM★★WORD-STRING EMPTY TO START★★
120  FOR J=1 TO 3:REM★★START OF A WORD★★
130  X=INT(26★RND(1)+1)
140  W$=W$+A$(X)
150  NEXT J:REM★★END OF A WORD★★
160  PRINT W$:REM★★PRINT THE WORD★★
170  NEXT K: REM★★GO BACK FOR NEXT WORD★★
180  GOTO 80
190  END
```

Program 26

Too many REMs spoil a program's appearance; do they add to its intelligibility?

```
PDY
XNM
HPI
EVW
EFT
KZT
IGM
KWL
QHW
AIY
ZBQ
MSH
FFA
ZYJ
BBX
JPT
FSV
BPG
GNR
EEP
```

How many times must you run to get a 'proper' word?

K Program 26.

UNIT 7
Handling numbers

7.1 Introduction

We have demonstrated that computers are not just number crunchers but in this Unit we take a closer look at their arithmetic capacity. We concentrate on fairly straight-forward arithmetic, so don't worry about finding it difficult. We're sure that you will be able to cope. We shall continue the 'let's see what happens if approach', and 'let's get the machine to tell us what is going on'. We hope that you will adopt the same approach with the machine that you use.

7.2 Averages and the arithmetic mean

'How long have you been taking over each Unit of the course, so far?' 'Well, on average, about 3 hours.' If we asked you how long it took you to complete a regular journey, such as going to work, you would answer in a similar manner. Sports enthusiasts use the terms goal average, and batting average, atlases abound with pictures of average rainfalls for the months of the year. We talk of average mark in a test or average age of a group of people, etc.

If we wished to calculate the average or arithmetic mean of the ages of a particular group, we would add up the ages for all of the members of the group and divide that sum by the total number of people in the group. To find the arithmetic mean then involves: adding up, counting and then dividing the sum by the count.

Example 1
Find the arithmetic mean of the following set of numbers:

6,7,2,5,4,4,9,8.

Solution
Their sum = 6+7+2+5+4+4+9+8 = 45.
There are 8 numbers.
So their arithemetic mean = 45/8 = 5.625.

SAQ 1
Find the arithmetic mean of the following set of numbers:

8,4,2,6,1,7,6,1,4.

Arithmetic mean
Example 2
Devise an algorithm and write a program to find the arithmetic mean of the numbers stored in these DATA statements as follows:

```
900   DATA 56,47,52,65,24,34,59,37,49,66
910   DATA 38,24,62,76,31,47,66,61,74,45
920   DATA 66,44,55,67,36,56,54,54,50,43
930   DATA 18,83,23,79,29,−9999
```

Solution
We will express the algorithm first of all in descriptive form.

1. Start.
2. Set counter to 1.

3. Set sum to 0.
4. Input the next mark.
5. If mark = −9999 then go to 9 otherwise carry on to 6.
6. Add mark to sum.
7. Add 1 to counter.
8. Go to 4.
9. Set total to counter−1.
10. Calculate average=sum/total.
11. Output average.

Figure 1   Descriptive algorithm for arithmetic mean

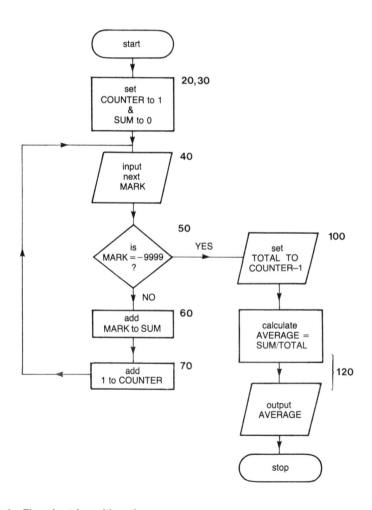

Figure 2   Flowchart for arithmetic mean

```
10   REM★★ARITHMETIC MEAN★★
20   LET C=1
30   LET S=0
40   READ M
50   IF M=-9999 THEN 100
60   LET S=S+M
70   LET C=C+1
80   GOTO 40
90   REM★★★★★★★★★★★★★★★★★★★★
100  LET N=C-1
110  REM★★★★★★★★★★★★★★★★★★★★
120  PRINT"AVERAGE=";S/N
130  REM★★★★★★★★★★★★★★★★★★★★
900  DATA  56,47,52,65,24,34,59,37,49,66
910  DATA  38,24,62,76,31,47,66,61,74,45
920  DATA  66,44,55,67,36,56,54,54,50,43
930  DATA  18,83,23,79,29,-9999
```

Program 1   Arithmetic mean

RUN
AVERAGE= 50.5714

K Program 1.

Exercise 1
Write a program to find the average length of the words in the 'Jude' DATA statements of Example 2 of Unit 5. You can do this by grafting a routine onto Program 1 of Unit 5 which already finds the lengths of words.

Exercise 2
Write a program to find the average score in a simulated experiment of tossing a die 100 times. Run it 10 times to see what range of results you get.

Simulation
The expected average score when throwing a die a large number of times is:

$$\frac{1+2+3+4+5+6}{6} = \frac{21}{6} = 3.5$$

However, in our runs of Exercise 2, we only hit exactly 3.5 once with values ranging from 3.24 to 3.76. That was from the results of 3,000 (30 × 100) throws so you might well ask, 'Is the random number generator biased?' (We did call it 'pseudo' anyway!) How many experiments do we need to convince us that it is, or is not, biased?

To explore that question fully we need to go into statistical theory that is beyond the scope of this course but we can at least find the mean of these means. All we have to do is to take data from the 30 runs of the program:
3.56,3.47,3.52,3.65,...
and enter them into the DATA statements of Program 1 above. This gives us the mean of the means.

You will notice below that we have entered only the decimal parts of the numbers in order to make our data entry a little easier, e.g. 56 instead of 3.56. (We can do this because all the numbers are 3. something.)

178

```
130  REM★★★★★★★★★★★★★★★★★★★★
900  DATA  56,47,52,65,24,34,59,37,49,66
910  DATA  38,24,62,76,31,47,66,61,74,45
920  DATA  66,44,55,67,36,56,54,54,50,43
930  DATA  −9999
940  END
RUN
AVERAGE= 51.2667
```

Figure 3

Thus the overall mean of 3,000 throws is 3.51 to 2 decimal places – a bit more convincing!

Simulation summarised

Simulation is rather a grand word for what we have just done. However, we wanted to emphasize that we can simulate a real life activity without getting deeply involved in statistics. We couldn't toss a die 3,000 times in classroom but with a computer we can collect and process data fairly rapidly.

If your curiosity has been aroused then try the following exercise.

Exercise 3

Write a program to find the average score in a simulated experiment of tossing 2 dice 100 times.

What would you expect the average score to be in this case and in experiments with 3, 4 . . . dice? Are your expectations justified by your experiments?

7.3 Range

While discussing the results of Exercise 2 on page 178, we quite naturally used the idea of range. We said that the values ranged from 3.24 to 3.76. The process involves finding the lowest and highest values of the set.

Example 3

Devise an algorithm and write a routine to find the maximum and minimum values of the numbers stored in the DATA statements in Example 2. Add this routine to the program to find the arithmetic mean as written as a solution to Example 2.

(If you feel confident enough, treat this Example as an exercise before working through our solution.)

Solution

You may feel we've been here before in Unit 4 when we found the lowest member of a list. We could use that approach again but to do so we would first have to put the data in a list form and then sort it twice with the interchange routine. That's a lot of work so we will look at a shorter approach: trying to find the lowest and highest marks as the data is read in.

We know how to read in the data (lines 10–50 in Program 1) but what do we do with it as each item is read?

- First we create two stores:
  M for top mark so far
  B for bottom mark so far.

- Then we read the first mark and put it into both B and M. After all it is the lowest and highest so far!
- Then we read each mark and if it is higher than M, put it into M or, if lower than B, put it into B. If neither, just read the next mark.

So a descriptive solution is:

Description
1. Start routine.
2. If counter=1 then write mark into top and bottom and go to 6 otherwise carry on to 3.
3. If mark > top then write mark into top and go to 6 otherwise carry on to 4.
4. If mark >=bottom then got to 6 otherwise carry on to 5.
5. Write mark into bottom.
6. End routine.

Figure 4

And a flowchart:

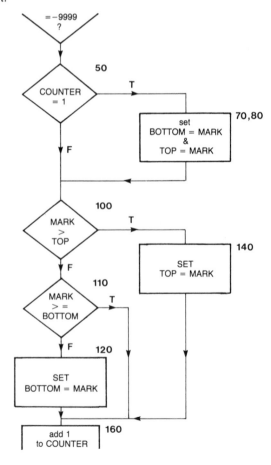

Figure 5.

180

Which do you find easiest to follow?

Where there are several branches in a program, the descriptive algorithm can be rather confusing. The two dimensional display of the flowchart may be more helpful. It's a matter of personal choice; you judge for yourself!

```
10   REM★★MAX AND MIN★★
20   LET C=1
25   LET S=0
30   READ M
40   IF M=−9999 THEN 190
50   IF C>1 THEN 100
60   REM★★★★★★★★★★★★★★★★★★
70   LET B=M
80   LET T=M
90   REM★★★★★★★★★★★★★★★★★★★
100  IF M>T THEN 140
110  IF M>=B THEN 160
120  LET B=M
130  GOTO 160
140  LET T=M
150  REM★★★★★★★★★★★★★★★★★★
160  LET C=C+1
165  LET S=S+M
170  GOTO 30
180  REM★★★★★★★★★★★★★★★★★★
190  PRINT"MAX=";T,"MIN=";B
200  REM★★★★★★★★★★★★★★★★★★
210  LET N=C−1
220  PRINT"AVERAGE=";S/N
230  REM★★★★★★★★★★★★★★★★★★
900  DATA 56,47,52,65,24,34,59,37,49,66
910  DATA 38,24,62,76,31,47,66,61,74,45
920  DATA 66,44,55,67,36,56,54,54,50,43
930  DATA 18,83,23,79,29,−9999
```

the program visits this backwater only the first time round the loop when C=1.

the decisions are made here

Program 2

```
RUN
MAX= 83          MIN= 18
AVERAGE = 50.5714
```

K Program 2.

Exercise 4
Write a program to draw up a frequency table for the data in Program 2, using categories:

0–9, 10–19, 20–29, . . .   90–99

Suggestion
You could use a score-list

S(0), S(10), S(20), ... S(100)

and for each mark read in, test whether it is less than the top of the second band (10), less than the top of the third band (20), etc. until you find

MARK < K true

then increment S(K−10). This is the approach we have used (see answer).

7.4 Number crunching

We have avoided anything other than fairly simple arithmetic so far in the course, and will continue to do so. But it would be wrong not to give a brief insight into the computer's arithmetic capacity. If your heart sinks at the sight of the following few pages, you will miss no vital programming information if you pass on to the next section on dry-running and tracing, but we hope you will give it a try. Our machine certainly does take the drudgery out of arithmetic.

Here is a simple program which calculates for the numbers 1 to 10 their squares (line 50), cubes (line 60) and reciprocals (line 70) and then tabulates the result.

```
 1  REM. . . .TABULATE THE SQUARES, CUBES AND
 2  REM. . . .RECIPROCALS FOR THE FIRST TEN
 3  REM. . . .NATURAL NUMBERS.
10  PRINT"N","N★N","N★N★N","1/N"
20  PRINT
30  FOR I=1 TO 10
40  LET N=I
50  LET S=I★I
60  LET C=I★I★I
70  LET R=1/I
80  PRINT N,S,C,R
90  NEXT I
100 END
```

Program 3

RUN

N	N★N	N★N★N	1/N
1	1	1	1
2	4	8	.5
3	9	27	.333333
4	16	64	.25
5	25	125	.2
6	36	216	.166667
7	49	343	.142857
8	64	512	.125
9	81	729	.111111
10	100	1000	.1

K Program 3. On the BBC Computer Program 3 overruns the screen.

Try:

```
10  PRINT"N";TAB(7);"N★N"; TAB(13);"N★N★N";TAB (21);"1/N"
80  PRINT;N;TAB(7);S;TAB(13);C;TAB(21);R
```

Raising to a power

We expect that you are familiar with the notation:

$4 \times 4 = 4^2$ (4-squared or 4 raised to the power 2)
$7 \times 7 \times 7 = 7^3$ (7-cubed or 7 raised to the power 3)
$10 \times 10 \times 10 \times 10 \times 10 = 10^5$ (10 raised to the power 5)

In BASIC raised to the power is shown as $\uparrow$ or simply $\wedge$. Any number N raised to the power P is shown as N $\uparrow$ P. P is called the exponent and would you believe it, raising to a power is called exponentiation.

Similarly for negative powers:

			N	P	N↑P
$\frac{1}{4} \times \frac{1}{4} = \frac{1}{4 \times 4} = 4^{-2}$			4	-2	$4 \uparrow (-2)$
$\frac{1}{7} \times \frac{1}{7} \times \frac{1}{7} = \frac{1}{7 \times 7 \times 7} = 7^{-3}$			7	-3	$7 \uparrow (-3)$
$\frac{1}{10} \times \frac{1}{10} \times \frac{1}{10} \times \frac{1}{10} \times \frac{1}{10} = \frac{1}{10 \times 10 \times 10 \times 10 \times 10} = 10^{-5}$			10	-5	$10 \uparrow (-5)$

Fractional powers (positive and negative) are also possible but we will not be concerned with them.

We can use the $\uparrow$ notation instead of $\ast$ in Program 3. Thus Program 3 re-written with $\uparrow$ becomes:

```
10   PRINT"N","N↑2","N↑3","N↑(-1)"
20   FOR N=1 TO 10
30   PRINT N,N↑2,N↑3,N↑(-1)
40   NEXT N
50   END
```

Program 4

(On the BBC Computer, you still need to space lines 10 and 30 as in Program 3.)

Sequences and their sums

Calculating the individual terms in a sequence, or the sum of the first N terms, is a very great labour without a computer. How long would it take you to evaluate the terms of

$$\frac{1}{1^2}, \ \frac{1}{2^2}, \ \frac{1}{3^2}, \ \cdots \ \frac{1}{N^2} \ ?$$

Well, it's very easy with Program 5.

```
10   PRINT"N". "N↑(-2)"
20   FOR N=1 TO 10
30   PRINT N,N↑(-2)
40   NEXT N
50   END
```
Program 5

N	$N \uparrow (-2)$
1	1
2	.25
3	.111111
4	.0625
5	.04
6	.0277778
7	.0204082
8	.015625
9	.0123457
10	.01

(Your computer may show numbers with E in them in column 2. This will be explained in section 7.6.)

K   Program 5.

Exercise 5
Write a program to find how many terms of the series

$$1, \frac{1}{2}, \frac{1}{3}, \frac{1}{4}, \ldots$$

are needed to make their sum exceed 2.4.

Exercise 6
Modify the program from Exercise 5 to find out how many terms are needed for

$$\text{sum} = 1 + \frac{1}{2^2} + \frac{1}{3^2} + \frac{1}{4^2} + \ldots$$

to exceed 1.5.

Exercise 7
Factorials are interesting numbers. Factorial $4 = 4 \times 3 \times 2 \times 1$ and is usually written 4! So

Factorial $7 = 7 \times 6 \times 5 \times 4 \times 3 \times 2 \times 1 = 7!$

Factorial $N = N \times (N-1) \times (N-2) \times \ldots \times 1 = N!$

Write a program to evaluate the factorial of any positive integer.

Exercise 8
We wrote a rather clumsy program to evaluate the yield (Y) on a deposit (D) at compound interest percentage (P) way back in Unit 1. A neater formula is $Y = D \times (1 + P/100)^T$

where T is the number of years of the investment.

Write a program to evaluate the yield, using this formula, for various deposits, percentages and time periods.

7.5 Dry running

Often we find that a program either does not work at all, or not to our complete satisfaction. If we have reasonable access to a computer we may sit at the machine until we trace the fault, but when all else fails we may be forced to sit down with pencil and paper and think hard. Stepping through an algorithm line by line with pencil and paper is called dry running.

We shall illustrate dry running by looking at Program 18 which was the solution to Exercise 5.

```
10   REM★★SUM OF RECIPROCALS★★
20   LET S=0
30   LET N=1
40   LET S=S+1/N
50   IF S>2.4 THEN 90
60   LET N=N+1
70   GOTO 40
90   PRINT"SUM=";S;"  THE NO. OF TERMS IS ";N
100  END
```

Program 18 (from Exercise 5)

```
RUN
SUM= 2.45   THE NO. OF TERMS IS 6
```

Tracing means finding and recording each step, the line number executed at that step and the values of the variables after that line has been executed. So, for Program 18 we need the headings:

step No.	line No.	N	S
1			
2			
etc			

We omit from the trace lines which don't affect the variables, i.e.:

REM   (line 10)
GOTO   (line 70)
PRINT   (line 90)

Apart from these, the program steps are as follows:

step No.	line No.	N	S
1	20	0	0
2	30	1	0
3	40	1	1

185

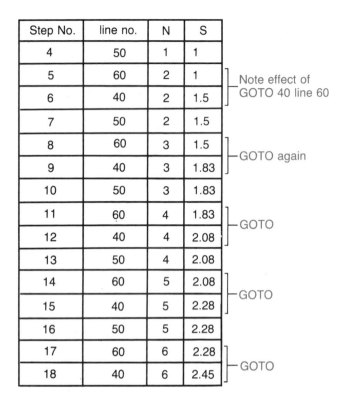

Step No.	line no.	N	S
4	50	1	1
5	60	2	1
6	40	2	1.5
7	50	2	1.5
8	60	3	1.5
9	40	3	1.83
10	50	3	1.83
11	60	4	1.83
12	40	4	2.08
13	50	4	2.08
14	60	5	2.08
15	40	5	2.28
16	50	5	2.28
17	60	6	2.28
18	40	6	2.45

Note effect of GOTO 40 line 60 (steps 5–6)

GOTO again (steps 8–9)

GOTO (steps 11–12)

GOTO (steps 14–15)

GOTO (steps 17–18)

Figure 6

Tracing

Most BASIC interpreters provide a TRACE command, but these often provide so much information that it is difficult to see the wood for the trees. A carefully designed trace routine of your own often works best. We shall not, therefore, show the TRACE command at work but will show you later in this Unit how to write your own trace into a program.

SAQ 2

Complete a dry-run on the following program, starting when line 20 has just been executed and continuing until the condition in line 50 is true. Draw up the table with the same headings as in the above example.

```
10   REM★★SUM OF SQUARES★★
20   S=0
30   N=1
40   S=S+N↑2
50   IF S>50 THEN 90
60   N=N+1
70   GOTO 40
90   PRINT "SUM=";S;"   NO. OF TERMS IS";N
100  END
```

Program 6

7.6 The representation of numbers

So far in the course we have left in abeyance a number of questions about the representation of numbers in our programs. We do not intend to consider the mathematics of number representation in computers in general but we need to tidy up our ideas about numbers.

In general terms computers must be able to process and store the following types of number:

(a) positive and negative whole numbers (integers or counting numbers);
(b) fractions and numbers which are partly whole and partly fractional (measuring numbers);
(c) very large and very small numbers;
(d) the number zero.

The single most important piece of advice that we can give you at this stage is that if a number has been involved in any sort of calculation within a program then consider it with a certain amount of suspicion. The reason for this statement is that numbers within a computer are stored and manipulated in binary form, that is to base 2, rather than to the base 10 with which we are familiar. In our familiar decimal notation you will recall that a number like $\frac{1}{3}$ or $\frac{1}{7}$ is incapable of exact expression, e.g. $\frac{1}{3} = 0.3333\ldots$ We assume that by adding on as many 3's to this number as we wish, we can achieve an acceptable level of accuracy in any particular problem. In the binary system, in just the same way, some numbers cannot be expressed exactly, e.g. in decimal form we can say that $\frac{1}{10} = 0.1$ exactly but when this number is changed into binary form it cannot be represented exactly.

Most BASIC interpreters allow for numbers to be expressed to an accuracy of six decimal digits. In decimal form then the number $3\frac{1}{10}$ could be represented as 3.10000 to six decimal digit accuracy. However, if this number had been the result of some calculation within a computer, we might find that the number output was 3.09999 or 3.10001. So, in general, you must always be suspicious of the least significant digit in any answer (i.e. the digit on the far right of the number).

Program 7 shows how this type of inaccuracy may occur. The FOR. . . NEXT loop adds 4.0, 4.1 and 4.25 into locations S, T and U one thousand times. Now 4.0 and 4.25 are exactly represented in binary form, but 4.1 is not. We can see that the result of this repetitive summation is exact in respect of 4.0 and 4.25, but not for 4.1 where the error is 0.04 in 4100.00. Obviously, we would avoid writing programs involving such repetitions wherever possible, but we hope that the program will act as a warning about possible inaccuracies.

```
10   REM★★ACCURACY DEMONSTRATION★★
20   LET S=0
30   LET T= 0
40   LET U=0
50   FOR I=1 TO 1000
60   LET S=S+4.0
70   LET T=T+4.1
80   LET U=U+4.25
90   NEXT I
100  PRINT S,T,U                        BBC: 100 PRINT;S,T,U
120  END
```

Program 7

RUN
4000   4100.04   4250

READY:

K̲ Program 7.

Small and large numbers
Six decimal digits do not allow us to cope with very small or very large numbers. So these numbers are represented in BASIC in exponential form.

Small numbers
0.000586321 means $\dfrac{586321}{1,000,000,000} = \dfrac{586321}{10^9}$

which could be expressed 586321×10^{-9}. We could also express 0.000586321 as $\dfrac{0.586321}{1000} = 0.586321 \times 10^{-3}$

In BASIC this last number would be written as $0.586321E-3$ or $0.586321E-03$.

Similarly,

$0.0234539 = 2.34539 \times 10^{-2} = 2.34539E-2$

and

$0.00000000959734 = 0.959734 \times 10^{-8} = 0.959734E-8$.

E stands for exponent, and the base for exponentiation is 10. So $E-4$ means move the decimal point 4 places to the left, and $E+9$ means move the decimal point 9 places to the right.

Large numbers
$12368500 = 1.23685 \times 10^7 = 1.23685E+7$
$935.432 = 0.935432 \times 10^3 = 0.935432E+3$
$959734000000000000000 = 0.959734E+21$

Most BASIC interpreters have a range of at least $E-32$ to $E+32$; but you should check the details of the particular system which you are using.

K̲ Find out how your computer represents small and large numbers with this program.

```
10   REM★★NUMBER DEMONSTRATION★★
20   PRINT"NUMBER","REPRESENTATION"
30   FOR I=-10 TO 10
40   PRINT "10↑";I,10↑I
50   NEXT I
```

Program 8

7.7   The INT-function for rounding
For some problems we need to round off the result of a calculation to the nearest whole number,

188

e.g.   6.6 to the nearest whole number is 7
      7.4 to the nearest whole number is 7.

This is especially true if we are not confident about the last figure accuracy of a decimal number,

e.g. 6.99999 or 7.00001 for 7.

The function INT(X+0.5) does this rounding for us as the following program demonstrates.

```
10   REM★★INT FOR ROUNDING★★
20   PRINT"X","INT(X)","INT(X+0.5)"
30   FOR I=−1.4 TO −2.6 STEP(−.1)
40   PRINT I, INT(I),INT(I+.5)          BBC: 40 P.;I,;INT(1);INT(1+.5)
50   NEXT I
60   END
```

X	INT(X)	INT(X+0.5)
−1.4	−2	−1
−1.5	−2	−1
−1.6	−2	−2
−1.7	−2	−2
−1.8	−2	−2
−1.9	−2	−2
−2	−2	−2
−2.1	−3	−2
−2.2	−3	−2
−2.3	−3	−2
−2.4	−3	−2
−2.5	−3	−2
−2.6	−3	−3

Program 9a

Changing line 30 to 30 FOR I=1.4 TO 2.6 STEP(.1) gives

X	INT(X)	INT(X+0.5)
1.4	1	1
1.5	1	2
1.6	1	2
1.7	1	2
1.8	1	2
1.9	1	2
2	2	2
2.1	2	2
2.2	2	2
2.3	2	2
2.4	2	2
2.5	2	3
2.6	2	3

Program 9b

K̲ Program 9a.

SAQ 3
What print-outs will we get from the above program if we change line 30 as follows:

(a)   30 FOR I=.4 TO 2.2 STEP(.2) ?
(b)   30 FOR I=.4 TO −.6 STEP(−.2) ?

7.8   The ABS-function

An arithmetic function related to the above ideas, is to find the modulus, or absolute value of a number. It sounds rather grand, but is very simple.

ABS(X) simply gives us the positive value of X.
e.g. ABS(23)=23, ABS(−23)=23.

The following program illustrates the function.

```
10   REM★★THE ABS-FUNCTION★★
20   PRINT"X","Y","X+Y","ABS(X+Y)"
30   FOR I=1 TO 4
40   READ X,Y
50   PRINT X,Y,X+Y,ABS(X+Y)          BBC: 50 PRINT;X,;Y,;X+Y,;ABS(X+Y)
60   NEXT I
100  DATA 5,7,5,−7,−5,7,−5,−7
```
Program 10

```
RUN
X                Y                X+Y          ABS(X+Y)
 5               7                12           12
 5              −7               −2            2
−5               7                2            2
−5              −7               −12           12
```

K̄   Program 10.

SAQ 4
What will the print-out table be if we change line 100 to
100 DATA 9,14,11,−2,−4,13,−7,−8 ?

7.9   Iteration

The process of making a guess at a value, testing it, making a better guess and testing again, etc., until we home in on an item or value is known as iteration. The essence of iteration involves:
- making an arbitrary start
- guessing how accurate this point is
- refining this in a sequence of repeated operations.

Square root by iteration
BASIC can do square roots directly as this program demonstrates:

```
10   FOR X=33 TO 63 STEP (10)
20   PRINT X,X ↑ (.5),SQR(X)          BBC: 20 PRINT;X;TAB(5);X ↑ (.5),SQR(X)
30   NEXT X
```
Program 11

(SQR(X) gives the square root of X provided that X> = 0.)

```
RUN
33          5.74456        5.74456
43          6.55744        6.55744
53          7.28011        7.28011
63          7.93726        7.93726
```

However, we shall also show you how to find a square root by an iterative method not because that's how you would normally do it but because it's an easy example through which to demonstrate iteration.

The method
If you want to square root a number N, then:

- take a guess at the square root, say G
- work out N/G
- then the average of G and N/G is an even better guess than your first one, i.e. it is closer to the unknown square root than your first guess.
- go back to the beginning using this new 'better' guess.

We shan't prove this here (it's in plenty of maths textbooks) but we shall show its working in a simple case.

To square root   N = 12
Guess   G= 2
Work out   N/G= 6
Take average $\dfrac{G+ N/G}{2} = \dfrac{2 + 6}{2} = 4$

So 4 is the new guess:

Guess G = 4
        N/G = 3
        $\dfrac{G + N/G}{2} = 3.5$

So 3.5 is the new guess.

In table form this looks like:

G	N/G	$\dfrac{G+N/G}{2}$
2	12/2=6	(2+6)/2=4
4	12/4=3	(4+3)/2=3.5
3.5	12/3.5=...	....

Figure 7

SAQ 5
To make sure that you have grasped the process draw up a table similar to that above, but make your first guess 1.

Iteration. . . stop

The question now is: 'How do we stop the process?' Well, we want to stop the process when the square of our guess becomes as close as possible to N. What do we mean by 'as close as possible'? The answer is that it's up to you. You're in charge! How accurate do you want the square root to be? If, for example, we wish to find the square root of 12 to 2 decimal places, then the difference between G★G and N would have to be

$$< 0.005$$

We don't need to know whether G★G is bigger or smaller than N – only the difference matters. So we are back to ABS. If

$$ABS(N-G★G) < 0.005$$

then stop, is what we are after.

Descriptive algorithm for square root iteration
1. Start.
2. Input the number whose square root is sought.
3. Input the accuracy required.
4. Input a guess at the square root.
5. If the guess is within the accuracy required then go to 8 otherwise continue with the next statement.
6. Make the guess more accurate.
7. Return to 5.
8. Output the square root value found.
9. Stop.

Figure 8

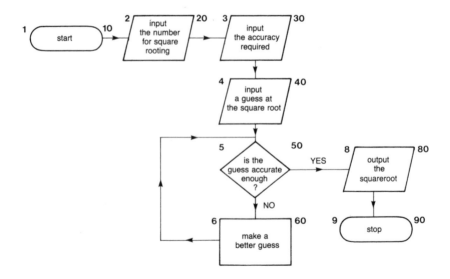

Figure 9 Flowchart for square root iteration

```
10   REM★★SQRT BY ITERATION★★
20   INPUT"NO. FOR SQUARE-ROOTING";N
30   INPUT"ACCURACY REQUIRED";A
40   INPUT"YOUR GUESS";G
50   IF ABS(N−G★G)<A THEN 80
60   LET G=.5★(G+(N/G))
70   GOTO 50
80   PRINT
81   PRINT"THE SQRT OF ";N;" IS ";G
90   END
```

Program 12   Square root iteration

```
RUN
NO. FOR SQUARE-ROOTING? 12
ACCURACY REQUIRED? .005
YOUR GUESS? 2

THE SQRT OF 12 IS 3.46429

RUN
NO. FOR SQUARE-ROOTING? 12
ACCURACY REQUIRED? .00005
YOUR GUESS? 2

THE SQRT OF 12 IS 3.4641
```

K Program 12.

Tracing the iterative process

Now the result of program 12 is not very startling. As we pointed out earlier on, we can find N directly with a computer. But we wanted a simple example to demonstrate iteration at work so we will now take a closer look at what is happening. We will put a trace into Program 12 as follows:

```
47   PRINT"OLD","NEW","ABS(N−G★G)"
55   PRINT G,
65   PRINT G,ABS(N−G★G)
```

Each pass round the loop (i.e. each iteration) lines 55 and 65 print out a report on how the calculation is going.

```
10   REM★★SQRT BY ITERATION★★
20   INPUT"NO. FOR SQUARE-ROOTING";N
30   INPUT"ACCURACY REQUIRED";A
40   INPUT"YOUR GUESS";G
47   PRINT"OLD","NEW","ABS(N−G★G)"
50   IF ABS(N−G★G)<A THEN 80
55   PRINT G,                          BBC: 55 PRINT;G;TAB(12);
60   LET G= 5★(G+(N/G))
65   PRINT G,ABS(N−G★G)        BBC: 65 PRINT;G;TAB(25);ABS(N−G★G)
70   GOTO 50
80   PRINT
81   PRINT"THE SQRT OF ";N;" IS ";G
90   END
```

Program 13   Iterative square root with trace

RUN
NO. FOR SQUARE-ROOTING? 12
ACCURACY REQUIRED? .005
YOUR GUESS? 2

OLD	NEW	ABS(N−G★G)	
2	4	4	
4	3.5	.25	3 loops only
3.5	3.46429	1.27602E−03	

THE SQRT OF 12 IS 3.46429

RUN
NO. FOR SQUARE-ROOTING? 12
ACCURACY REQUIRED? .0005 ——— increasing the accuracy tenfold still only
YOUR GUESS? 2   takes 4 loops

OLD	NEW	ABS(N−G★G)
2	4	4
4	3.5	.25
3.5	3.46429	1.27602E
3.46429	3.4641	9.53674E−07

THE SQRT OF 12 IS 3.4641

K̲ Program 13.

RUN
NO. FOR SQUARE-ROOTING? −67 ————— if we give it a negative number
ACCURACY REQUIRED? .005
YOUR GUESS? 8

OLD	NEW	ABS(N−G★G)
8	−.1875	67.0352
−.1875	178.573	31955.3
178.573	89.0989	8005.61
89.0989	44.1734	2018.29
44.1734	21.3283	521.898
21.3283	9.09349	149.692
9.09349	.862795	67.7444
.862795	−38.3959	1541.25
−38.3959	−18.3255	402.823
−18.3255	−7.33468	120.797
−7.33468	.900008	67.81
.900008	−36.7719	1419.17
−36.7719	−17.4749	372.373
−17.4749	−6.82043	113.518
−6.82043	1.5015	69.2545
1.5015	−21.5603	531.847
−21.5603	−9.22637	152.126
−9.22637		

it doesn't like it, and we have
to pull out the plug!

194

Exercise 9

Change the square root program above to produce cube roots. If G is a guess at the cube root of N then $\frac{1}{2}(G + N/G^2)$ will be a better guess.

Assignment 7

1. If g is a guess at the solution of the quadratic equation $x^2+bx+c = 0$, then a better guess is $-c/(b+g)$. Devise an algorithm and write a BASIC program to find the solution of any quadratic equation.

    Notes:

    1. By solution we mean a value of x which makes the left-hand side of the equation equal to zero.

    2. When testing your algorithm choose values of b and c such that $b^2>4c$.

2. Pythagoras' theorem was about right-angled triangles, remember. It does however generate some special whole number (integer) triples, e.g.

    $3^2 + 4^2 = 5^2$

    $5^2 + 12^2 = 13^2$

    Devise an algorithm and BASIC program to find out how many such integer triples there are for numbers <100.

    Hint: you will need to use the INT(X+0.5) function in this program.

Objectives of Unit 7

Calculate (manually) an arithmetic mean. ☐

Write a program to calculate arithmetic means. ☐

Write a program to find the largest and smallest item in a data list. ☐

Use ★, / and ↑ in programs. ☐

Dry run a program. ☐

Interpret numbers in E notation. ☐

Use INT(X+.5) for rounding. ☐

Use ABS(X). ☐

Write programs for iterative routines to include terminating procedures. ☐

Insert trace print lines in a program. ☐

Answers to SAQ's and Exercises

SAQ 1

Sum = 8 + 4 + 2 + 6 + 1 + 7 + 6 + 1 + 4 = 39
There are 9 numbers.
So the arithmetic mean is 39/9 = 4.333. . .

Exercise 1

```
10  REM★★AVERAGE LENGTH★★
20  LET S=0
30  LET C=1
40  READ W$
50  IF W$="ZZZZ" THEN 160
60  LET L=LEN(W$)
70  LET S=S+L
80  LET C=C+1
90  GOTO 40
100 REM★★★★★★★★★★★★★★★★★★★★★★★★★
110 DATA THE, HORSE, STOOD, STILL, TILL, HE, HAD, FINISHED, THE, HYMN
120 DATA WHICH, JUDE, REPEATED, UNDER, THE, SWAY, OF, A, POLYTHEISTIC
130 DATA FANCY, THAT, HE, WOULD, NEVER, HAVE, THOUGHT, OF, HUMOURING
140 DATA IN, BROAD, DAYLIGHT, ZZZZ
150 REM ★★★★★★★★★★★★★★★★★★★★★★★
160 LET N=C-1
170 LET A=S/N
180 PRINT"AVERAGE LENGTH OF THE WORDS IS ";A
190 END
```
Program 14

AVERAGE LENGTH OF THE WORDS IS 4.64516

K Program 14.

Exercise 2

```
10  REM★★MEAN OF 100 THROWS★★
20  REM★★ OF 1 DIE★★
30  RANDOMIZE
50  LET S=0
60  FOR I=1 TO 100                    BBC: 60 use RND(6)
70  LET X=INT(6★RND(1)+1)
80  LET S=S+X
90  NEXT I
100 PRINT"AVERAGE SCORE=";S/100
110 END
```
Program 15

K Program 15.

Exercise 3

```
10  REM★★MEAN OF 100 THROWS★★
20  REM★★OF 2 DICE★★
30  RANDOMIZE
50  LET S=0
60  FOR I=1 TO 100
70  LET X=INT(6★RND(1)+1) ⎤
75  LET Y=INT(6★RND(1)+1) ⎦————————— BBC: use RND
80  LET S=S+X+Y
```

196

```
90   NEXT I
100  PRINT"AVERAGE SCORE=";S/100
100  END
```

Program 16

K Program 16.

Exercise 4

```
10   REM★★HISTOGRAM★★
20   DIM S(100)
30   FOR K=0 TO 100 STEP (10):S(K)=0:NEXT K
40   REM★★★★★★★★★★★★★★★★★★★★★★
50   READ M
60   IF M=−9999 THEN 150
70   REM★★★★★★★★★★★★★★★★★★★★★★
80   K=10
90   IF M<K THEN 120 ───────────────── K for score category
100  K=K+10                            or class interval
110  GOTO 90
120  S(K−10)=S(K−10)+1 ─────────────── correct category found.
130  GOTO 50                           Increment counter for
140  REM★★★★★★★★★★★★★★★★★★★★★★        that category.
150  FOR K=0 TO 100 STEP (10)
160  PRINT K,S(K)
170  NEXT K
180  REM★★★★★★★★★★★★★★★★★★★★★★
190  DATA 56,47,52,65,24,34,59,37,49,66
200  DATA 38,24,62,76,31,47,66,61,74,45
210  DATA 66,44,55,67,36,56,54,54,50,43
220  DATA 18,83,23,79,29,−9999
```

Program 17

```
RUN
0        0
10       1
20       4
30       5
40       6
50       8
60       7
70       3
80       1
90       0
100      0
```

K Program 17.

Exercise 5

```
10   REM★★SUM OF RECIPROCALS★★
20   LET S=0
30   LET N=1
40   LET S=S+1/N
50   IF S>2.4 THEN 90
```

197

```
60  LET N=N+1
70  GOTO 40
90  PRINT"SUM=";S;"  THE NO. OF TERMS IS  ";N
100 END
```
Program 18

```
RUN
SUM= 2.45   THE NO. OF TERMS IS 6
```

K Program 18.

Exercise 6

```
10  REM★★SUM OF N ↑ (−2)★★
20  S=0
30  N=1
40  S=S+N ↑ (−2)
50  IF S>1.5 THEN 90
60  N=N+1
70  GOTO 40
90  PRINT "SUM=";S,"NO. OF TERMS=";N
100 END
```
Program 19

```
RUN
SUM= 1.5118   NO. OF TERMS= 7
```

You can, of course, change line 50 to explore the number of terms needed for the sum to exceed other values, e.g.

```
50  IF S>1.6 THEN 90
RUN
SUM= 1.6005   NO. OF TERMS= 22 ——————— for 1.6
```

```
50  IF S>1.61 THEN 90
RUN
SUM= 1.61104   NO. OF TERMS= 29 ——————— for 1.61
```

```
50  IF S>1.62 THEN 90
RUN
SUM= 1.62024   NO. OF TERMS= 40 ——————— for 1.62
```

```
50  IF S>1.63 THEN 90
RUN
SUM= 1.63012   NO. OF TERMS= 67 ——————— for 1.63
```

What a good starting point these and similar programs would make to lessons about limits and convergence of number series!

K Program 19.

Exercise 7

```
10  REM. . . .FACTORIALS
20  PRINT"TO END THE RUN, ENTER −9999"
30  PRINT
```

```
40   INPUT"NEXT FACTORIAL";N
50   IF N=−9999 THEN 130
60   LET F=1
70   FOR I=1 TO N
80   LET F=F★I
90   NEXT I
100  PRINT N,F
110  PRINT
120  GOTO 40
130  END
```

Program 20

```
RUN
TO END THE RUN, ENTER −9999

NEXT FACTORIAL? 1
 1              1

NEXT FACTORIAL? 3
 3              6

NEXT FACTORIAL? 5
 5              120

NEXT FACTORIAL? 7
 7              5040

NEXT FACTORIAL? 9
 9              362880

NEXT FACTORIAL? 11
 11             3.99168E+07 ──── what's happened here?
                              see the section on number representation.

NEXT FACTORIAL? −9999

>READY
```

Ⓚ Program 20.

SAQ 2

Step No.	Line No.	N	S
1	20	0	0
2	30	1	0
3	40	1	1
4	60	2	1
5	40	2	5
6	60	3	5
7	40	3	14
8	60	4	14

9	40	4	30
10	60	5	30
11	40	5	55

Exercise 8

```
10  REM★★COMPOUND INTEREST★★
20  PRINT"ENTER DEPOSIT,PERCENTAGE,TIME"
30  INPUT D,P,T
40  PRINT"TIME","YIELD"
50  FOR I=1 TO T
60  PRINT I,D★(1+P/100)↑I
70  NEXT I
80  END
```

Program 21

```
ENTER DEPOSIT,PERCENTAGE,TIME
 500 , 11.5 , 5
 TIME           YIELD
 1              557.5
 2              621.612
 3              693.098
 4              772.804
 5              861.677
```

K Program 21.

SAQ 3

(a)
X	INT(X)	INT(X+0.5)
.4	0	0
.6	0	1
.8	0	1
1	1	1
1.2	1	1
1.4	1	1
1.6	1	2
1.8	1	2
2	2	2

(b)
X	INT(X)	INT(X+0.5)
.2	0	0
0	0	0
−.2	−1	0
−.4	−1	0
−.6	−1	−1

SAQ 4

RUN
X	Y	X+Y	ABS(X+Y)
9	14	23	23
11	−2	9	9
−4	13	9	9
−7	−8	−15	15

SAQ 5

9	N/G	$\dfrac{G+N/G}{2}$
1	12	6.5
6.5	1.8	4.15
4.15	2.89	3.52
3.52	3.41	3.46 etc

Exercise 9

```
10  REM★★CUBEROOT ITERATION★★
20  INPUT"NUMBER FOR CUBEROOTING";N
30  INPUT"ACCURACY REQUIRED";A
40  LET G=N/2 ───────────────── the machine makes the first guess at N/2
43  LET C=1
50  IF ABS(N−G★G★G) <A THEN 80
60  LET G=0.5★(G+N/(G★G))
67  LET C=C+1
70  GOTO 50
80  PRINT"THE NO. OF LOOPS=";C
81  PRINT"THE CUBEROOT OF ";N;"=";G
90  END
```

Program 22

```
RUN
NUMBER FOR CUBEROOTING? 28
ACCURACY REQUIRED? .005
THE NO. OF LOOPS= 14
THE CUBEROOT OF 28 = 3.03641

READY:

RUN
NUMBER FOR CUBEROOTING? 10101
ACCURACY REQUIRED? .005
THE NO. OF LOOPS= 28
THE CUBEROOT OF 10101 = 21.6166

READY:
RUN
NUMBER FOR CUBEROOTING? −937
ACCURACY REQUIRED? .005
THE NO. OF LOOPS= 21
THE CUBEROOT OF −937 =−9.78542

READY:
```

K Program 22.

UNIT 8
Introduction to data processing

8.1 Introduction

In this Unit we shall emphasize again how important it is to impose some sort of order on data. In particular, we shall analyse in detail one method of ordering data: the interchange procedure for sorting. Having sorted the data we shall then show how to search through it quickly using the bisection search procedure. Finally we shall look at how to handle data in tabular form.

These activities will also give us a chance to see how subroutines can help us perform many of those little repetitive tasks which can occur in programs of any size.

8.2 Sorting

In Unit 4 we spent some time discussing the procedure for finding the lowest value item in a list. We did this by an interchange procedure that put the lowest item into position 1 on the list. We said that we could repeat the procedure for the rest of the list, placing the second lowest value into position 2, etc., and we left you with the problem of sorting the whole list as an assignment. Because of the interchange sort's importance, we are now going to look at it in greater detail.

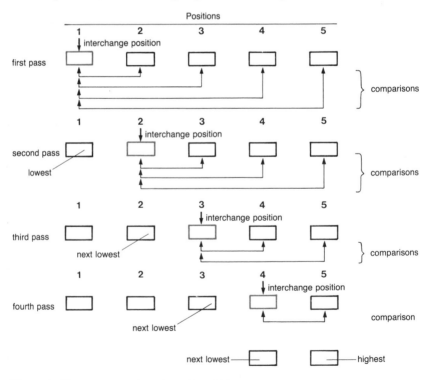

Figure 1 The sort procedure for a list of 5 items

204

Figure 1 illustrates the procedure for placing the items into locations 1 to 5 with the lowest item in 1, the next lowest in 2 and so on.

First pass. On the first pass all items are compared with the item in position 1 and the lowest is then placed in position 1.

Second pass. Position 1 can now be ignored and the procedure repeated on positions 2 to 5. This will find the next lowest which is placed in position 2.

Third pass. Now positions 1 and 2 can be ignored since they contain 'lowest' and 'next to lowest'. The procedure is repeated on positions 3 to 5. This finds the third lowest which goes in position 3.

Fourth pass. This is performed on items 4 and 5 only and results in the 4th lowest going into the fourth position. The remaining item must be the highest and will already be in the fifth position so no further passes are needed.

We can summarise the sort procedure as:

loop number	point interchange	remaining sub-sequence	
		start	end
1	1	2	5
2	2	3	5
3	3	4	5
4	4	5	5

Figure 2a   Four sorts in a list of 5 items

Or, more generally, if we want to sort a list of N items:

loop number	interchange point	remaining sub-sequence	
		start	end
1	1	2	N
2	2	3	.
3	3	4	.
.	.	.	.
.	.	.	N
.	.	.	.
K	K	K+1	.
.	.	.	.
.	.	.	N
.	.	.	N
N−1	N−1	N	N

Figure 2(b)   (N−1) sorts in a list of N items

Since each pass involves a repetitive series of comparisons, it is an obvious candidate for a FOR . . . NEXT . . . loop. Then we need a further loop to decide which loop we are going round:

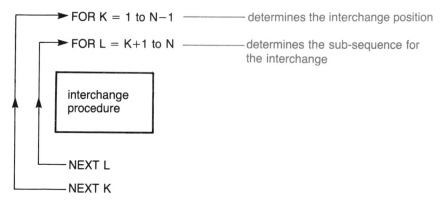

Figure 3   The nested loops of interchange sorting

SAQ 1
Use the interchange sort to place the following in order. Show the numbers stored at each location after each run

6, 1, 4, 0, 2, 3, 7, 8

The program is:

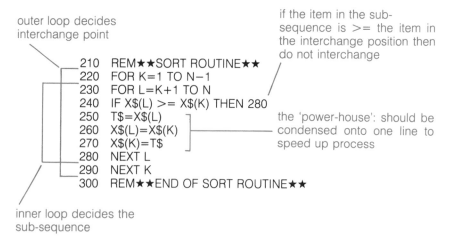

outer loop decides interchange point

if the item in the sub-sequence is >= the item in the interchange position then do not interchange

```
210  REM★★SORT ROUTINE★★
220  FOR K=1 TO N−1
230  FOR L=K+1 TO N
240  IF X$(L) >= X$(K) THEN 280
250  T$=X$(L)
260  X$(L)=X$(K)
270  X$(K)=T$
280  NEXT L
290  NEXT K
300  REM★★END OF SORT ROUTINE★★
```

the 'power-house': should be condensed onto one line to speed up process

inner loop decides the sub-sequence

Program 1   Interchange sort

Using the sort program
The sort program can be used whenever it is needed. Here is one particular use: to sort a list of names into alphabetical order.

lines 50–80   read in the data
lines 210–300   carry out the sort
lines 410–450   print out the sorted list
the data has been stored in line 900

```
10  REM★★SORT ROUTINE★★
20  CLEAR 100
30  DIM X$(100)
50  I=1
60  READ X$
70  IF X$="ZZZZ" THEN 190                    ———— reading in the data
80  X$(I)=X$:I=I+1:GOTO 60
180 REM★★★★★
190 N=I−1:REM★LENGTH OF LIST
200 REM★★★★★
210 REM★★SORT ROUTINE★★★★★★
220 FOR K=1 TO N−1
230 FOR L=K+1 TO N
240 IF X$(L) >= X$(K) THEN 280
250 T$=X$(L)
260 X$(L)=X$(K)                              ———— sort routine
270 X$(K)=T$
280 NEXT L
290 NEXT K
300 REM★★END OF SORT ROUTINE★★
400 REM★★★★★
410 PRINT"FINAL SORTED LIST"
420 FOR P=1 TO N
430 PRINT X$(P);TAB(6★P);                    ———— printing out the result
440 NEXT P
450 PRINT
500 REM★★★★★
900 DATA TONY,SAM,PETE,JOE,BILL,ZZZZ
```

Program 2   Using the sort routine

```
RUN
FINAL SORTED LIST
BILL   JOE   PETE   SAM   TONY
```

8.3 Subroutines

By the time you have reached this stage you will begin to distinguish the wood from the trees. You will be aware that programs have an overall structure and are assemblies of smaller parts like the paragraphs of an essay. It is usual to break a program down into its constituent parts, and to write and test each part separately. Certain operations are often repeated several times throughout a program. The structure of a program may be simplified and tidied up by including these repetitive operations as subroutines.

We shall illustrate subroutines by taking a final look at the sort procedure. We are going to insert two extra trace print lines into the program so that we can see what is happening at each of the three stages of the sort routine:

Sort routine	**Trace print line to show**
1. Input.	The list as taken in.
2. Sort.	The list after each sub-sequence.
3. Output.	The final, sorted, list.

Figure 5 shows the overall structure and how we can use one PRINT subroutine for all three PRINT operations.

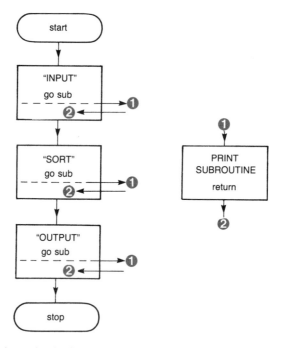

Figure 5   Print sub-routine in the sort program

GOSUB

In BASIC to go to a subroutine we say:

GOSUB

followed by the line number of the start of the subroutine. Each subroutine must end with the statement

RETURN

which will return control to the next line in the main body of the program after the appropriate GOSUB statement. Thus in the following program segment line 30 transfers control to line 200 and lines 200 and 210 are executed. The 220 returns control to line 40 for the program to continue in the normal way.

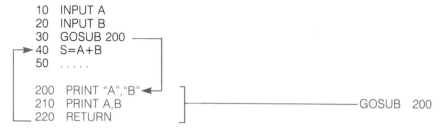

```
 10  INPUT A
 20  INPUT B
 30  GOSUB 200
 40  S=A+B
 50  .....

200  PRINT "A","B"
210  PRINT A,B
220  RETURN
```

GOSUB 200

SAQ 2

What is the value of B after this program has been run: (a) if 5 is inputted; (b) if 3 is inputted?

```
10  INPUT A
20  IF A<5 THEN 40
30  GOSUB 70
40  B=A★A
50  PRINT B
60  END
70  A=1/A
80  RETURN
```

Program 3

Here is the sort program with a print subroutine (lines 500 – 550) which is used each time the program executes line 194, line 280 and line 420.

```
 10  REM★★SORT ROUTINE★★
 20  CLEAR 100
 30  DIM X$(100)
 50  I=1
 60  READ X$
 70  IF X$="ZZZZ" THEN 190
 80  X$(I)=X$:I=I+1:GOTO 60
180  REM★★★★★★★★★★★★★★★★★★★★★★★★★
190  N=I−1:REM★LENGTH OF LIST
192  PRINT"LIST AT START"
194  GOSUB 510   → OUT
196  PRINT       ← IN              ── First trace
200  REM★★★★★★★★★★★★★★★★★★★★★★★★★
210  REM★★SORT ROUTINE★★★★★★
220  FOR K=1 TO N−1
225  PRINT"PASS NO.";K
230  FOR L=K+1 TO N
240  IF X$(L) >= X$(K) THEN 280
250  T$=X$(L):X$(L)=X$(K):X$(K)=T$
280  GOSUB 510   → OUT
285  NEXT L      ← IN              ── Second trace
287  PRINT
290  NEXT K
300  REM★★END OF SORT ROUTINE★★
400  REM★★★★★★★★★★★★★★★★★★★★★★★★★
410  PRINT"FINAL SORTED LIST"
```

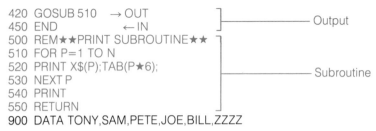

```
420 GOSUB 510    → OUT ⎤
450 END          ← IN  ⎦──────────── Output
500 REM★★PRINT SUBROUTINE★★ ⎤
510 FOR P=1 TO N            |
520 PRINT X$(P);TAB(P★6);   |
530 NEXT P                  |──────── Subroutine
540 PRINT                   |
550 RETURN                  ⎦
900 DATA TONY,SAM,PETE,JOE,BILL,ZZZZ
```

Program 4   Print subroutine in sort program

```
RUN
LIST AT START                                          printed by GOSUB at
TONY        SAM       PETE      JOE       BILL ⎤────── line 194

PASS NO. 1
SAM         TONY      PETE      JOE       BILL ⎤
PETE        TONY      SAM       JOE       BILL |
JOE         TONY      SAM       PETE      BILL |
BILL        TONY      SAM       PETE      JOE  ⎦

PASS NO. 2
BILL        SAM       TONY      PETE      JOE  ⎤      each block printed
BILL        PETE      TONY      SAM       JOE  |      by GOSUB at line
BILL        JOE       TONY      SAM       PETE ⎦      280 on the four occa-
                                                     sions the program
PASS NO. 3                                           executes the loop
BILL        JOE       SAM       TONY      PETE ⎤     controlled by K
BILL        JOE       PETE      TONY      SAM  ⎦

PASS NO. 4
BILL        JOE       PETE      SAM       TONY ⎤─┘

FINAL SORTED LIST                                      printed by GOSUB at
BILL        JOE       PETE      SAM       TONY ⎤────── line 420
```

Examples on subroutines

The purpose of a subroutine is to simplify and shorten long programs. By its very nature then, it is difficult to get short meaningful programs which illustrate subroutines without their often being a little contrived. We need a program where the same or similar function is repeated at different points in the program.

Example 1

The game of dice ('craps' in the USA) provides a simple example. A pair of dice is thrown twice and the total score on each throw is noted. If the two scores are the same, the game ends. If they are different, the dice are thrown again. Write a program to simulate the game which prints out the number of throws required to obtain equal scores and what that score was.

Solution

```
10  REM★★2 EQUAL THROWS★★
20  RANDOMIZE
```

```
30  C=1
40  GOSUB 130:REM★★FIRST THROW★★
50  S1=S ◄─────────────────────────────┐   the subroutine produces
60  GOSUB 130:REM★★SECOND THROW★★ ├──generally different values
70  S2=S ◄─────────────────────────────┘   of S for the 'main' program.
80  IF S1=S2 THEN 100
90  C=C+1:GOTO 40
100 PRINT"EQUAL SCORE ";S1;" IN ";C;" THROWS"
110 END
120 REM★★DICE ROLLING SUBROUTINE★★
130 D1=INT(6★RND(1)+1):D2=INT(6★RND(1)+1) ┐
140 S=D1+D2:RETURN                          ┘── subroutine
```

Program 5   Simulation of 'craps'

```
RUN
EQUAL SCORE 7 IN 9 THROWS
RUN
EQUAL SCORE 8 IN 21 THROWS
RUN
EQUAL SCORE 8 IN 7 THROWS
RUN
EQUAL SCORE 5 IN 4 THROWS
RUN
EQUAL SCORE 10 IN 22 THROWS
RUN
EQUAL SCORE 10 IN 7 THROWS
```

Exercise 1

(a) Write a segment of program to print a line of dashes "--------" across the screen or printer, probably 40 for the screen and 60 for the printer. (BBC screen = 40.)

(b) Write one line of program to print a 'submarine' or $<=>$, at any point across the screen or printer where the variable S determines the position.

(c) Write a program to print on successive lines:
    (i)   a line of dashes;
    (ii)   a submarine at any point;
    (iii)   another line of dashes;
    with the line printing in (i) and (iii) in a subroutine.

Exercise 2

Now you must admit that the solution to Exercise 1 looks like a vessel in a canal, so why not a submarine as we are concerned with subroutines? Instead of battleships in a 2-dimensional sea, we have a submarine in a 1-dimensional canal. Anyway, we have the picture for a simple game.

Write a program to generate a random number between 1 and 38 for a screen, or 1 and 58 for a printer. (Or, of course, any width convenient for your machine.) The submarine is going to take up the last three positions of the width (38, 39, 40 or 58, 59, 60). Use the random number to print the submarine in random positions along the canal.

Exercise 3

The essence of the game we are going to play with the machine will be clear from

Exercise 2. The computer generates a random number and invites you to find the submarine by guessing a number between 1 and 40, or 1 and 60. If you guess the correct position, i.e. between S and S+2 if S is the random number (remember the submarine takes up 3 places in the line), then the machine records a 'hit' and the game ends. If you don't find the submarine, the machine will record a 'miss' and invite you to try again. Write a program to do this.

(We advise you to write the program to give yourself the option to stop playing before you find the submarine, because it is infuriating to have to try every position across the screen just to stop the program running. You could just pull the plug out, and then it would sink!?)

8.4 Searching

The submarine problem gives us a good lead into discussions about searching data. The only methodical way to find the submarine was to search the canal successively position by position starting from one end. How much easier it would have been had the program responded with 'too high' or 'too low', as appropriate, after each guess. No doubt you can immediately think of a procedure for 'homing-in' on the submarine as quickly as possible!

Similarly, if dictionaries, telephone directories, encyclopedias and library catalogues were not arranged in alphabetical order, think how difficult it would be to find the desired information.

But if we've gone to a lot of trouble to sort our data into numerical or alphabetical order, then we need an efficient search technique to find any given item. If we consult a dictionary or telephone directory for an item, we don't start looking at the first page and work methodically through the volume page by page until the item is found. We take a rough guess, e.g. if the name begins with 'P' then we try to open the directory at just over half-way through it, and start looking from that point.

Bisection search
A 'rough' guess is too imprecise a term for a computer. However we can specify guessing points as follows:

- divide the range of items into half and ask 'is the item above or below the half-way mark?'
- if it is below then we define a new range with the middle item now acting as the upper limit;
- if above then the middle item becomes our lower limit;
- either way we discard half the old range and repeat our halving or bisection procedure with the new range.

So the bisection search is, in outline:

Is 7 in the list 1,2,3,4,5,6,7,8,9,10?

List in order:

1	2	3	4	5	6	7	8	9	10

Halve list.

1	2	3	4	5	6	7	8	9	10

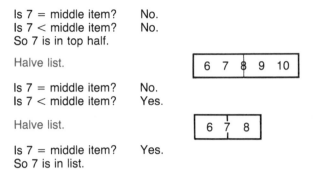

Is 7 = middle item? No.
Is 7 < middle item? No.
So 7 is in top half.

Halve list.

Is 7 = middle item? No.
Is 7 < middle item? Yes.

Halve list.

Is 7 = middle item? Yes.
So 7 is in list.

That outline illustrates the principle of the bisection search but in practice we need to distinguish between the values of the items in a list and the indexes of those items.

Example 2
An ordered list contains the items A, F, I, M, P, T, U, Z. Use the bisection search procedure to find whether or not P is in the list.

We call P, Query – the value we wish to enquire about:

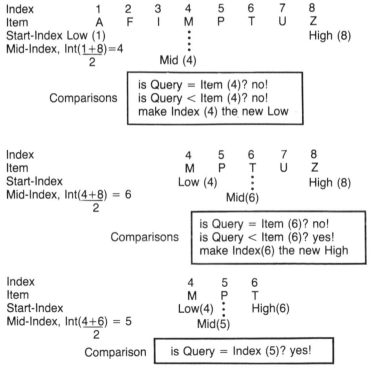

Figure 6 Bisection search

Exercise 4

Carry out the bisection search procedure on the list in Example 2 but looking for the letter I.

We only had to make 3 comparisons to home-in on the item 'P' in Example 2, but they were a bit long-winded, and the whole procedure may seem to have little advantage over simply searching straight through the list. The effectiveness of the method is not really apparent in short lists. We will demonstrate its power in searching longer lists later, but first we still have some loose ends to tie up.

Some problems with bisection search

(a) How to stop

Example 3

Carry out the same procedure as before, but search for the letter 'Q'.

The method would proceed exactly the same as before as far as the 3rd comparison, so we'll pick up the story there.

Query = Q

Index	4	5	6
Item	M	P	T
Start-Index	Low(4)	:	High(6)

Mid-Index, $\text{Int}\dfrac{(4 + 6)}{2} = 5$ Mid(5)

Comparisons

| is Query = Item(5)? no! |
| is Query < Item(5)? no! |
| make Index(5) the new Low |

Index	4	5	6
Item		P	T
Start-Index		Low(5)	High(6)

Mid-Index, $\text{Int}\dfrac{(5 + 6)}{2} = 5$ Mid(5)

Comparisons

| is Query = Item(5)? no! |
| is Query < .... we have done this before?! |

So we don't seem able to stop. Q is not there but we are stuck looking for it between P and T. We have already met the problem of stopping the process in the last example. If the indexes Low and High have moved so close that they are at adjacent positions, and Query is not yet found, then Query is not a member of the list. That is the end and outcome of the search. So the end is either when the Query has been found, or when Low and High occupy adjacent indexes (High − Low = 1).

(b) How to start

To start the process seemed straightforward enough. We make Index (1)=Low and Index(N)=High. Trouble would occur however if Item(1) and Item(N) were not the lowest and highest possible values.

E.g. consider the following list which does not include letters before C or after S:

214

1	2	3	4	5
C	F	G	P	S
Low				High

If Query was A or B or higher than S, then the process would not work. The easiest solution is to ensure that the items at the ends of the list will always have the extreme values, e.g. in a list of names make Item(1)=AAAA and Item(N)=ZZZZ.

We will now outline the algorithm in flowchart form.

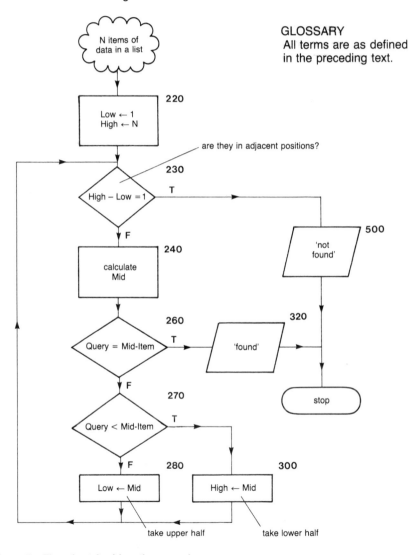

GLOSSARY
All terms are as defined in the preceding text.

Figure 7   Flowchart for bisection search

215

All we have to do now is to write the program:

```
10   REM★★BISECTION SEARCH★★
20   CLEAR 100
30   DIM N$(20):DIM T$(20)
40   I=1
50   READ N$(I),T$(I)
60   IF N$(I)="ZZZZ" THEN 100
70   I=I+1:GOTO 50
90   REM★★★★★★
100  N=I:REM★WE ARE USING ZZZZ THIS TIME★
110  REM★★★★★★
150  INPUT"QUERY NAME";Q$                    BBC: 150 omit;
200  REM★★START OF SEARCH★★★★★★
210  PRINT" L";TAB(5);" H";TAB(10);" M";TAB(15);"N$(M)"
220  L=1:H=N                                 BBC: 210 insert; after PRINT
230  IF H−L=1 THEN 500
240  M=INT((L+H)/2)
250  PRINT L;TAB(5);H;TAB(10);M;TAB(15);N$(M)
260  IF Q$=N$(M) THEN 320                     BBC: 250 insert; after PRINT
270  IF Q$<N$(M) THEN 300
280  L=M:GOTO 230                             210 and 250 are trace print
300  H=M:GOTO 230                             lines only
320  REM★★END OF SEARCH★★★★★
330  PRINT Q$;"'S TELE NO. IS ";T$(M)
350  GOTO 600
500  PRINT Q$;" IS NOT IN THE LIST"
600  INPUT"DO YOU WISH TO LOOK FOR ANOTHER NAME":R$
610  IF R$="YES" THEN 150
620  END                                      BBC: 600 omit;
900  DATA AAAA, 0000
910  DATA BENNY, 1234
920  DATA COPPER, 9832
930  DATA DRAPER, 1980
940  DATA EDDIE, 7294
950  DATA GWYNNE, 5821
960  DATA HETTY, 8632
970  DATA MORLEY, 7832
980  DATA PROSSER, 1383
990  DATA SMYTHE, 1147
1000 DATA WEEKS, 5529
1010 DATA WILSON, 9936
1020 DATA ZZZZ, 9999
```

Program 6   Bisection search program

```
RUN
QUERY NAME? MORLEY
  L    H    M    N$(M)
  1   13    7    HETTY
  7   13   10    SMYTHE
  7   10    8    MORLEY
MORLEY'S TELE NO. IS 7832
```

DO YOU WISH TO LOOK FOR ANOTHER NAME?
QUERY NAME? WEEK
```
L    H    M    N$(M)
1    13   7    HETTY
7    13   10   SMYTHE
10   13   11   WEEKS
```
WEEK IS NOT IN THE LIST

8.5 Tables

When we want to store a lot of information there are various methods open to us. One is lists (see Unit 4), which are sometimes called one-dimensional arrays. A second method is tables or two-dimensional arrays.

Suppose you want to store the following data:

	1st qtr	2nd qtr	3rd qtr	4th qtr
Car sales	20	70	80	40
Servicing	10	14	18	11
Petrol	30	45	50	30

Figure 8   Income for Main Road Service Station (£,000's)

Now you could put this in one list but it would be hard to use. The first four items would be income for car sales, the next four for servicing, etc. Alternatively you would have three lists: one for car sales, one for servicing and one for petrol. But BASIC allows you to have a two dimensional table named by any of the 286 variable names, e.g.:

T(,)

Comparison of lists and tables
Lists need one index to describe a position in the list. Tables need two, which are usually called sub-scripts not indices (or indexes, as we have called them).

List
L(1), L(2), L(3) . . .   L(I) . . .
```
                 └──── index of this item = 3
```

Array
```
A(1,1)    A(1,2)    A(1,3)
A(2,1)    A(2,2)    A(2,3)
A(3,1)    A(3,2)    A(3,3)
          └──────────────── this item needs two sub-scripts:
                            3 to tell us it is in row 3;
                            2 to tell us it is in column 2.
```

Tables

- A table must contain either all string variables, or all numerical variables. (Numbers can of course be stored as strings, and their values found by the VAL-function.)

- We use one of the 286 variable names allowed in our minimal-BASIC scheme to describe the table as a whole, e.g. A table, B$ table, M3$ table.

Generally, a table comprises:

	col.1	col.2	col.3	col.4
row 1	r1c1	r1c2	r1c3	. . . .
row 2	r2c1	r2c2	r2c3	. . . .
row 3	r3c1	r3c2	r3c3	. . . .
etc	. . . .	. . . .	. . . .	. . . .

Figure 9   The rows and columns of a table

For the service station data, T needs 3 rows and four columns and so contains 12 items:

$T(1,1)$ $T(1,2)$ $T(1,3)$ $T(1,4)$

$T(2,1)$ $T(2,2)$ $T(2,3)$ $T(2,4)$

$T(3,1)$ $T(3,2)$ $T(3,3)$ $T(3,4)$

So

$T(2,1) = 10$

$T(3,3) = 50$ etc.

This is very similar to the idea of tables which you have previously met. There we said that a file consists of a series of records each of which consists of fields. In table form this would look like:

	Field 1	Field 2
	Name	Telephone number
Record 1	BENNY	1234
Record 2	COPPER	9823
Record 3	DRAPER	1850
Record 4	EDDIE	7294

Or, more generally:

	Field 1	Field 2	Field 3	etc
Record 1	R1F1	R1F2	R1F3	. . . .
Record 2	R2F1	R2F2	R2F3	. . . .
Record 3	R3F1	R3F2	R3F3	. . . .
etc	. . . .	. . . .	. . . .	. . . .

If the telephone numbers table is called T$ then the individual items will be labelled:

	Field 1	Field 2
	Name	Telephone number
Record 1	T$(1,1)=BENNY	T$(1,2)=1234
Record 2	T$(2,1)=COPPER	T$(2,2)=9823
Record 3	T$(3,1)=DRAPER	T$(3,2)=1950
Record 4	T$(4,1)=EDDIE	T$(4,2)=7294

- The whole table is called T$ table.
- Each item in the table is described by two subscripts. Thus 1950 (3rd row, 2nd column) is

T$(3,2)

- The 3 and 2 describe the position of item T$(3,2), not its value. Its value is 1950. So we say

T$(3,2) = 1950

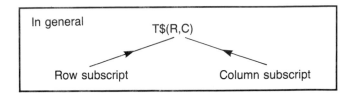

In general   T$(R,C)

Row subscript   Column subscript

Example 4
The N$-table overleaf has 9 values as shown. What are their variable names?

R \ C	1	2	3
1	BENNY	COPPER	DRAPER
2	EDDIE	GWYNNE	HETTY
3	MORLEY	PROSSER	SMYTHE

N$(,)

Solution

BENNY = N$(1,1)   COPPER = N$(1,2)   DRAPER = N$(1,3)

EDDIE = N$(2,1)   GWYNNE = N$(2,2)   HETTY = N$(2,3)

MORLEY = N$(3,1)   PROSSER = N$(3,2)   SMYTHE = N$(3,3)

SAQ 3
In the following A$ table identify the variables and their values as in Example 4.

ARCHER	BENNY	COPPER
DRAPER	EDDIE	FRAME
GWYNNE	HETTY	KEMP
LAMB	MORLEY	NOAKES
PROSSER	SMYTHE	TAIT

Tables and nested loops
If FOR. . . NEXT loops and lists seemed to be made for each other, then even more so do nested FOR. . . NEXT loops and tables seem complementary.

For example, suppose you want to read:

ARCHER,BENNY,COPPER,DRAPER,EDDIE,FRAME,GWYNNE,HETTY, KEMP,LAMB,MORLEY,NOAKES,PROSSER,SMYTHE,TAIT,WEEKS

into a table, N$, with 4 rows and 4 columns. (We need a string array because we are storing string data.) This can be done with a READ statement in two nested loops:

```
60   FOR I=1 TO 4
90   FOR J=1 TO 4
80   READ N$(I,J)
90   NEXT J
100  NEXT I
```

This process is carried out in full by lines 10 to 100 of Program 7.

It's all very well to store the value in a table, but of course we cannot see the result of this until we print it out. The second half of the program prints the table values out in a column with I and J accompanying them so that you can identify clearly how I and J are used.

```
10   REM★★TABLE READ AND PRINT★★
20   CLEAR 200
30   DIM N$(20,5)
```
— DIM statement for 2–D array. We are asking for space for 20 rows and 5 columns.

```
40   REM★★READ ROUTINE★★★★★★★★★★
60   FOR I=1 TO 4
70   FOR J=1 TO 4
80   READ N$(I,J)
90   NEXT J
100  NEXT I
110  REM★★PRINT ROUTINE★★★★★★★★★★
115  PRINT "I",  "J","N$(I,J)"
130  FOR I=1 TO 4 ─────────────────── rows
140  FOR J=1 TO 4─────────────────── columns
150  PRINT I,J,N$(I,J)                    BBC: 150P.;I,;J,N$(I,J)
160  NEXT J
180  NEXT I
190  GOTO 270
240  REM★★★★★★★★★★★
250  DATA ARCHER,BENNY,COPPER,DRAPER,EDDIE,FRAME,GWYNNE,HETTY
260  DATA KEMP,LAMB,MORLEY,NOAKES,PROSSER,SMYTHE,TAIT,WEEKS
270  END
```

Program 7   Reading data into a 4 × 4 array.

RUN

I	J	N$(I,J)
1	1	ARCHER
1	2	BENNY
1	3	COPPER
1	4	DRAPER
2	1	EDDIE
2	2	FRAME
2	3	GWYNNE
2	4	HETTY
3	1	KEMP
3	2	LAMB
3	3	MORLEY
3	4	NOAKES
4	1	PROSSER
4	2	SMYTHE
4	3	TAIT
4	4	WEEKS

SAQ 4
The following amendments are made to Program 7. Write out what the output table
will look like.

```
60   FOR I=1 TO 3
70   FOR J=1 TO 5
130  FOR I=1 TO 3
140  FOR J=1 TO 5
```

Table output

The output of Program 7 is not very satisactory since we want to see the table in table form. To do this we delete line 115 and insert a new print routine:

```
130   FOR I=1 TO 5                    the first column starts at position 1−1=0
140   FOR J=1 TO 3
150   PRINT TAB(10★(J−1));N$(I,J);
160   NEXT J
170   PRINT                            columns 10 characters wide
180   NEXT I
190   GOTO 270
```

Program 8

The output then is:

ARCHER	BENNY	COPPER
DRAPER	EDDIE	FRAME
GWYNNE	HETTY	KEMP
LAMB	MORLEY	NOAKES
PROSSER	SMYTHE	TAIT

Assignment 8

1.   A salesman has 4 product lines. The value (in £) of his firm orders for one week are shown in the table.

day \ product	1	2	3	4	totals
1	500	300	20	25	e
2	600	700	40	0	f
3	200	550	60	20	g
4	250	450	100	5	h
5	400	200	100	11	i
totals	a	b	c	d	t

Write a program which will help him analyse his week's work by giving:

   (i)   his day totals (e,f,g,h,i)
  (ii)   his product totals (a,b,c,d)
 (iii)   his overall weekly total (t).

2.   Write a program to extend the submarine game to a 10 × 10 grid. If the guess is close to the submarine then the program should give a 'near miss' clue. You decide what is meant by 'close'.

Objectives of Unit 8

Now that you have completed this Unit, check that you are able to:

Use the interchange sort (manually) on a set of data ☐

Write two nested program loops to perform the interchange sort ☐

Follow GOSUB in programs ☐

Write GOSUBS into programs ☐

Use the bisection search (manually) on a set of data ☐

Write a program for the bisection search ☐

Put data into two dimensional arrays ☐

Write a program to read data into a two dimensional array ☐

Write a program to print data out of a two dimensional array ☐

Write a program to find the row sums and the column sums in a two dimensional array ☐

Answers to SAQ's and Exercises

SAQ 1

```
0  6  4  1  2  3  7  8
0  1  6  4  2  3  7  8
0  1  2  6  4  3  7  8
0  1  2  3  6  4  7  8
0  1  2  3  4  6  7  8
0  1  2  3  4  6  7  8
0  1  2  3  4  6  7  8
```

FINAL SORTED LIST
```
0   1   2   3   4   5   6   7   8
```

SAQ 2
(a) $B = 1/25$

(b) $B = 9$ (GOSUB is not used in this case.)

Exercise 1
(a) 10 FOR I=1 TO 60   *BBC: use 40 in line 10*
     20 PRINT"−";
     30 NEXT I
     40 PRINT   *Program 11*
or in one line:
     FOR I=1 TO 60:PRINT"−";:NEXT I:PRINT *BBC: use 40*

(b) PRINT TAB(S);"<=>"

(c) 10 INPUT S
     20 GOSUB 100
     30 PRINT TAB(S);"<=>"

223

```
40    GOSUB 100
50    END
100   FOR I=1 TO 60:PRINT"-";:NEXT I:PRINT          BBC: use 40
110   RETURN
```
Program 12

The value that we give S will determine the position of the submarine along the canal, and we get picture like:

```
------------------------------------------------------------
                        <=>
------------------------------------------------------------
```

Exercise 2

```
10    REM★★SUBMARINE★★
20    RANDOMIZE
50    S=INT(58★RND(1)+1)                            BBC: 50 S=RND(38)
60    GOSUB 510
70    PRINT TAB(S);"<=>"
80    GOSUB 510
90    END
500   REM★★PRINT SUBROUTINE★★
510   FOR I=1 TO 60:PRINT"-";:NEXT I:PRINT          BBC: use 40
520   RETURN
```
Program 13

RUN
```
------------------------------------------------------------
                      <=>
------------------------------------------------------------
```
RUN
```
------------------------------------------------------------
   <=>
------------------------------------------------------------
```
RUN
```
------------------------------------------------------------
                                        <=>
------------------------------------------------------------
```

Exercise 3

```
10    REM★★SUBMARINE★★
20    RANDOMIZE
30    REM★★PRINT CHALLENGE★★★
40    GOSUB 300                          → 1
50    PRINT"A NUMBER FROM 1 TO 60 MIGHT FIND ME"
60    GOSUB 300                          → 2
70    REM★★RANDOM POSITION OF SUB★★          subroutine used 8 times
80    S=INT(58★RND(1)+1)
90    PRINT
100   INPUT"TRY ANOTHER NUMBER";X
110   IF X<S THEN 190
120   IF X>S+2 THEN 190
130   REM★★A HIT★★
140   GOSUB 300                          → 3
```

224

```
150  PRINT TAB(S);"HIT"
160  GOSUB 300                        → 4
170  GOTO 320
180  REM★★A MISS★★
190  GOSUB. 300                       → 5
200  PRINT"YOU MISSED"
210  GOSUB 300                        → 6
220  INPUT"DO YOU STILL WANT TO PLAY";R$
230  IF R$="YES" THEN 90
240  PRINT"SPOILSPORT!! I WAS HERE":PRINT
250  GOSUB 300                        → 7
260  PRINT TAB(S);"<=>"
270  GOSUB 300                        → 8
280  GOTO 320
290  REM★★PRINT SUBROUTINE★★
300  FOR I=1 TO 60:PRINT"—";:NEXT I:PRINT ⎤ subroutine prints just one
310  RETURN                                ⎦ line of dashes
320  END
```

Program 14

(BBC use 40 for line length in lines 50 and 300. Omit; in lines 100 and 220)

```
RUN
-------------------------------------------------------------
A NUMBER FROM 1 TO 60 MIGHT FIND ME
-------------------------------------------------------------

TRY ANOTHER NUMBER? 27
-------------------------------------------------------------
YOU MISSED
-------------------------------------------------------------
DO YOU STILL WANT TO PLAY? YES
TRY ANOTHER NUMBER? 60
-------------------------------------------------------------
YOU MISSED
-------------------------------------------------------------
DO YOU STILL WANT TO PLAY? NO
SPOILSPORT!! I WAS HERE
-------------------------------------------------------------
    <=>
-------------------------------------------------------------
```

Exercise 4

1	2	3	4	5	6	7	8
A	F	I	M	P	T	U	Z

⋮

Mid (4)

```
┌─────────────────────────────────┐
│ Query = Item (4)? No.           │
│ Query < Item (4)? Yes.          │
│ make Index (4) the new high     │
└─────────────────────────────────┘
```

```
A    F    I    M
1    2    3    4
     ⋮
```

Mid-Index $= \text{Int}(\frac{1+4}{2}) = 2$

```
┌─────────────────────────────────────┐
│ Query = Item (2)? No.               │
│ Query < Item (2)? No.               │
│ make Index (2) the new low          │
└─────────────────────────────────────┘
```

```
2    3    4
F    I    M
     ⋮
```

```
┌─────────────────────────────────────┐
│ Query = Item (3)? Yes.              │
│ Therefore I is in list              │
│                                     │
└─────────────────────────────────────┘
```

SAQ 3

A$(1,1) = ARCHER	A$(1,2) = BENNY	A$(1,3) = COPPER
A$(2,1) = DRAPER	A$(2,2) = EDDIE	A$(2,3) = FRAME
A$(3,1) = GWYNNE	A$(3,2) = HETTY	A$(3,3) = KEMP
A$(4,1) = LAMB	A$(4,2) = MORLEY	A$(4,3) = NOAKES
A$(5,1) = PROSSER	A$(5,2) = SMYTHE	A$(5,3) = TAIT

SAQ 4

RUN

I	J	N$(I,J)
1	1	ARCHER
1	2	BENNY
1	3	COPPER
1	4	DRAPER
1	5	EDDIE
2	1	FRAME
2	2	GWYNNE
2	3	HETTY
2	4	KEMP
2	5	LAMB
3	1	MORLEY
3	2	NOAKES
3	3	PROSSER
3	4	SMYTHE
3	5	TAIT

(Note that WEEKS was not read into the table. A 5×3 table will only read the first 15 items.)

226

UNIT 9
File-handling

Warning (BBC Computer)

In this Unit we only introduce very simple file-handling examples. These do not reveal an important point about OPENOUT on the BBC Computer.

On many computers, OPENOUT means 'open for output' as stated on page 231. On the BBC Computer, OPENOUT means 'create a new file'. So, on the BBC Computer you must never use OPENOUT to address an existing file. If you do this, you will destroy the file's structure.

If you want to read from or write to an existing BBC Computer file, use OPENIN for both jobs. So,

OPENOUT creates new files:
OPENIN   reads and writes to existing files.

9.1 Saving programs

The course so far has largely been concerned with a system of only 3 devices, viz. keyboard, processor and monitor. That system is volatile, i.e. when you switch off the power your programming efforts are lost. If you wish to run a program again you will have to type it in again. But all microcomputers provide facilities for saving a program on ordinary cassette tapes. Once the program is on cassette, you can switch off your computer and still be able to re-run the program whenever you want in the future.

There are two occasions on which you will wish to store programs:
(a) when you have a complete program that you want to keep; and
(b) to save part of a program which you are developing. If you save every time you have a screen-full, you will never lose too much when you have an accident with the part currently in your computer. When the complete program has been entered and saved, you can always erase your intermediate part-programs.

The process of saving
First you have to give the program a name which the computer will use to locate your program. Systems differ in how long and what characters may be included in the file-name. Usually up to 6 characters are allowed at least, and usually the name has to start with a letter of the alphabet. You will have to check up on these details for the particular system that you are using.

Suppose you want to save a program called PROGNAME. The procedure will be something like:

Either
- Connect the cassette tape recorder to your computer.
- Key SAVE "PROGNAME" on your computer without pressing RETURN.
- Start the tape recorder running in record mode.
- Press RETURN on the computer.
- Once the program is saved, turn off the recorder.
  (This is the procedure on the BBC Computer.)

Or
- Connect the cassette tape recorder to your computer.
- Start the tape recorder running in record mode.
- Key SAVE and press RETURN.
- The computer asks you for FILENAME? Key PROGNAME (or whatever name you are using) without " " and press RETURN.

The process of loading
Having saved a program you may wish to use it at a later date. It can be loaded back into the machine with a LOAD command. A typical interaction would be:

Either
- Connect the cassette recorder to your computer.
- Key LOAD "PROGNAME" without pressing RETURN.
- Set the tape recorder running in play mode.
- Press RETURN.
- Switch off the recorder when loading is complete.
  (This is the procedure on the BBC Computer.)

Or
- Connect the recorder to your computer.

- Key LOAD and press RETURN.
- The computer responds with FILENAME? Key PROGNAME (no " ")
  without pressing RETURN.
- Set the recorder running in play mode.
- Press RETURN.
- Switch off the recorder when loading is complete.

9.2 LPRINT

Sooner or later you will want a copy on paper of a program or data. Copy printed on paper is usually referred to as 'hard copy'.

So far in the course we have written all our programs so that all the responses you see on your screen would be printed onto paper if your computer were attached to a printer. You have seen these responses being printed out in the runs which we have shown from our computer. This was done to help you to trace the runs of all parts of the programs. But we would not normally wish to have all of the screen responses printed out on paper. For example, in the run of Program 13 of Unit 7, we would want printed out on paper the final result perhaps, but not all of the input prompts:

ACCURACY REQUIRED? etc

These would be needed by the user to set up the run on the screen, but not to be printed out as a permanent record.

LPRINT allows us to direct output to the line-printer.

Similarly LLIST will print the program currently in memory at the line-printer.

Some systems allow LRUN which outputs to the line-printer all that is seen on the screen during the run of a program.

BBC: see page 251 for details of how to use a printer on the BBC Computer.

9.3 Sequential files

We have used the term 'file' several times throughout the course, to mean 'a collection of data items'. However, when a program is saved we refer to its having a file-name, and we think of both saved programs and data as files.

Data
So far we have either input data from the keyboard during the course of a program's execution, or read from DATA statements which formed part of the program. On several occasions we have made a program handle different sets of data by over-writing or substituting new DATA statements for old ones. This latter method can be quite effective for a small computer system without file-handling facilities. But if we wish to handle collections of data of meaningful size, we need the facility to be able to store this data on either tape or disk. We need to be able to store new data on a file on cassette or disk and to read data from these files to use in program runs.

Incompatibility of systems
Most of the main micro-computer systems differ from each other in the finer details

of how file-handling is achieved. We will concentrate on the general principles as far as possible, and try to distil out those elements which are common to most systems. Our examples will be kept as simple as possible. But it is most likely that you will have to make minor changes to our programs for them to run on your own particular system.

Sequential files

As a simplification we shall only consider sequential file-handling. Sequential files are where we read in every item of data from the file in the sequence in which it was originally created. This is, of course, the only type of file that you can use on a tape storage system since a tape has to be read sequentially.

9.4 Create and access

Create refers to a program's activity of writing data from the program in the computer's memory to a peripheral device: in our case either tape or disk. Access is when data is read from the peripheral device to the program in memory.

Because you cannot 'see' what's stored on tape or disk, the activities of create and access must be complementary. You do not know whether your program to create has been successful until you've written an access program to read the data back in. Only then can you see it on the screen or printer.

It is possible to create and access simultaneously by using two tape recorders but, in order to keep this Unit as simple as possible, we shall keep create and access as separate as possible.

Create

To create a new file, or to write into an existing one, we have to tell the computer:
- the name of the file;
- that we wish to OPEN the file for output to it;
- then we write out to it;
- then we CLOSE it;

Notice that:
- during the create run, the computer needs a temporary number for that file to identify it during execution;
- that between OPEN and CLOSE, the computer is under control of the tape recorder.

So creating a program is something like this on most microcomputers:

```
1000 REM★★CREATE A DATA.FILE★★
1010 OPEN "O", £2, "DATA1"          1010 BBC: A=OPENOUT "DATA1"
```

```
1060 CLOSE £2                        1060 BBC: CLOSE#A
```

Notes

OPEN "O"
or
OPENOUT — tells the computer to open a file in output mode ("O" for output).

£2 or #A — our internal (to the program) file number which we will use to refer to the file as long as it is open.* Some computers allow a range of file numbers but we will stick to £2 for create (A for BBC Computer).

"DATA1" — the file-name on the cassette or disk under which the data will be stored.

CLOSE £2
or
CLOSE #A — this closes the file and puts an 'end of file marker' (EOF) on the tape.

So let's see this in use.

Example 1a
Write a program to create a data file of 10 names.

Solution

```
1000 REM★★CREATE A DATA FILE★★
1010 OPEN "O", £2, "DATA1"
1020 FOR I=1 TO 10
1030 READ N$
1040 PRINT £2, N$
1050 NEXT I
1060 CLOSE £2
1090 PRINT "DATA1 HAS BEEN SAVED"
9000 DATA ARCHER, BENNY, COPPER, DRAPER, EDDIE, FRAME, GWYNNE,
     HETTY
9010 DATA KEMP, LAMB, MORLEY, NOAKES, PROSSER, SMYTHE, TAIT,
     WEEKS
```

input at the keyboard or loaded in from file

high line numbers because create comes at the end of a program after some processing

write into file

Program 1   Create a data file

```
BBC: 1010 A=OPENOUT "DATA1"
     1040 PRINT #A,N$
     1060 CLOSE #A

RUN
DATA1 HAS BEEN SAVED
```

before pressing RET the recorder would have to be activated (PLAY/RECORD) and switched off here.

Once we have opened the file for output (line 1010) we can write to it. Here we used it as follows:

```
1020 FOR I=1 TO 10
1030 READ N$
1040 PRINT £2, N$          1040 BBC: PRINT #A, N$
1050 NEXT I
```

---

* Some books use # instead of £.

The only new bit here is PRINT £2, N$. This writes the value N$ into the file £2. (You can see now why we wanted a number for the file to use during the program.)

At the end of all that the 10 names (ARCHER, BENNY, etc.) are all on the tape under the file-name "DATA1". If you switched off the computer, they would still be there.

Access

Now you want the data back to use. For this you need an access program. This has the following structure:

```
10 REM★★ACCESS A DATA FILE★★
20 OPEN "I", £1, "DATA1"           20 BBC: B= OPENIN "DATA1"
30 IF EOF (1) THEN 100             30 BBC: IF EOF#B= −1 THEN 100
```

```
        use
       of file
```

```
100 CLOSE £1                       100 BBC: CLOSE #B
```

Notes

OPEN"I" or OPENIN	tells the computer to open the file in input mode ("I" for input).
£1 or #B	our internal (to the program) file number.
"DATA1"	the name of the file that the computer is to look for on the tape or disk.
EOF(1) or EOF	tells the computer to look for the end of file marker.
CLOSE £1	tells the computer to close the file number 1.

In use the program works as follows:

Example 1b

Write a program to access the data file "DATA1" which was created in Example 1a and to print out the 10 names in the file.

```
10 REM★★ACCESS A DATA FILE★★
20 OPEN "I", £1, "DATA1"           20 BBC: B=OPENIN "DATA1"
30 IF EOF (1) THEN 100             30 BBC: IF EOF#B= −1 THEN 100
40 INPUT £1, A$                    40 BBC: INPUT #B, A$
50 PRINT A$
60 GOTO 30
100 CLOSE £1                       100 BBC: CLOSE #B
```

Program 2   Access a data file

RUN ———

——— before pressing RET the recorder
would have to be activated (PLAY only)

```
ARCHER
BENNY
COPPER
DRAPER
EDDIE
FRAME
```

232

GWYNNE
HETTY
KEMP
LAMB
————————————————————————————— and switched off here.

Once we have opened the file, we input the data in it with:

40 INPUT £1, A$ 40 BBC: INPUT #B, A$

Then we can use the data in any other program. In this case, we simply want to print it so we write:

50 PRINT A$

Exercises preamble

A fairly serious defect of Programs 1 and 2 is that they both work only for a specifically named file, viz, 'DATA1'. Now if a file-handling program is going to be of general use, we don't want to have to edit the program just to create or access data from a file of different names. We can overcome this by entering the file name into a variable store location, F$, in the following example.

INPUT"NAME OF THE DATA FILE";F$

OPEN "O",£2,F$ (BBC : A=OPENOUT(F$))

Also it was rather artificial to read into a file from a DATA statement. Let's write some programs which remedy these two points.

Exercise 1

Modify Program 1 to write a sequence of names to a file directly from the keyboard, and allow the file thus created to have a variable name.

Exercise 2

Modify Program 2 to access the file created in Exercise 1 and to print out the list.

Exercise 3

Write a program to access the file created in Exercise 1 and to search through it to find and print out all those names whose initial letter is 'N'.

Exercise 4

Write a program to access the file created in Exercise 1 and to enter the names into a list, and to print out the list with indexes.

9.5   Files in flowcharts

The solution to Exercise 4 holds the key to the development of future programs. It's our old friend the list again, which makes all the difference! Having got the data into list form we can do much more with it. Before we do, however, let's try to summarise the position we've reached.

The program solution to Exercise 1 may be summarised as in Figure 1.

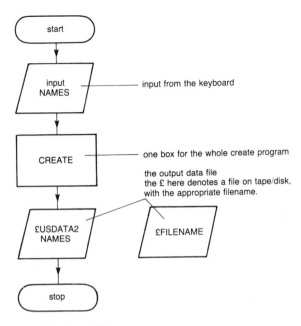

Figure 1   Flowchart for 'Create a file'

The flowchart solution for Exercise 4 is given in Figure 2.

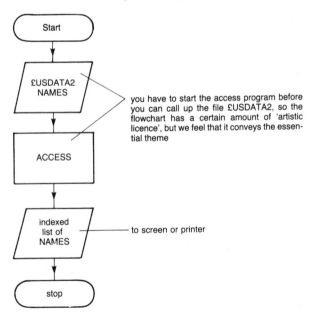

Figure 2   Access a file and index as a list

9.6 Sorting filed data

The list of names in answer to Exercise 2 is just asking to be sorted! We have an access routine and we developed a sort routine in Unit 8. All we have to do now is to link the two together. Before we do let's sketch the algorithm.

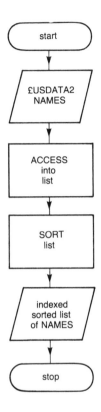

Figure 3   Access and sort

The program is simply three routines (access, sort and print) that you have already met, joined together.

```
10   REM★★ACCESS AND SORT★★
20   DIM X$(50)
30   C=0
40   INPUT "NAME OF THE DATA FILE";G$
50   OPEN "I", £1, G$
60   IF EOF (1) THEN 100
70   C=C+1
80   INPUT £1, X$(C)
90   GOTO 60
100  CLOSE £1
110  REM★★END OF ACCESS★★
```

```
40  BBC: omit;
50  BBC: B=OPENIN (G$)
60  BBC: IF EOF#B= −1
         THEN 100
      access routine
80  BBC: INPUT #B, X$(C)
100 BBC: CLOSE #B
```

```
130 REM★★N IS THE LENGTH OF THE LIST★★
140 N=C
200 REM★★★★★★
210 REM★★SORT ROUTINE★★★★★★
220 FOR K=1 TO N−1
230 FOR L=K+1 TO N
240 IF X$(L) >= X$(K) THEN 280
250 T$=X$(L)                                      sort routine
260 X$(L)=X$(K)
270 X$(K)=T$
280 NEXT L
290 NEXT K
300 REM★★END OF SORT ROUTINE★★
400 REM★★★★★★
410 PRINT"FINAL SORTED LIST"
420 FOR P=1 TO N
430 PRINT P, X$(P)                                print routine
440 NEXT P
450 PRINT
500 REM★★★★★★
```

Program 3   Access and sort

```
RUN
NAME OF THE DATA FILE? USDATA2
FINAL SORTED LIST
```

1	ASHTON
2	BANKS
3	BARR
4	BURNS
5	CAREY
6	COMPTON
7	DOYLE
8	EDGE
9	GRANT
10	HOWSON
11	ICKERY
12	NASH
13	NEILS
14	NUNN
15	PRIEST
16	PURVISS
17	SCALES
18	SHIPTON
19	TEELE
20	TURNER
21	WATERS
22	WATTS
23	WELLS
24	WEST

Exercise 5

We don't necessarily wish to print out the list as we did for demonstration purposes in Program 3, but we definitely would want the sorted data to be saved in a data file for future use.

Modify Program 3 to write the sorted data list to a file, SDATA, say.

How will you test that it is successful?

Exercise 6

Having created a file of sorted data you will sooner or later wish to search through it quickly.

Combine the list-access routine of Program 3 with the bisection search routine of Unit 8 to make this file-search utility program.

Exercise 7

Write a program to access a file and input the data into a table.

You are in charge of the dimensions of the table and the data you use.

9.7 Merge

We've created, accessed, sorted and searched files. What else is there to do? Well, very seldom does a data file which is doing useful work, stay static for long. We usually want to add or delete items, or make amendments to it. The rest of this Unit will be spent considering how to add and delete items to and from a file.

No doubt you have already visualised how you would go about these tasks, and we hope that you follow up your ideas. We will develop a fairly standard approach. To add items to a file we will merge two files together. You've done this if you have ever played cards. You have a hand which you have sorted and have spread out fan-like before you. You pick up another card and slot it into its appropriate place in your hand.

The process of merging involves a master file (sorted into order) and a list of new items to go in (also sorted into order).

Master file	New items (=work file)
AMES	
COLES	DAVIS
GREGG	
HOPE	
IVES	
JAMES	LAMB
MUNN	NORRIS
PRICE	PEARCE
ROSS	
SYMES	TATE

But before we develop a program for the merge, we must anticipate and remove one problem: the extremes of the master file. Both in the bisection search (Unit 8) and in Exercise 6 we found it necessary to ensure that the master file included the extremes. So we now develop a program routine to ensure that this will be so.

The extremes of the master file

The following routine takes any sorted file (G$) and places "AAAA" as the first item and "ZZZZ" as the last.

```
10  REM★★ACCESS A DATA FILE★★
20  DIM M$(50)                              lowest item made AAAA
30  C=1:M$(C)="AAAA" ─────────────────── before accessing the file
40  INPUT "NAME OF THE DATA FILE";G$        40  BBC: omit;
50  OPEN "I", £1, G$                        50  BBC: B=OPENIN(G$)
60  IF EOF(1) THEN 100                      60  BBC: IF EOF#B= −1
70  C=C+1                                        THEN 100
80  INPUT £1, M$(C)                         80  BBC: INPUT #B, M$(C)
90  GOTO 60
100 CLOSE £1                                100 BBC: CLOSE #B
110 REM★★★★★★
120 N=C+1:M$(N)="ZZZZ" ─────────────── highest made ZZZZ after
130 REM★★★★★★                            closing the file
140 FOR I=1 TO N
150 PRINT I, M$(I)
160 NEXT I
```

Program 4   Adding AAAA and ZZZZ to a file

```
RUN
NAME OF THE DATA FILE? SDATA3
```

```
1       AAAA ─────────────────────── lowest item
2       AMES ┐
3       COLES│
4       GREGG│
5       HOPE │
6       IVES ├──────────────────── original file SDATA3
7       JAMES│
8       MUNN │
9       PRICE│
10      ROSS │
11      SYMES┘
12      ZZZZ ─────────────────────── highest item
```

The merge program

A picture of the overall process is shown in Figure 4. Once again there is a certain amount of artistic license. The program does not really have two starting points, but as you will see when the program is run, there are two quite distinct entry points for the two input files.

The essential point to remember is that SDATA3 and SDATA4 have been sorted into alphabetical order before entry into the program. This was done using programs developed earlier in this Unit.

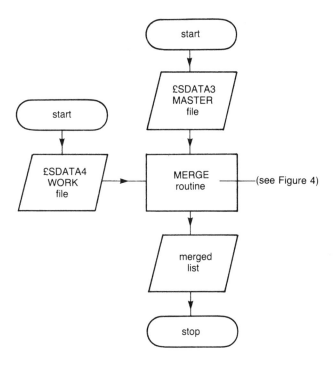

Figure 4   Merge routine in outline

The merge routine

The central idea is:

- if the item in the Master file is lower in order than the item from the Work file
- then write the item from the Master file into the New file;
- otherwise write the item from the Work file into the New file.

W$ next item in Work file
M$ Master
New-list into which they both
write (C$ in the program)

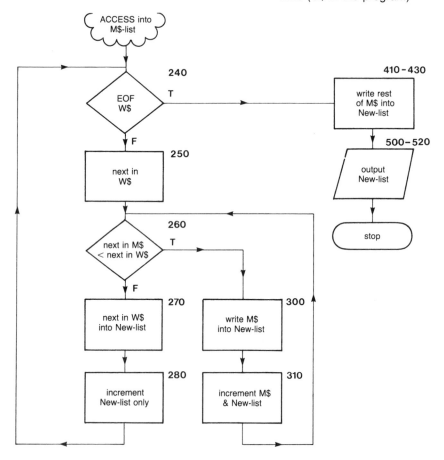

Figure 5   The merge routine in detail

```
10   REM★★ACCESS A DATA FILE★★
20   DIM M$(50):DIM C$(50) ─────────── C$ will be the New-list
30   C=1:M$(C)="AAAA"
40   INPUT"NAME OF THE DATA FILE";G$          40  BBC: omit;
50   OPEN "I", £1, G$                         50  BBC: B=OPENIN(G$)
60   IF EOF(1) THEN 100                       60  BBC: IF EOF#B= −1
70   C=C+1                                            THEN 100
80   INPUT £1, M$(C)
```

```
90  GOTO 60
100 CLOSE £1
110 REM★★★★★★★★
120 N=C+1:M$(N)="ZZZZ"
130 REM★★★★★★★★
140 FOR I=1 TO N
150 PRINT I, M$(I)
160 NEXT I
200 REM★★MERGE★★★★★★★★
210 I=1:K=1
220 INPUT"NAME OF THE WORK FILE";H$
230 OPEN "I", £1, H$
240 IF EOF(1) THEN 400
250 INPUT £1, W$
260 IF M$(I)<W$ THEN 300
270 C$(K)=W$——write Work-item to C$ (K)
280 K=K+1
290 GOTO 240
300 C$(K)=M$(I)–write Master-item to C$ (K)
310 K=K+1:I=I+1
320 GOTO 260
400 CLOSE £1
410 C$(K)=M$(I)
420 K=K+1:I=I+1
430 IF I<= N THEN 410
440 REM★★★★★★★★
500 FOR L=2 TO K-2
510 PRINT L, C$(L)
520 NEXT L
```

accessing Master file, M$, (c)
and inserting AAAA and
ZZZZ at ends
80   BBC: INPUT #B,M$(C)
100 BBC: CLOSE #B

print out of Master file
before merge

220 BBC: omit;
230 BBC: A=OPENIN(H$)
240 BBC: IF EOF#A= −1
    THEN 400
250 BBC: INPUT#A,W$

— merge

400 BBC: CLOSE #A

K is one too high at 430
and we don't want "ZZZZ"
either; hence K−2

Program 5   The complete merge program

Runs of merge program
First using SDATA3 as the Master file:

RUN
NAME OF THE DATA FILE? SDATA3

1	AAAA
2	AMES
3	COLES
4	GREGG
5	HOPE
6	IVES
7	JAMES
8	MUNN
9	PRICE
10	ROSS
11	SYMES
12	ZZZZ

NAME OF THE WORK FILE? SDATA4

2	AMES
3	COLES

4	DAVIS
5	GREGG
6	HOPE
7	IVES
8	JAMES
9	LAMB
10	MUNN
11	NORRIS
12	PEARCE
13	PRICE
14	ROSS
15	SYMES
16	TATE

Second using SDATA4 as the Master file:

RUN
NAME OF THE DATA FILE? SDATA4

1	AAAA
2	DAVIS
3	LAMB
4	NORRIS
5	PEARCE
6	TATE
7	ZZZZ

NAME OF THE WORK FILE? SDATA3

2	AMES
3	COLES
4	DAVIS
5	GREGG
6	HOPE
7	IVES
8	JAMES
9	LAMB
10	MUNN
11	NORRIS
12	PEARCE
13	PRICE
14	ROSS
15	SYMES
16	TATE

We have run the program using data files SDATA3 and 4 as Master file. You can see that it doesn't really matter which one we call the Master and which the Work file. (It is interesting to note that entering the smaller of the two first (SDATA4) takes up slightly less room in the memory.)

If we wanted the New-list in a data file, we would have to add a create routine to the end of the program, instead of 500–520, perhaps.

242

9.8 Deletion

Deletion may seem a very different process from addition and merging but it can be achieved by modifying the merge program only very slightly.

First, the items for deletion are collected into a Work file.

Then:

- if the item in the Master list = that in the Work list then do not write the Master list item into the New-list;
- otherwise do write the Master list item into the New list.

We will not give a flowchart in this case, but hope that you can follow the changes to the merge program as shown in the delete program below. In this case a moment's thought will convince you that the Work and Master lists are no longer interchangeable.

Master file (SDATA)
AHSTON
BANKS
BARR
BURNS
CAREY
COMPTON
DOYLE
EDGE
GRANT
HOWSON
ICKERY
NASH
NEILS
NUNN
PRIEST
PURVISS
SCALES
SHIPTON
TEELE
TURNER
WATERS
WATTS
WELLS
WEST

Work file (SDATA5)
= deletions to be made

BURNS
DOYLE
NASH
TEELE
WATTS

colour = changes from merge program

```
10   REM★★ACCESS A DATA FILE★★
20   DIM M$(50):DIM C$(50)
30   C=1:M$(C)="AAAA"
40   INPUT "NAME OF THE DATA FILE";G$        40  BBC: omit;
50   OPEN "I", £1, G$                        50  BBC: B = OPENIN(G$)
60   IF EOF(1) THEN 100                      60  BBC: IF EOF#B= −1
70   C=C+1                                        THEN 100
80   INPUT £1, M$(C)                         80  BBC: INPUT #B, M$(C)
90   GOTO 60
100  CLOSE £1                                100 BBC: CLOSE #B
```

243

```
110 REM★★★★★★★
120 N=C+1:M$(N)="ZZZZ"
130 REM★★★★★★★★
140 FOR I=1 TO N
150 PRINT I, M$(I)
160 NEXT I
200 REM★★DELETE★★★★★★★★
210 I=1:K=1
220 INPUT"NAME OF THE WORK FILE";H$
230 OPEN "I", £1, H$
240 IF EOF(1) THEN 400
250 INPUT £1, W$
260 IF M$(I) = W$ THEN 330  ──────────→
300 C$(K)=M$(I) ─
310 K=K+1:I=I+1
320 GOTO 260
330 I=I+1 ─
340 GOTO 240
400 CLOSE £1
410 C$(K)=M$(I)
420 K=K+1:I=I+1
430 IF I<=N THEN 410
440 REM★★★★★★★★
500 FOR L=2 TO K-2
510 PRINT L, C$(L)
520 NEXT L
```

220 BBC: omit;
230 BBC: B= OPENIN(H$)
240 BBC: IF EOF#B= −1
    THEN 400
250 BBC: INPUT #B,W$
if master item = Work item
do nothing, just go for the
next Master item
otherwise write Master item into
New list

400 BBC: CLOSE #B

Program 6   Deletion program

RUN
NAME OF THE DATA FILE? SDATA

```
1            AAAA
2            ASHTON
3            BANKS
4            BARR
5            BURNS
6            CAREY
7            COMPTON
8            DOYLE
9            EDGE
10           GRANT
11           HOWSON
12           ICKERY
13           NASH
14           NEILS
15           NUNN
16           PRIEST
17           PURVISS
18           SCALES
19           SHIPTON
20           TEELE
21           TURNER
```
─────── Master list

```
22          WATERS
23          WATTS
24          WELLS
25          WEST
26          ZZZZ
NAME OF THE WORK FILE? SDATA5
2           ASHTON
3           BANKS
4           BARR
5           CAREY
6           COMPTON
7           EDGE
8           GRANT
9           HOWSON
10          ICKERY
11          NEILS          ——————New list . . . the old Master with
12          NUNN                  five items deleted
13          PRIEST
14          PURVISS
15          SCALES
16          SHIPTON
17          TURNER
18          WATERS
19          WELLS
20          WEST
```

Postscript

Our file-handling techniques have been fairly rough and ready. We've aimed at simplicity rather than sophistication.

You will have noticed that we have 'written out to' and 'read in from' files one field at a time. The INPUT£ and PRINT£ statements can handle more than one variable, but great care must be taken over details to ensure success.

We have also had only one file open at any time. This means that the data must be read into the computer's memory for processing before being outputted again. If the file is large the machine must have a large memory to hold the file. To overcome this we would have to have input and output files open simultaneously; and to read in from one, process and output to the other within one routine. To have two files open simultaneously, entails having two recording devices in use at the same time. This is luxury many will not be able to afford.

Despite all these simplifications we have managed to leave you with programs to carry out the basic file-handling operations.

Assignment 9

1. Write a program to create a library Master loan file in alphabetical order by borrower's name, with records of the form:

    BORROWER   DATE DUE   BOOK TITLE

(a)   Write a routine to merge new records with this Master file.

(b)   Write a routine to access and search through the file to find those books which are overdue.

2.   Write a program to access a table of numerical values, to complete row and column sums, and to create a new file to include this extra information.

Objectives of Unit 9

Check that you are able to write programs in a form suitable for your micro-computer to:

Create a data file (open for output)   ☐

Access a data file (open for input)   ☐

Sort a data file   ☐

Add new items to a data file (merge)   ☐

Delete items from a data file   ☐

Answers to Exercises

Exercise 1

```
1000  REM★★CREATE A DATA FILE★★
1010  INPUT "NAME OF THE DATA FILE";F$      1010  BBC: omit;
1020  OPEN "O", £2, F$                      1020  BBC: A=OPENOUT (F$)
1030  INPUT"NEXT NAME";N$                   1030  BBC: omit;
1040  IF N$="ZZZZ" THEN 1070
1050  PRINT £2, N$                          1050  BBC: PRINT #A, N$
1060  GOTO 1030
1070  CLOSE £2                              1070  BBC: CLOSE #A
1080  PRINT F$;" HAS BEEN SAVED"
```

Program 7

```
NAME OF THE DATA FILE? USDATA2
NEXT NAME? BARR
NEXT NAME? SHIPTON
NEXT NAME? HOWSON
NEXT NAME? WELLS
NEXT NAME? CAREY
NEXT NAME? WEST
NEXT NAME? NEILS
NEXT NAME? ASHTON
NEXT NAME? NASH
NEXT NAME? TURNER
NEXT NAME? COMPTON
NEXT NAME? BURNS
```

NEXT NAME? EDGE
NEXT NAME? NUNN
NEXT NAME? PRIEST
NEXT NAME? DOYLE
NEXT NAME? SCALES
NEXT NAME? WATERS
NEXT NAME? GRANT
NEXT NAME? BANKS
NEXT NAME? PURVISS
NEXT NAME? TEELE
NEXT NAME? WATTS
NEXT NAME? ICKERY
NEXT NAME? ZZZZ
USDATA2 HAS BEEN SAVED

Exercise 2

```
10 REM★★ACCESS A DATA FILE★★
20 INPUT"NAME OF THE DATA FILE";G$        BBC: 20 omit;
30 OPEN "I". £1, G$                       BBC: 30 B=OPENIN(G$)
40 IF EOF(1) THEN 80                      BBC: 40 IF EOF#B= −1
50 INPUT £1, A$                                   THEN 80
60 PRINT A$                               BBC: 50 INPUT #B, A$
70 GOTO 40
80 CLOSE £1                               BBC: 80 CLOSE #B
```

Program 8

```
RUN
NAME OF THE DATA FILE? USDATA2
BARR
SHIPTON
HOWSON
WELLS
CAREY
WEST
NEILS
ASHTON
NASH
TURNER
COMPTON
BURNS
EDGE
NUNN
PRIEST
DOYLE
SCALES
WATERS
GRANT
BANKS
PURVISS
TEELE
WATTS
ICKERY
```

Exercise 3

```
10 REM★★ACCESS A DATA FILE★★
20 INPUT"NAME OF THE DATA FILE";G$
30 OPEN "I", £1, G$                        30 BBC: B=OPENIN(G$)
40 IF EOF(1) THEN 90                        40 BBC: IF EOF#B= −1
50 INPUT £1, A$                                      THEN 90
60 IF LEFT $(A$,1)<>"N" THEN 40            50 BBC: INPUT #B, A$
70 PRINT A$
80 GOTO 40
90 CLOSE £1                                 90 BBC: CLOSE #B
```

RUN
NAME OF THE DATA FILE? USDATA2
NEILS
NASH
NUNN

Program 9

Exercise 4

```
10 REM★★ACCESS A DATA FILE★★
20 DIM A$(50) ─────────────────── dimension the list
30 C=0 ──────────────────────── initialise the index for the list
40 INPUT"NAME OF THE DATA FILE";G$    40 BBC: omit;
50 OPEN "I", £1, G$                   50 BBC: B=OPENIN(G$)
60 IF EOF(1) THEN 100
70 C=C+1 ───────────────────── increment only if EOF marker
80 INPUT £1, A$(C)                    is not found
90 GOTO 60                            60 BBC: IF EOF#B= −1
100 CLOSE £1                                THEN 100
110 REM★★N IS TOTAL NO. IN THE LIST★★ ─ so the final count of C is the
120 N=C:REM★★★★★★★★             length of the list
130 FOR I=1 TO N                      80 BBC: INPUT #B, A$(C)
140 PRINT I, A$(I)                    100 BBC: CLOSE #B
150 NEXT I                            140 BBC: PRINT; I, A$(I)
```

RUN   *Program 10*
NAME OF THE DATA FILE? USDATA2

1	BARR
2	SHIPTON
3	HOWSON
4	WELLS
5	CAREY
6	WEST
7	NEILS
8	ASHTON
9	NASH
10	TURNER
11	COMPTON
12	BURNS
13	EDGE
14	NUNN

15	PRIEST
16	DOYLE
17	SCALES
18	WATERS
19	GRANT
20	BANKS
21	PURVISS
22	TEELE
23	WATTS
24	ICKERY

Exercise 5

Instead of the print routine of lines 410–500 of Program 3, we have to write a create routine as follows:

```
300 REM★★END OF SORT ROUTINE★★
400 REM★★★★★★★★
410 REM★★CREATE A DATA FILE★★
420 INPUT"NAME FOR THE DATA FILE";F$
430 OPEN "O", £2, F$              430 BBC: A = OPENOUT (F$)
440 FOR P=1 TO N
450 PRINT £2, X$(P)               450 BBC: PRINT #A, X$(P)
460 NEXT P
470 CLOSE £2                      470 BBC: CLOSE #A
480 PRINT F$;" HAS BEEN SAVED"
500 REM★★★★★★★★
```

Program 11

```
RUN
NAME OF THE DATA FILE? USDATA2
NAME FOR THE DATA FILE? SDATA
SDATA HAS BEEN SAVED
```

To test whether it has been successful we can load and run the access program for the file SDATA.

```
NAME OF THE DATA FILE? SDATA
ASHTON
BANKS
BARR
BURNS
CAREY
COMPTON
DOYLE
EDGE
GRANT
HOWSON
ICKERY
NASH
NEILS
NUNN
PRIEST
PURVISS
```

SCALES
SHIPTON
TEELE
TURNER
WATERS
WATTS
WELLS
WEST

Exercise 6

```
10  REM★★ACCESS FOR SEARCH★★
20  DIM N$(50)
30  C=0
40  INPUT "NAME OF THE DATA FILE";G$
50  OPEN "I", £1, G$
60  IF EOF(1) THEN 100
70  C=C+1
80  INPUT £1, N$(C)
90  GOTO 60
100 CLOSE £1
110 REM★★N IS THE LENGTH OF THE LIST★★
120 N=C:REM★★★★★★★
150 INPUT"QUERY NAME";Q$
200 REM★★START OF SEARCH★★★★★★★★
220 L=1:H=N
230 IF H−L=1 THEN 500
240 M=INT((L+H)/2)
260 IF Q$=N$(M) THEN 320
270 IF Q$<N$(M) THEN 300
280 L=M:GOTO 230
300 H=M: GOTO 230
320 REM★★END OF SEARCH★★★★★★★
330 PRINT"YES ";Q$;" IS IN THE LIST"
350 GOTO 600
500 PRINT Q$;" IS NOT IN THE LIST"
600 PRINT"END OF SEARCH"
```

40 BBC: omit;
50 BBC: B=OPENIN(G$)
60 BBC: IF EOF#B= −1
       THEN 100
— access
80 BBC: INPUT #B, N$(C)
100 BBC: CLOSE #B

}— bisection search

}— print routine

Program 12

```
RUN
NAME OF THE DATA FILE? SDATA ———————— The sorted data file. (We
QUERY NAME? HOWSON                     couldn't use the bisection
YES HOWSON IS IN THE LIST              search on the unsorted file.)
END OF SEARCH
RUN
NAME OF THE DATA FILE? SDATA
QUERY NAME? SMITH
SMITH IS NOT IN THE LIST
END OF SEARCH
```

Note: We have combined an access program with the bisection search program of
Unit 8, and it works. To make the program foolproof, however, we must be careful
about its limits: remember N$(1)="AAAA" and N$(N)="ZZZZ" in Unit 8! We deal
with the problem in Program 5.

250

Exercise 7

```
10   REM★★ACCESS A DATA FILE★★
20   DIM A$(30,30)
30   INPUT"NO. OF ROWS AND COLUMNS";R,C
40   INPUT"NAME OF THE DATA FILE";G$
50   OPEN "I", £1, G$
60   IF EOF(1) THEN 100
70   FOR I=1 TO R
72   FOR J=1 TO C
80   INPUT £1, A$(I,J)
85   NEXT J
90   NEXT I
95   GOTO 60
100  CLOSE £1
110  REM★★★★★★★
120  REM★★PRINT OUT THE TABLE★★★
130  FOR I=1 TO R
140  FOR J=1 TO C
150  PRINT TAB(10★(J−1));A$(I,J);
160  NEXT J
170  PRINT
180  NEXT I
```

```
50 BBC: B=OPENIN(G$)
60 BBC: IF EOF#B= −1
       THEN 100
access and input into
table combined
80 BBC: INPUT #B,A$(I,J)


100 BBC: CLOSE #B
```

───── table print out

Program 13

Run on SDATA

```
RUN
NO. OF ROWS AND COLUMNS? 6 , 4
NAME OF THE DATA FILE? SDATA
```

ASHTON	BANKS	BARR	BURNS
CAREY	COMPTON	DOYLE	EDGE
GRANT	HOWSON	ICKERY	NASH
NEILS	NUNN	PRIEST	PURVISS
SCALES	SHIPTON	TEELE	TURNER
WATERS	WATTS	WELLS	WEST

BBC Computer with a printer

To print everything that appears on the screen during a program run, press CTRL and key B. (This switches the printer on.) To turn the printer off, press CTRL and key C.

To make a program print selected parts of the output to the printer, add the statement VDU2 into your program before the relevant PRINT statement. This will direct all PRINT output to the printer until the program meets the statement VDU3 which turns the printer off again.

INDEX

254

Course comments
Please let us know what you think of this course to help us improve future editions of it. We would especially like to know of any problems you have had in getting particular programs to run on your micro.

Make of microcomputer M27

Name ....

Address ....

....

....

Correspondence tuition

Are you studying by yourself and need help?

If you are, enrol now with NEC as a correspondence student on 30 Hour BASIC. We will give you a correspondence tutor with experience of your make of microcomputer. He will then take you through the course, marking and commenting on your assignments and giving you any advice you need on getting the programs in 30 Hour BASIC to run on your micro.

To enrol, send us the following details:

Name ....

Address ....

....

Postcode ....

Tel. No. ....

Date of birth ....

Microcomputer you are using ....
M027

Course fee: £50 (44 if you already have a copy of 30 Hour BASIC).

Also available

Cassettes

Two cassettes of the main programs in 30 Hour BASIC. Price £5.95 inc. p & p and VAT each. (Suitable for use with the BBC Computer only.)

Free notes

30 Hour BASIC needs small adaptations for use on certain microcomputers. If you are having problems getting our programs to work on your machine, send us a stamped addressed envelope with the make and model of your microcomputer written clearly on the inside of the envelope flap. We'll send you a sheet of notes on getting 30 Hour BASIC programs to run on your computer.

National Extension College,
18 Brooklands Avenue, Cambridge CB2 2HN.